Denner,

Hope you enjoy!

The Military Industrial Complex at 50

Edited by David Swanson

Charlottesville, VA

First edition—2011

Also by David Swanson
WHEN THE WORLD OUTLAWED WAR (2011)
WAR IS A LIE (2010)
DAYBREAK: UNDOING THE IMPERIAL PRESIDENCY
AND FORMING A MORE PERFECT UNION (2009)
THE 35 ARTICLES OF IMPEACHMENT (Introduction, 2008)

• • •

Swanson, David, 1969 Dec. 1-

The Military Industrial Complex at 50

Book design by David Swanson

Cover Image by Barbara Stanley

Printed in the USA

First Edition / December 2011

ISBN: 978-0-9830830-7-8

MIC50.org

Contents

Introduction — David Swanson..5

I. WHERE WE FIND OURSELVES
Your Local Military Industrial Complex — David Swanson......................23
The Eisenhower, Jefferson, King Debate — Wally Myers..........................34
An ICBM Launch on World Peace Day — Ann Wright..............................50
Jeju Island, South Korea — Ann Wright...55
CIA's Push for Drone War Driven by Internal Needs — Gareth Porter....59

II. JOBS OR WARS
Pitfalls of Military Keynesianism — Dave Shreve..65
Destructive Economic Impact of Military Spending — Robert Naiman...83
The Military As a Jobs Program — Ellen Brown...92
Civilizing the Military — Ellen Brown...98
We the 99% Demand a Different Budget — David Swanson...................102

III. NOTHING IS SAFE
How Private Warmongers and the
     Military Infiltrated Universities — Steve Horn and Allen Ruff...........108
War Is Not Healthy for Civil Liberties — Jeff Fogel...............................122
How Much Does the Military Spend Saving Souls? — Chris Rodda.......129
What War Does to Law — Ben Davis...138
Thinking Critically About Mass Media — Robert Jensen.........................152
Militarism and the Economics of Extinction — Clare Hanrahan...........161
Atomic Appalachia and the
     Militarized Southeast — Clare Hanrahan and Coleman Smith..........170
The Extra Casualties of War — Mia Austin Scoggins.............................199

IV. NON-COOPERATION WITH EVIL

Crazy Horse Back on the War Path — Bruce Gagnon.............................211

Whistleblowing, and How to Get More of It — Karen Kwiatkowski.......224

Leading With Integrity — Bunny Greenhouse...232

A Soldier's Roadmap to a Peaceful Future — Paul Chappell....................243

V. WHAT TO DO

Questions — Tony Russell...266

Moving from a War Economy
   to a Peace Economy — Mary Beth Sullivan...267

Time for an Economic Bill of Rights — Ellen Brown...............................280

What Needs Changing — Jonathan Williams...285

Activism and the M.I.C. — Ray McGovern...294

Imperial Collapse in the Middle East — Helena Cobban.........................302

It Would Grind to a Halt Tomorrow — Lisa Savage.................................312

Stop Deceptive Military Testing in Schools — Pat Elder.........................318

Ready to Rumble for Jobs,
   Not War and More Weapons? — Judith Le Blanc..................................328

Political Passivity, Anti-Authoritarianism,
   and Building a Base — Bruce Levine...332

VI. SING

When Bradley Comes Marching Home — John Heuer
   with Stu Hutchison, Wally Myers, and Pete Seeger............................352

Appendix: Sample Resolution...354

Notes...356

Introduction

By David Swanson

This book is the most comprehensive collection I've seen explaining what the military industrial complex is, where it comes from, what damage it does, what further destruction it threatens, and what can be done and is being done to chart a different course.

The book is almost entirely a collection of remarks presented at a truly amazing event, a conference held in Charlottesville, Virginia, in 2011 to mark 50 years since President Dwight D. Eisenhower found the nerve in his farewell speech in 1961 to articulate one of the most prescient, potentially valuable, and tragically as yet unheeded warnings of human history:

Until the latest of our world conflicts, the United States had no armaments industry. American makers of plowshares could, with time and as required, make swords as well. But now we can no longer risk emergency improvisation of national defense; we have been compelled to create a permanent armaments industry of vast proportions. Added to this, three and a half million men and women are directly engaged in the defense establishment. We annually spend on military security more than the net income of all United States corporations.

This conjunction of an immense military establishment and a large arms industry is new in the American experience. The total influence — economic, political, even spiritual — is felt in every city, every Statehouse, every office of the Federal government. We recognize the imperative need for this development. Yet we must not fail to comprehend its grave implications. Our toil, resources and livelihood are all involved; so is the very structure of our society.

In the councils of government, we must guard against the acquisition of unwarranted influence, whether sought or unsought, by the military-industrial complex. The potential for the disastrous rise of misplaced power exists and will persist.

We must never let the weight of this combination endanger our liberties or democratic processes. We should take nothing for granted. Only an alert and knowledgeable citizenry can compel the proper meshing of the huge industrial and military machinery of defense with our peaceful methods and goals, so that security and liberty may prosper together.

The collection that follows will persuade most readers that the "total influence" of the military industrial complex (MIC) has become far more total, that the disastrous rise of misplaced power is no longer merely a potential event, that our liberties and democratic processes are in a state of collapse, and that Ike himself was disastrously misinforming the citizenry when he claimed that the very monster he warned of had been "compelled" by the need for "defense."

The MIC at 50 conference, held September 16th to 18th, 2011, was the most universally praised and appreciated conference I've been a part of. As is evident in the chapters that follow, the speakers learned from, synthesized, and inspired each other in the course of the three days. We could do worse than to schedule many more such gatherings.

But, truth be told, although I helped to organize, spoke at, and fully participated in the conference, I got more out of the speakers' remarks by reading through them while editing this book. You may be better off possessing this book than having attended. Many attendees requested that this book be produced, and my hope is that the book you are now holding in your hands or electronically scrolling through will meet their expectations.

This is a book that can be read straight through as the argument builds from analysis to action. I've kept the remarks for the most part in the order in which they were delivered. This is also a book that can be read perfectly well by jumping to the sections that interest you first. This was the agenda for the conference:

Friday, September 16, 2011, at the Haven, 112 W Market Street, Charlottesville, Va.

6:00 Authentic Afghan Dinner

Welcome by Charlottesville Mayor Dave Norris

6:30 MIC in Cville and VA — David Swanson

7:00 Dramatic Dialogue with Eisenhower, Jefferson, and Martin Luther King Jr.

7:45 Voices of Conscience — Ann Wright

8:30 Free MIC50 Cake for All, provided by Camino Restaurant

Saturday and Sunday, September 17 and 18, 2011, at The Dickinson Fine and Performing Arts Center at Piedmont Virginia Community College, 501 County Road 338, Charlottesville, Va. 22902-7589.

Saturday

8:30 Federal Budget and Impact of MIC on the Economy — Robert Naiman and Dave Shreve

9:45 Budget Activity — Lisa Savage

10:30 BREAK

10:45-12:30

Are Weapons Corporations People? — George Friday

MIC and Civil Liberties — Jeff Fogel

What War Does to Law — Ben Davis

LUNCH

1:15 War Media — Robert Jensen

2:00 MIC and the Environment — Claire Hanrahan and Coleman Smith

2:45 Extra Casualties: The Human Cost of War — Mia Austin Scoggins

3:30 BREAK

3:45 MIC and Weapons Proliferation, Global Hostility — Bruce Gagnon

4:30 Whistleblowing — Karen Kwiatkowski and Bunny Greenhouse

5:15 Why Peace is Possible and How We Can Achieve It — Paul Chappell

Sunday

9:30-11:30

Conversion to a Peace Economy — Mary Beth Sullivan

What Needs Changing — Jonathan Williams

LUNCH

12:15 Activism — Ray McGovern, Helena Cobban, Lisa Savage

1:45 BREAK

2:00 Action Planning

3:00 Panel With All Conference Speakers Together

4:00 Anti-Authoritarian Activism — Bruce Levine

Two speakers we had planned to include, Judith Le Blanc and Ellen Brown, were unable to attend but have nonetheless contributed articles to this collection. I've actually included three short articles from Brown, two of which were prepared specifically for this project. A few of the articles below — Ann Wright's, Robert Jensen's, and Paul Chappell's — are not exactly the remarks they presented but are articles they produced on the same topic at about the same time. I've also added to the collection four excellent articles from friends of ours who were not part of the conference but whose insights mesh well with and expand on the rest of this discussion: Gareth Porter, Pat Elder, Chris Rodda, and an article by Steve Horn and

Allen Ruff. I've been unable to include anything from two people who did participate and make valuable contributions, George Friday and Dave Norris. Friday did stellar work as a facilitator as well as a presenter.

George Friday worked for the Piedmont Peace Project, was a founding member and Executive Director of the Independent Progressive Political Network, was a founding member and is on the executive committee of Move to Amend (the national coalition to strip corporations of their claim to be "persons"); and is former co-chair of United for Peace and Justice.

The first section of the book below, on "Where We Find Ourselves," is intended to paint a portrait of the MIC at age 50. My opening article is a portrait of the MIC in the state of Virginia. This should fairly closely resemble a similar portrait that might be constructed for any other part of the United States. I provide a guide at the end of the article to assist in such research.

The second article is actually a play, written by Wally Myers for the MIC50 conference and performed on opening night. The play puts the military industrial complex into historical context by means of an imagined discussion among Charlottesville local Thomas Jefferson, Dwight Eisenhower, and Martin Luther King, Jr. Myers has made this play available to be performed anywhere. It consists almost entirely of quotations, with some sections ~~crossed through~~ and amended (in parentheses). The play leaves you with the deep understanding that militarism as we know it did not always exist and need not remain with us forever.

In Ann Wright's two articles, she provides, first, an overview of MIC expansion underway right now in the Pacific. Then Wright narrows in on one particular location, typical of many around the globe, where local people are resisting U.S. military base construction. Gareth Porter concludes this section with a new but typical example of how the MIC creates its own momentum for war; a massive bureaucracy that lives off the work of death will seek to continue and expand it for its own sake. This is what Eisenhower was afraid of. It is what we all should be treating as a national emergency.

Section II on "Jobs Not Wars" places the military industrial complex in the context of the national economy and the federal budget. Dave Shreve's contribution reads like an academic paper from an economics professor, and so it is, or rather an economics historian. What's that, you ask? Well, it's something that held the attention of our whole auditorium. When you've read this, if you're like me, you will have learned a better history of the presidencies of Eisenhower and of Lyndon Johnson, and you'll have come to understand why deficit spending can be good, and why military cuts alone without conversion and reallocation of the funds can be economically bad even if morally desirable. Conversion will be a major topic later in this book. By conversion I mean the redirection, retooling, and retraining of portions of the MIC into civilian or nonviolent industries. Shreve fleshes out the mechanics of exactly how it is that military spending does less for job creation and retention than other spending. He leaves you with an acute understanding of how military spending resembles burying cash in the earth and then hiring people to dig it up again.

Shreve, like many of the speakers at the conference, references an extremely valuable study published by Robert Pollin and Heidi Garrett-Peltier in 2007 and updated in the years following. As Shreve points out, this study looked at the benefits of spending money and found that spending money on the military produced fewer jobs than spending the same money in each of several other industries or even on tax cuts for household consumption. Shreve further points out that a corollary lesson can be derived from the study in the context of cutting rather than spending funds: "All cuts would reduce employment levels and harm the economy, but cuts to military spending would raise unemployment and dampen economic activity less than corresponding cuts to education, transportation, and other non-military outlays."

Robert Naiman's article comes from the perspective of someone closely following the actions of our government in Washington, D.C. Naiman saw good news in the agenda of the now-failed Supercommittee in Congress. Of course, the economic impact of military cuts is less damaging than other cuts, but still damaging economically. To be economically beneficial the money has to be spent elsewhere or be directed into tax cuts for consumers. But the possibility of cutting military spending has always been the missing ingredient in this recipe, and Naiman is right that it is now on the table in a way we have not seen for many years. As we'll encounter below, Bruce Gagnon and Judith Le Blanc present a more pessimistic view than Naiman of both the Supercommittee and of the automatic cuts set to follow its failure. But the promise Naiman points to lies, in the short term, as Le Blanc agrees, in the possibility of forcing the automatic cuts to actually hit the military, and in the long term, in the fact that cutting the military is now part of the public discussion in Washington.

It is only the barest of beginnings. "A trillion dollars in cuts" sounds big to most of us, but we should bear in mind that cuts "over ten years" are only a tenth as large as they sound when looked at "over one year," and that cuts to "projected spending" are cuts to dreamed up future budgets and not necessarily to actual current spending. Nonetheless, in December 2011 senators from both big political parties introduced numerous amendments to the National Defense Authorization Act aimed at cutting pieces of the military, including overseas bases. The analysis found in these pages suggests a need to press this agenda forward, to in fact demand cuts rather than falling into the common liberal habit of shouting against any cuts to anything on principle. We want "Jobs Not Wars," not "Jobs Not Cuts."

Ellen Brown summarizes the economic case, showing that current practice is driven by corrupt politics, secrecy, and profit-driven wars, not by economic sense. She points the way toward economic conversion, which will be taken up more fully later in this book. Her second article looks within the military itself for a better model for the economy as a whole, one that would — ironically — shrink the military. I end the section with a short note pointing to a useful tool you can find online for creating a visual image of how you would like our public spending to be reprioritized.

The third section, on "Nothing Is Safe," explains how the "total influence" is, indeed, not just economic, but also "political, even spiritual." These articles show how the military industrial complex threatens higher education, civil liberties, freedom of and from religion, the rule of law, informed public communications, the natural environment, and the war makers themselves. Steve Horn and Allen Ruff's article outlines the new "long war university" or what might be less charitably called the chickenhawk farm. These authors name names, and those they name are worth keeping a close eye on. Jeff Fogel's article places the stripping away of civil liberties during the current "global forever war" in the context of a long tradition, while perfectly clarifying what is radically new in the latest attacks on our freedom. Chris Rodda's article details the fortune the U.S. military spends trying to turn its troops and their children into evangelical Christians. One of the contractors hired for the work explains that soldiers are easy to convert:

> *Deployment and possibly deadly combat are ever-present possibilities. They are shaken. Shaken people are usually more ready to hear about God than those who are at ease, making them more responsive to the gospel.*

That and the oversight-free contracts explains the contractors' motivations, but what explains the military's? Is it somehow advantageous to military commanders for soldiers to practice obedience to a Lord and to believe death not to be real?

Ben Davis's article examines how war is used to pervert domestic law and violate international law, and how new areas of secrecy and obscurity hide the very question of legality. At the same time, Davis inspires us to resist this trend.

Robert Jensen's article looks at the corporate media's over-reliance on official sources, and redefines propaganda not in terms of what it includes but of what it leaves out. If propaganda is persuasive discourse that excludes many points of view and inconvenient facts in order to mislead, then — Jensen points out — propaganda may be the norm for advertising and marketing as well as corporate news. We may have a deeper problem than sporadic sales-campaigns for new wars.

Clare Hanrahan's article presents a devastating tally of militarism's damage to the natural environment. Every section of the United States holds people who believe theirs must be the most militarized area. Clare Hanrahan's and Coleman Smith's article makes a strong case for the Southeast to claim that title, even while describing a pattern of environmental destruction that is not far removed from the rest of the country.

Not only are most war casualties in U.S. wars non-Americans and a large percentage of them children and the elderly, but Mia Austin Scoggins documents the fact that most U.S. casualties are of types not officially recognized. Veterans, their children, their spouses, and their friends, suffer from poisons encountered during wars, from disabilities, PTSD, suicide, and murder. The documented damage is overwhelming, the ripple effects immeasurable.

Hanrahan raises the concern that environmentalists do not tend to join forces with pacifists even though war and militarism do more damage to the natural environment than perhaps anything else. But is this unique to environmentalists, or does it apply to every article in this section of the book? Do civil libertarians, media reform advocates, or proponents of economic justice or representative government, or even most advocates for veterans join together to oppose war making? I think it's safe to say: only when no other options can be found, and maybe not even then. Why take on the military industrial complex when you're already struggling against a much less formidable opponent?

Well, here's why: by uniting in a mass movement to overcome the military industrial complex and the plutocracy it fosters we could all be stronger in each of our individual areas.

In Section IV on "Noncooperation With Evil" are four tremendous presentations that lead us in the direction of resistance to the military industrial complex, in our thinking and in our daily lives, including for people who are in some way part of the MIC. Bruce Gagnon takes us back to the proto-MIC of the nineteenth century and then forward to plans being made for a possible first strike on China by a U.S. space plane, showing a consistent drive for profit and control that creates wars and war technology, and that has also driven the current assaults by war profiteers on our Social Security, Medicare, and Medicaid. Perhaps the most disturbing of the many questions Gagnon raises is this: if our top industrial export is weapons, what must our foreign policy be in order to keep sales up?

Karen Kwiatkowski and Bunny Greenhouse are whistleblowers from the Bush era who see the struggle for integrity in our government as having grown even more difficult in the Obama era. Kwiatkowski, also a Republican candidate for Congress, draws on Smedley Butler and President Eisenhower as models for whistleblowers, but urges potential whistleblowers to speak out earlier than those men did in their careers. Greenhouse is someone who did speak out in the midst of a successful career and paid a price for it but has no regrets. Her story illuminates the typical subservient behavior of individuals in the U.S. military, and the rest of our government, by recounting an extremely rare example of ordinary honesty.

Paul Chappell's article is an interview of Chappell that very roughly approximates his moving presentation at the conference. This is an excellent place to start in understanding or explaining to others how military spending, including on hundreds of foreign bases, doesn't go beyond what's needed to keep us safe, but on the contrary is making us less and less safe all the time.

Section V on "What to Do" is where the book becomes truly engaging and cheerful — not necessarily optimistic, but rather beyond optimism or pessimism and into the world of activism. Here are both solutions and models for how to achieve them. Tony Russell's questions set the stage.

Mary Beth Sullivan outlines the path to economic conversion. She recounts some of the movement's recent history. The idea of converting military industries to civilian purposes has been popular and nearly even successful in recent decades, up to about 20 years ago. Our current Secretary of "Defense" Leon Panetta, who now describes a teeny reduction in a massively bloated military budget as "doomsday," was a backer, 20 years ago, of a bill in Congress that would have begun the conversion process. Sullivan reminds us of the role played by current presidential candidate Newt Gingrich in blocking that bill on behalf of Lockheed Martin. Ellen Brown lays out a new bill of rights that we need to establish as well as a key step to get us there: taking public control of money now created by private banks.

Jonathan Williams strives to answer key questions for activists: "How do we win? How do we get our demands met? We need power. But what is power? How do we get it?" Williams answers these questions like a good community organizer, focusing on leadership development, relationship building, and the organizing of people power, and applying these lessons to the problem of the MIC. Some 20 to 50 percent of members of the U.S. military who have been deployed to Iraq or Afghanistan suffer from post traumatic stress disorder (PTSD). Williams describes a campaign that is organizing on military bases to remove these troops from the ranks of those available to send into wars.

Ray McGovern provides essential food for activism: inspiration. Helena Cobban pushes us to think our way out of U.S. exceptionalism, which she says has not provided us with privilege but made us less secure and less well off. Lisa Savage presents a model campaign organized in Maine to advance peace and economic conversion, and speaks to the question of communicating with a wider audience. Pat Elder presents a model campaign developed in Maryland and already mentioned by Williams, aimed at preventing the military from testing students and using the test results for recruitment without prior permission. Le Blanc focuses on exactly where our activism is needed now as regards our senators and misrepresentatives in Congress.

The final speech at the conference, and the final article here, is by Bruce Levine. Some participants, after listening to Bruce, told me we'd saved the best for last. This is a book, so you can feel free to read him first. Levine presents some surprising causes of inaction and solutions to fueling activism through recovery from "corporatocracy abuse" and "battered people's syndrome," allowing us to develop "anti-authoritarianism, individual self-respect, collective self-confidence, courage, determination, and solidarity."

Section VI consists of a song that we sang to conclude the three-day event. Never underestimate the power of singing.

The primary product of the military industrial complex is, of course, war, but this is not a book about war, not exactly. For one thing, U.S. wars are fought in other countries, not here. But this was not an international conference. Over 90 percent of the people killed in U.S. wars are not from the United States, yet their loved-ones' voices were not a part of this conference. This was predominantly a gathering of U.S. residents in the U.S. to talk about what can be done in the U.S. As such, it can be repeated in other U.S. cities. Do try this at home. Yet, as with most peace movement events, this was a gathering of speakers and participants overwhelmingly motivated by the desire to avoid killing foreign human beings. We talked about other things. We talked about the arguments that would bring into the room in theory all of the people who were not there in reality, the people who care about the environment or the economy or civil liberties but not (or not so much) about halting the mass-murder of non-Americans. The argument that Bruce Gagnon makes most explicitly in these pages, for peace activists to shift to talking about jobs instead of peace, stands, from a certain angle, in conflict with the inspiring case that Ray McGovern and Lisa Savage make for pursuing the justice that is in your heart regardless of outcome or with an awareness that the impact may be distant, indirect, and undetectable. In my view this conflict is best resolved by pursuing both strategies: preaching the immorality of war *and* explaining how the MIC deprives us of jobs. Since when is having two arguments for one change in policy a weakness? We can't move funding away from wars if people believe that wars are just. And we can't get everyone's attention focused on the topic of war until we explain the relationship to their own well being. We will have to explain this to more and more people as wars change their appearance, drones replace soldiers, and what Ben Davis describes below as "dark matter" expands.

This conference was held and this book published in the context of an Obama presidency that is accelerating the advance of the military industrial complex, but is perceived in many quarters as doing the exact opposite. President Obama has increased the size, cost, privatization, and global presence of the U.S. military. He has, with his War on Libya, established the prerogative to take the nation into war against the will of the United States Congress. He has created drone warfare on a significant scale. He has enlarged and formalized due-process-free imprisonment, and cemented in place warrantless spying and the power to abuse prisoners. He has expanded the use of assassination, including of U.S. citizens. President Obama has radically expanded claims of state secrets to protect the crimes of his predecessor, and made greater use of the Espionage Act to punish whistleblowers than all previous administrations combined. Obama has formalized, legalized, systematized, and normalized what was illicit under Bush. He has pursued base construction and expansion of missile "defense" systems to the detriment of U.S. relations with China, North Korea, Russia, Iran, and Pakistan, among other nations. Like all presidents during this permanent war, Obama is a war president. Unlike all other Nobel Peace Prize recipients, Obama praised war in his acceptance speech.

In November 2012, U.S. voters are likely to face a choice for president between two major party candidates both of whom favor outrageous spending on war preparation, with the range of debate likely at best to extend from spending 60% of discretionary spending on the military to 70%. This spending benefits a very small and very wealthy elite, but does serious damage to 99% of us.

The MIC50 conference was held the same weekend as the initial unnoticed action by Occupy Wall Street. Some of us had supported the planning for that action and, as you'll see in the remarks below, had for a long time been planning to start occupying Freedom Plaza in Washington, D.C., on October 6, 2011 — an occupation still underway as I write this in December. The first widely seen pepper spraying incident at Occupy Wall Street was a week after the MIC50 conference, and the mass arrest on the Brooklyn Bridge was on October 1st. Helena Cobban's remarks below point to a major inspiration for the occupation of both D.C. and Wall Street, namely Tahrir Square in Cairo, Egypt, where a popular movement had overthrown a president in January 2011.

We must vote, just as Egyptians must vote, but voting alone will get us nowhere good. Our government will halt the foreclosures on our homes only after we have halted the foreclosures on our homes. Our government will forgive student debt only after we have blocked its payment. Our government will regulate Wall Street only after we have divested from it. And our government will stop dumping our hard-earned pay into wars we don't want and cannot survive only when we have made that path (that running of the gauntlet of K Street's opposition) easier for every type of misrepresentative than continuing on the current trajectory. Shifting our demand from "Jobs Not Cuts" to "Jobs Not Wars" is an important and valuable step. But simultaneously working on our vision for a better community could result in the future in the ability to dream so big that our dearest wish, in an extravagantly over-wealthy country, is no longer merely for jobs.

The following articles will stimulate your thinking. I have tried to leave each author/speaker their own style and voice. I've kept endnotes, turned footnotes into endnotes, and turned hyperlinks into endnotes or removed them.

I want to thank Jason Leopold of *PubRecord.org* for permission to reprint Chris Rodda's article, and the same Jason Leopold but this time of *TruthOut.org* for permission to reprint Steve Horn and Allen Ruff's. Gareth Porter's article was originally published by Inter Press Service.

The authors' photos were taken during the conference by and donated by Tom Cogill, with the exception of those of Jeff Fogel, Bunny Greenhouse, and Karen Kwiatkowski. Those three were provided by the authors.

The image on the front cover was created by Barbara Stanley of Skipper Graphics. The image of Jefferson, Eisenhower, and King was created by Wally Myers. The images in Dave Shreve's and Mia Austin Scoggins' articles were provided by the authors. The pie charts in my article on "We the 99% Demand a Different Budget" were produced by an online tool programmed by Karl Anliot.

A great deal of credit goes to John Heuer for bringing the idea for this conference to Charlottesville, building on a prior event held in Greensboro, North Carolina. Tony Russell and Jon Kessler did much of the planning in Charlottesville, along with Linda Lisanti, Brandon Collins, Ryan DeRamus, Bill Lankford, Hisham Ashur, Virginia Rovnyak, and Kirk Bowers, along with many others. Wally Myers, Clare Hanrahan, and Coleman Smith were also involved in the planning. Countless wonderful people helped out during the three days of the conference itself. The Charlottesville Center for Peace and Justice was an early and big supporter. Further support came from the Eisenhower Chapter (NC Triangle) of Veterans for Peace, Peace First, Augusta Coalition for Peace and Justice, Amnesty International Group 157, Richmond Peace Education Center, Foreign Policy in Focus, The Good Earth, The Political Club of Piedmont Virginia Community College (PVCC), Jeff Clements, John Heuer, Sherry Stanley, Phyllis Albritton, Ann Wright, and anonymous but generous donors. The Camino Restaurant donated delicious food and cake. Sha Llel donated the audio equipment and made the technology run smoothly enough to hardly be noticed. The Haven and PVCC were very hospitable venues. Mayor Dave Norris, City Council Member Kristin Szakos, and then candidate but now City Council Member-Elect Dede Smith participated in the conference, and we appreciated their support. Three is a majority on a city council of five, and we look forward to strong steps toward economic conversion.

David Swanson is the author of *When the World Outlawed War, War Is A Lie*, and *Daybreak: Undoing the Imperial Presidency and Forming a More Perfect Union*. He blogs at davidswanson.org and warisacrime.org and works for the online activist organizations rootsaction.org and democrats.com.

I. WHERE WE FIND OURSELVES

Your Local Military Industrial Complex

By David Swanson

So, here we are 50 years and 8 months tomorrow from the day on which President Dwight Eisenhower, on his way out of office, warned: "In the councils of government, we must guard against the acquisition of unwarranted influence, whether sought or unsought, by the military industrial complex. The potential for the disastrous rise of misplaced power exists and will persist." I don't think we're here to propose Eisenhower or anyone else as a perfect model of all virtues. But what he said that day 50 years ago, in a very flawed and imperfect speech, was one of the most prescient predictions and potentially valuable warnings ever offered on the face of this earth. I say potentially because we have yet to heed it.

Yesterday the Dean of Arts and Sciences at the University of Virginia, Meredith Woo, posted on her blog that our new war in Libya was admirable and Jeffersonian. In fact, she compared it to Jefferson's war in the same location, which she held up as "a pristine example" of a "just war." In her descriptions of that long ago war and the current one she devoted not one word to the killing, maiming, or traumatizing of innocent people. She made no case for the necessity of either war, except to claim that the first one was fought in self-defense several thousand miles away against a band of pirates who had never approached U.S. shores and whom Woo scornfully mocked as unworthy adversaries. Woo's entire case is that our Libyan wars have not yet been as bad as our Afghanistan and Iraq wars. Well those are sure high standards! What a proud UVA alumnus I am today! And wouldn't it have been nice to see a little opposition to the Iraq and Afghanistan wars from UVA's administration prior to this cheerful celebration of the Libya War as not being as bad as the other ones, which — by the way — are still raging?

This past Sunday the Charlottesville *Daily Progress* printed a column called "A Stimulus Package Conservatives Could Support," but there was nothing conservative, and nothing Eisenhower would have tolerated, in the column. I tried to find some points in this column that I could say the author got right, but the best I could come up with was this: giving her the benefit of the doubt, I suspect that the author, Amity Shlaes, spelled her own name correctly.

Her idea for improving our economy is to increase military spending, including in particular through the Defense Advanced Research Projects Agency (DARPA).

DARPA is the same agency that has moved on from mechanical killer elephants and telepathic warfare to exploding frisbees, cyborg wasps, and Captain America no-meals and no-sleep soldiers, as well as far more useful things that could have been developed outside the military, like the internet and GPS. But DARPA has 240 employees. Let's double it. Heck, let's triple it. We've still got statistically the exact same unemployment rate we started with. Or let's add a half a million employees to the military, as Shlaes proposes. If we could afford to do that, we could afford to add many more employees elsewhere, because the military is the least efficient way to create jobs. In fact, we could scale back military spending to a level higher than 10 years ago, put that money into non-military industries and tax cuts, and see a net gain of millions of jobs, even after finding new jobs for everyone who lost one in the military industrial complex. We could seriously reduce unemployment and it wouldn't cost us a dime. That fact only seems startling if we lose touch with how much we're spending on the military and what a waste it is.

But Shlaes has other arguments. First of all, the military knows how to manage youth, she says. But does it? The leading cause of death in the U.S. military right now is suicide. I understand that once you're dead you're no longer unemployed, but surely that can't be what Shlaes had in mind as a solution to youth unemployment. We tried to bring to this conference a young widow of a soldier whose pleas for help after seven tours in our current wars went unanswered by the military. He took his life, and his wife publicly described the lengthy process that had led to that tragedy. She was then so viciously harassed that she canceled her conference participation and went into hiding. I suppose that's one way to manage young people.

Secondly, Shlaes argues, the military is already on all the campuses. That's certainly true in Charlottesville. Recruiting offices are already open everywhere, she explains. True enough. The military can spend tons of money quickly, she assures us. Well, that's as true as anything could be. But it doesn't change the fact that you could have many more jobs just as quickly by other means. Feeding the military industrial complex because it's large and hungry is how Congress Members think; it's not how we need to think.

Oh, but it's not large, says Shlaes. It's only 5 percent of gross domestic product, less than President Reagan managed, and less than during Vietnam, Korea, or World War II.

But think about this argument. If the country becomes wealthier (I know it doesn't seem wealthier, but 400 billionaires have as much money as half the country; there's wealth, it's just concentrated), Anyway, as I was saying, if a country becomes wealthier it should spend more money, at a steady percentage of GDP, on its military, not because it needs to, but because it can, and because — even though almost anything else would produce more jobs — this will produce some jobs.

Shlaes' statistics are debatable as well. Chris Hellman recently compiled all the U.S. national security spending through various departments, including the so-called "intelligence" agencies, Homeland Security, etc., and arrived at $1.2 trillion per year. According to the National Priorities Project we're dumping 59% of discretionary spending into the military each year. According to the *St. Petersburg Times* this week, U.S. troops are in 148 countries. We could cut 80% of this madness and still be the world's top military spender. In the process we could avoid all of the damage we are going to hear about during this conference not only to our economy, but also in terms of weapons proliferation, foreign relations, civil liberties, the natural environment, the rule of law, and — lest we forget — the killing of large numbers of human beings.

Shlaes asserts without argument that an ever larger military deters wars. Eisenhower warned, and the evidence is extensive, that a larger military creates wars. And that larger military is all over Charlottesville and Virginia. The *Daily Progress*, which does a far better than average job of covering peace advocacy, nonetheless willingly prints propaganda for the military industrial complex. It also carries a lot of advertisements for the military industrial complex. And those advertisements are purchased with our tax dollars, funneled through the Congress, into the Pentagon, and on over to so-called private corporations taking no-bid, uncompeted contracts to enjoy what for some are booming economic times. BAE Systems, which often runs a green full-page ad in the *Daily Progress*, paid a $400 million fine last year to the U.S. government to settle charges of having bribed Saudi Arabia to buy its weapons. The U.S. government, however, continued dumping billions into BAE.

Charlottesville, as many of you may know, is home to the National Ground Intelligence Center (NGIC), now north of town but previously downtown in what became the SNL Financial building. The new location for the center also accommodates units of the National Geo-Spatial Intelligence Agency and the DIA, the Defense Intelligence Agency. The University of Virginia has built a research park next door.

Ray McGovern was just reminding me of the role the NGIC played in selling the Iraq War. When the experts at the Department of Energy refused to say that aluminum tubes in Iraq were for nuclear facilities, because they knew they could not possibly be and were almost certainly for rockets, and when the State Department's people also refused to reach the "correct" conclusion, a couple of guys down here at NGIC were happy to oblige. Their names were George Norris and Robert Campus, and they received "performance awards" (cash) for the service. Colin Powell used their claims in his U.N. speech despite the warning of his own staff that they weren't true. NGIC also hired MZM Inc. to assist with war lies for a good chunk of change, and MZM then gave a well-paid job to NGIC's deputy director Bill Rich Jr., and for good measure Bill Rich III too. MZM was far and away the top "contributor" to former Congressman Virgil Goode's campaigns, and he got them a big contract in Martinsville before they went down in the Duke Cunningham scandal. Rich then picked up a job with a company called Sparta, which, like MZM, was conveniently located in the UVA research park.

There's a Judge Advocate General's Legal Center attached to UVA Law School as well. Then there's the Virginia National Guard, which does tend to guard nations, just not this one.

Local want ads offer jobs "researching biological and chemical weapons" at Battelle Memorial Institute (located in the UVA Research Park). As you may know, researching such weapons is rarely if ever done without producing or at least possessing them.

Other jobs are available producing all kinds of weaponry for all kinds of governments at Northrop Grumman. Then there's Teksystems, Pragmatics, Wiser, and many others with fat Pentagon contracts. Employers also recruit here for jobs in Northern Virginia with Concurrent Technologies Corporation, Ogsystems, the Defense Logistics Agency, and many more.

From 2000 to 2010, 161 military contractors in Charlottesville pulled in $919,914,918 through 2,737 contracts from the federal government. Over $8 million of that went to Mr. Jefferson's university, and three-quarters of that to the Darden Business School. And the trend is ever upward. The 161 contractors are found in various industries other than higher education, including nautical system and instrument manufacturing; blind and shade manufacturing; printed circuit assembly; real estate appraisers; engineering services; recreational sports centers; research and development in biotechnology; new car dealers; internet publishing; petroleum merchant wholesalers; and a 2006 contract with Pig Daddy's BBQ.

Piedmont Virginia Community College, which has been good enough to allow our conference to rent its facilities tomorrow and Sunday, has a new program aimed at qualifying more students for military so-called intelligence work.

And Charlottesville is relatively military-free as areas of Virginia go. Were the state of Virginia to ban participation in wars of aggression, weapons sales to brutal dictatorships, and the manufacture of aggressive and illegal weapons, the Military Industrial Complex would be obliged to help itself to many billions of public dollars just to cover the cost of moving operations to the other 49 states or abroad.

I think Shepherd Johnson is here tonight. If you give him a ride through Virginia he'll point out current and former, public and secret, military facilities behind just about every hill. With his help, I've compiled a list of highlights.

The Pentagon and all of its surrounding weapons corporation headquarters are in Virginia. The Chairman of the Joint Chiefs of Staff lives in Quarters Six at Fort Myer in Arlington. The Army and Air Force chiefs of staff live on "Generals Row," also in Fort Myer.

Norfolk is home to the world's largest naval base. NATO is there too. And until last month, so was the United States Joint Forces Command.

The Army maintains major commands in Virginia as well, including the United States Army Combined Arms Support Command at Fort Lee, and the United States Army Training and Doctrine Command at Fort Eustis.

The Air Force has its Air Combat Command at Langley Air Force Base. Langley and Eustis combine to form the Joint Base Langley—Eustis.

The Port of Hampton Roads is a Sea Port of Embarkation (SPOE). Also in Tidewater, Va., is Lamberts Point at Norfolk. So are two large shipyards, found in Newport News (Northrop Grumman) and Portsmouth, there to service the aforementioned largest Naval Base in the world.

But the military is spread throughout the state. Out in Radford is a major munitions plant. Up in Warrenton are four military sites, at least one of them used by the CIA.

Let's not forget the Navy. There are SEAL teams at Little Creek and (team 6) at Dam Neck. These are military forces operating at the secret command of the President.

In Peter's Mountain near Gordonsville, is an AT&T site that many believe the military used to use and probably still does.

The Defense Intelligence Agency used to train "psychic spies" (men who'd stare at goats if they were smart enough to recognize one) at a place in Nelson county called the Monroe Institute.

The Army prepares for war in Virginia at Fort Belvoir, Fort Eustis, Fort Lee, Fort Monroe, Fort Myer, and Fort Story, the Navy at the Navy

Amphibious Base Little Creek, the Naval Surface Warfare Center Dahlgren, Naval Station Norfolk, Norfolk Naval Shipyard, Oceana Naval Air Station (the cause of all that noise pollution in the air at Virginia Beach), and the Naval Weapons Station Yorktown. Meanwhile, the Marines are based in Quantico, as is the FBI Academy.

The NSA is in Chesapeake and just across the West Virginia line. The CIA is at Camp Peary, a.k.a. the Farm, right next to Colonial Williamsburg, where CIA warriors and foreign warriors are trained. The "intelligence community" may not have much intelligence or community, but it has a lot of Virginia real estate, including the Office of the Director of National Intelligence at Tyson's Corner, right next to the National Counter-Terrorism Intelligence Center, which is not far from the headquarters of the Central Intelligence Agency, which has additional offices in the Reston-Herndon area.

Then there's the National Reconnaissance Office in Chantilly, the National Geo-Spatial Intelligence Agency in Springfield, and the U.S. Army Intelligence and Security Command (INSCOM) National Ground Intelligence Center here in Charlottesville (the command is headquartered at Fort Belvoir). The DIA is headquartered at Bolling Air Force Base in Washington, D.C., but has an office building in Clarendon.

The U.S. Marine Corps' so-called "intelligence" activity (and its prison for whistleblowers from Smedley Butler to Bradley Manning) is at Quantico. The Office of Naval Intelligence is located in Suitland, Md., but has a training center located at Dam Neck and known as the Navy Marine Maritime Intelligence Center. And over at Langley Air Force Base is the 480th Intelligence, Surveillance and Reconnaissance Wing. The Virginia National Guard (emphasis on "National") is located all over Virginia, including just down Avon Street. The National Geospatial Intelligence Agency is in Herndon.

Mount Weather in Northern Virginia is set up to host our federal government underground in times of emergency, as was its predecessor across the West Virginia line, the Greenbrier, which now offers tours of Congress's potential second-home underground or let's you rent the space out for parties with "a James Bond, M.A.S.H., or spy theme."

The "private" military corporations in Virginia are legion. Down in Lynchburg, Areva manufactures fuel rods for nuclear reactors. Virginia is home to SAIC, Dyncorp, Mantech, MPRI, and CACI. Xe (Blackwater) is moving to Arlington from its location just across the North Carolina line, a location at which the Virginia Beach Police train, and from which many Blackwater employees commute to live in Virginia Beach. L3 Flight International Aviation is in Newport News.

A company called American Type Culture Collection in Manassas supplied the biological materials for anthrax to Saddam Hussein. And then, of course, when it was clear Iraq had no more anthrax, the pretense that it did was somehow a justification to bomb a nation full of human beings, 99.9 percent of whom had never shaken hands with Donald Rumsfeld.

Then there's Virginia's congressional delegation, which splits its time between Virginia and D.C.

Eisenhower was talked out of saying "military industrial congressional complex," but the meaning nonetheless came through. The Fifth District has flip-flopped between the two big political parties in the last two elections without the slightest impact on its representation in terms of war and military spending. In the midst of this hysterical debate over debt and deficits in Washington this summer the House passed a bigger military spending bill than ever, with almost no comment, and the Senate is working on passing it right now with no notice in the news and not a single outraged rally from the tea party.

We are drawn almost irresistibly to imagining that whatever harm all this military activity does to the world or to our future safety, at the very least it means jobs, it brings money into Virginia from Washington, D.C. And in fact, unlike many states, Virginia does get back more federal money than it puts in. But it puts in a heck of a lot, and gets it back in the least economically beneficial manner possible.

At costofwar.com you can find a number ticking ever upwards showing what the nation has spent thus far on its two largest current wars, both of which a majority of Americans have favored ending for some time now. The figure is now over $1.2 trillion. If you click on Virginia and then Charlottesville, you get $105 million as the amount in taxes that Charlottesville has paid for the wars in Afghanistan and Iraq. That doesn't include future costs of interest, veterans care, the impact on fuel prices, or lost opportunities.

But our wars are a small part of the $1.2 trillion we spend each year on the military. We've spent $1.2 trillion on these two wars over a decade, but we spend $1.2 trillion each and every year on the military. So, each year, Charlottesville dumps $105 million into the military industrial complex. Sure, it gets some of it back. But the City of Charlottesville has a budget of $130 million. I bet the mayor could think of some useful things that could be done with an extra $105 million or even a little bit of it. Federal funding for block grants and other programs is being cut all the time. Don't let anybody tell you military spending is not a local issue. It would be hard to do worse, morally or economically, than handing that money over to the war machine.

Nations with less wealth than ours have higher standards of living, life expectancies, infant survival rates, education levels, vacation days, retirement security, and progress toward green energy. There's no technological reason we can't run everything in this country on clean energy. There's no law of physics preventing us from providing free top-quality education for all who want it from pre-school through college. There's no medical reason we can't have universal health coverage. What's standing in the way is a broken political system, and what is breaking it is in large part the military industrial complex.

Find Your Own Local Military Industrial Complex

Violators of law: http://www.contractormisconduct.org

Government contracts: http://www.governmentcontractswon.com

More on government contracts: http://www.fedspending.org

Still more: http://www.militaryindustrialcomplex.com

The cost of wars: http://costofwar.com

The economic cost of military spending: http://www.peri.umass.edu/fileadmin/pdf/published_study/spending_priorities_PERI.pdf

David Swanson is the author of *When the World Outlawed War, War Is A Lie,* and *Daybreak: Undoing the Imperial Presidency and Forming a More Perfect Union.* He blogs at davidswanson.org and warisacrime.org and works for the online activist organizations rootsaction.org and democrats.com.

Saving the Soul of America: The Eisenhower, Jefferson, King Debate

By Wally Myers

Host: Ladies and gentlemen, citizens and guests, welcome. Recent polls show that two out of three Americans think that our government is going in the wrong direction. Many of us feel confused and conflicted, not knowing what or who to believe. Surrounded by a fog of deceit we long for some beacon of clarity. We feel the storms of war thundering before us, blowing away our rights with the gale winds of fear, and burning down the edifice of our morality with the lightening fires of hate. Yet this human tragedy is as old as war itself; but fought now with weapons newly spawned in the laboratories of devastation.

America must come to realize that the fog of lies and the storms of war are our own creation — our creation of our own destruction. And they have a history. They have a direction. They have a conclusion. To find the clarity to guide us in a different direction we recall the past so as not to repeat its deadly conclusion. We evoke the past to foresee the future, ever mindful that it is we who choose the direction and bring it into being and nurture it.

Tonight we evoke three leaders who have shaped our history. And now, please welcome Dwight David Eisenhower, the Commander of the Allied military forces in World War II Europe and the President who stopped the war in Korea.

Please welcome the sage of Monticello Thomas Jefferson, the author of the Declaration of Independence, Governor of Virginia, Ambassador to France, founder of the University of Virginia, and our third President.

Please welcome the Reverend Doctor Martin Luther King Jr., the leader of the civil rights movement and the pioneer of nonviolent resistance in America.

Thank you, gentlemen, for coming in this, our time of darkness. America appears to be going in the wrong direction, and so we seek your counsel. We will follow the political debate format. So, audience, please hold your applause to the very end. Gentlemen, we call on each of you to tell of the dangers for America that you faced. President Eisenhower, would you begin with the dangers posed by the Military Industrial Complex.

Opening Statements

Eisenhower: Thank you. "~~Until the latest of our world conflicts~~, (Before World War II) the United States had no armaments industry. American makers of plowshares could, with time and as required, make swords as well. But now we can no longer risk emergency improvisation of national defense; we have been compelled to create a permanent armaments industry of vast proportions. Added to this, three and a half million men and women are directly engaged in the defense establishment. We annually spend on military security more than the net income of all United States corporations.

"This conjunction of an immense military establishment and a large arms industry is new in the American experience. The total influence — economic, political, and even spiritual — is felt in every city, every State house, and every office of the Federal government. We recognize the imperative need for this development. Yet we must not fail to comprehend its grave implications. Our toil, resources and livelihood are all involved; so is the very structure of our society.

"In the councils of government, we must guard against the acquisition of unwarranted influence, whether sought or unsought, by the Military Industrial Complex. The potential for the disastrous rise of misplaced power exists and will persist.

"We must never let the weight of this combination endanger our liberties or democratic processes. We should take nothing for granted. Only an alert and knowledgeable citizenry can compel the proper meshing of the huge industrial and military machinery of defense with our peaceful methods and goals, so that security and liberty may prosper together.

"Akin to, and largely responsible for the sweeping changes in our industrial-military posture, has been the technological revolution during recent decades.

"In this revolution, research has become central; it also becomes more formalized, complex, and costly. A steadily increasing share is conducted for, by, or at the direction of, the Federal government.

"The prospect of domination of the nation's scholars by Federal employment, project allocations, and the power of money is ever present and is gravely to be regarded. Yet, in holding scientific research and discovery in respect, as we should, we must also be alert to the equal and opposite danger that public policy could itself become the captive of a scientific technological elite.

"It is the task of statesmanship to mold, to balance, and to integrate these and other forces, new and old, within the principles of our democratic system — ever aiming toward the supreme goals of our free society."[1]

Host: Thank you President Eisenhower. It appears that the danger of misplaced power has grown more grave. In our time the Military Industrial Complex is in charge — bribing statesmen, financing academic research, and perverting technological innovation by waging more and more wars for higher and higher profits.

President Jefferson, as one of the founding fathers, we are interested in your perspective on the dangers that faced America at its beginning.

Thomas Jefferson: Thank you all for being here tonight. "Men by their constitutions are naturally divided into two parties: those who fear and distrust the people and wish to draw all powers from them into the hands of the higher classes, namely the aristocrats; and those who identify themselves with the people, have confidence in them, cherish and consider them as the most honest and safe, namely the democrats."[2]

"What has destroyed liberty and the rights of man in every government which has ever existed under the Sun is the generalizing and concentrating all cares and powers into one body, no matter whether of the autocrats of Russia or France, or the aristocrats ~~of a Venetian Senate~~ (within our own borders, or of our Federal Government.)"[3]

"(In my time) our country ~~is now~~ (was already) taking so steady a course as to show by what road it will pass to destruction, ~~to wit~~ (namely): by consolidation of power first, and then corruption, its necessary consequence."[4]

"(To avoid that) I wish, ~~therefore,~~ to see maintained that wholesome distribution of powers established by the constitution for the limitation of government with foreign concerns limited to the Federal Government and home concerns to the States. Never should we see all offices transferred to Washington, where, further withdrawn from the eyes of the people they may more secretly be bought and sold as at market."[5]

"(Furthermore,) I hope we shall crush in its birth the aristocracy of our moneyed corporations which dare already to challenge our government to a trial of strength and bid defiance to the laws of our country."[6]

Host: Thank you President Jefferson. It appears that the race for the consolidation of power continues to tear apart the restraints of the Constitution. Even business has turned into a battlefield with powerful corporations devouring their competition. In the same manner our news has been consolidated to a point where our democratic institutions are in peril.

Jefferson: Newspapers, why "truth itself becomes ~~suspicious~~ (suspect) by being put into that polluted vehicle. (I'm afraid that) advertisements contain the only truths to be relied on in a newspaper."[7]

Host: Not any more, even advertizing is a source of mind control. Technology has now grown to a point where we can record and replay events. But even that advancement has failed to protect truth. Unfortunately the art of deceit has grown into the science of propaganda. And those who profit from deceit are free to use that dark science.

Rev. King, as the winner of the Nobel Peace Prize, we are interested in your thoughts about our involvement in so many wars.

Martin Luther King: (I am honored to be here. I believe that) "every man lives in two realms, the internal and the external. The internal is that realm of spiritual <u>ends</u> expressed in art, literature, morals, and religion. The external is that complex of devices, techniques, mechanisms, and instrumentalities by <u>means</u> of which we live. Our problem today is that we have allowed the internal to become lost in the external. We have allowed the *means by* which we live to outdistance the *ends for* which we live. So much of modern life can be summarized in that arresting dictum of the poet Thoreau: 'Improved means to an unimproved end.' This is the serious predicament, the deep and haunting problem confronting modern man. If we are to survive today, our moral and spiritual 'lag' must be eliminated. Enlarged material powers spell enlarged peril if there is not proportionate growth of the soul. When the 'without' of man's nature subjugates the 'within,' dark storm clouds begin to form in the world."[8]

"~~It will~~ (To establish that balance within politics we must) look across the seas and see individual capitalists of the West investing huge sums of money in Asia, Africa, and South America, only to take the profits out with no concern for the social betterment of the countries, and say, 'This is not just.' ~~It will~~ (We must) look at our alliance with the landed gentry of Latin America and say, 'This is not just.' The Western arrogance of feeling that it has everything to teach others and nothing to learn from them is not just. A true revolution of values will lay hands on the world order and say of war, 'This way of settling differences is not just.' This business of burning human beings with napalm, of filling our nation's homes with orphans and widows, of injecting poisonous drugs of hate into the veins of peoples normally humane, of sending men home from dark and bloody battlefields physically handicapped and psychologically deranged, cannot be reconciled with wisdom, justice, and love. A nation that continues year after year to spend more money on military defense than on programs of social uplift is approaching spiritual death."[9]

Host: Thank you Rev. King. The storm clouds of war darken with the growing collusion between the government and corporations. In the name of security, aggression is called defense; and exploitation is called national interest while the cries for justice of an impoverished world remain silenced by corporate news. Gentlemen, thank you all for your opening statements. Please enter into a conversation with each other.

Conversation

Jefferson: General Eisenhower, you spoke of the necessity of vast arms industries conjoined with an immense military establishment. And you hope that statesmen can balance this with democracy and freedom. As I mentioned in my opening statement that I too "feared for our government due to the strength and defiance of corporations" and that was in 1816. I imagine that arms industries would be vastly more dangerous. As for an immense military establishment, even "a standing army endangers our lives and liberties."[10]

You say that we can no longer risk emergency improvisation for national defense; rather we require this Military Industrial Complex. I see that "our resources will be exhausted whenever a speck of war is visible in our horizon, instead of being reserved for ~~what is really to take place~~ (real needs.)"[11]

Gentlemen, "liberty is dangerous." We must be brave and confident that we can meet our security needs. Dr. Franklin said it well, "Those who would give up essential liberty to purchase a little temporary safety deserve neither liberty nor safety."

Eisenhower: The "technological revolution is largely responsible for the necessity for the Military Industrial Complex" within the present world structures. On the other hand, "I hate war as only a soldier who has lived it can, only as one who has seen its brutality, its futility, its stupidity."[12]

And like President Jefferson, I recognize the futility and waste of war. "That every gun that is made, every warship launched, every rocket fired signifies, in the final sense, a theft from those who hunger and are not fed, those who are cold and are not clothed.

"This world in arms is not spending money alone. It is spending the sweat of its laborers, the genius of its scientists, and the hopes of its children. This is not a way of life at all, in any true sense. Under the cloud of threatening war, it is humanity hanging from a cross of iron."[13]

King: (I have felt that connection.) "A few years ago there was a shining moment in the struggle against poverty. It seemed as if there was a real promise of hope for the poor — both black and white — through the Poverty Program. Then came the build-up in Vietnam, and I watched the program broken and eviscerated as if it were some idle political play thing of a society gone mad on war, and I knew that America would never invest the necessary funds or energies in rehabilitation of its poor so long as Vietnam continued to draw men and skills and money like some demonic, destructive suction tube. So I was increasingly compelled to see the war as an enemy of the poor and to attack it as such."[14]

Jefferson: "All men know that war is a losing game to both parties."[15] It is the greatest scourge of mankind. It not only robs the present but the future generations. If it were incumbent on every generation to pay its own debts as it goes, that would prevent one-half the wars of the world. I predict future happiness for Americans if ~~they~~ (we) can prevent the government from wasting the labors of the people under the pretense of ~~taking care of~~ (protecting) them.

King: Gentlemen, "we will not build a peaceful world by following a negative path. It is not enough to say 'We must not wage war.' It is necessary to love peace and sacrifice for it."[16] President Eisenhower, what is your peace plan?

Eisenhower: I think "there are a few clear precepts which govern the conduct of world affairs. First: No people on earth can be held, as a people, to be enemy, for all humanity shares the common hunger for peace and fellowship and justice. Second: No nation's security and well-being can be lastingly achieved in isolation but only in effective cooperation with fellow-nations. Third: Any nation's right to form a government and an economic system of its own choosing is inalienable. Fourth: Any nation's attempt to dictate to other nations their form of government is indefensible. And fifth: A nation's hope of lasting peace cannot be firmly based upon any race in armaments but rather upon just relations and honest understanding with all other nations. I believe that these principles define a way toward true peace."[17]

King: I agree with those principles; but, did your administration live by them? Didn't you treat the communist as enemies? Didn't you try to isolate them? Did you allow Vietnam to choose its government or its economic system? Did you restrict the armaments race?

Eisenhower: I believe those principles would have lead to true peace; but, "the Soviet government held a vastly different vision of the future. In the world of its design, security was to be found, not in mutual trust and mutual aid but in force: huge armies, subversion, and rule of neighbor nations.

The goal was power superiority at all costs. Security was to be sought by denying it to all others. The result has been tragic for the world and, for the Soviet Union, it has also been ironic."[18]

Host: Fifty tragic years later the irony falls on us, for now our government has taken the place of the Soviets — by our security at all costs with military expenditures almost as large as all other nations combined, by our superiority with over 700 military bases in over 120 countries around the world, by our dominance from economic coercion, and by our subversion with covert mercenaries. President Eisenhower, America has become the new Soviet Union. President Jefferson, America has become the new British Empire.

King: "Gentlemen, we cannot achieve peaceful ends by violent means. We need a new method to resolve our conflicts." Nonviolent resistance is a new political dynamic pioneered by Mohandas Gandhi to attain independence from Great Britain; and used in the Civil Rights movement here in America.

"In a real sense nonviolence seeks to redeem the spiritual and moral lag that I spoke of earlier as the chief dilemma of modern man. It seeks to secure moral ends through moral means. Nonviolence is a powerful and just weapon. Indeed, it is a weapon unique in history, which cuts without wounding and ennobles the man who wields it.

"The nonviolent resisters can summarize their message in the following simple terms: we will take direct action against injustice despite the failure of governmental and other official agencies to act first. We will not obey unjust laws or submit to unjust practices. We will do this peacefully, openly, cheerfully because our aim is to persuade. We adopt the means of nonviolence because our end is a community at peace with itself. We will try to persuade with our words, but if our words fail, we will try to persuade with our acts. We will always be willing to talk and seek fair compromise, but we are ready to suffer when necessary and even risk our lives to become witnesses to truth as we see it.

"I believe in this method because I think it is the only way to reestablish a broken community. It is the method which seeks to implement the just law by appealing to the conscience of the great decent majority who through blindness, fear, pride, and irrationality have allowed their consciences to sleep."[19]

Jefferson: Reverend King, I'm shocked! Are you telling me that India broke free of Great Britain without a fight! That the American Colonies could have had independence without the Revolutionary War. With due respect, sir, I do not believe it.

Host: President Jefferson, a lot of progress has been made in the two hundred years since your presidency. As Rev. King said, nonviolent resistance is a new political dynamic pioneered by Mohandas Gandhi beginning in South Africa in 1906. He later used it to attain Indian independence from Great Britain; and it was Rev. King who used it in the Civil Rights movement here in America, which led to desegregation in the United States. These principles of peace have succeeded in so many contexts as to make war obsolete.

King: "Mahatma Gandhi embodied in his life certain universal principles that are inherent in the moral structure of the universe, and these principles are as inescapable as the law of gravitation."[20]

Jefferson: Rev. King, I have a dream. In my version of the Declaration of Independence, I deplored slavery as a "cruel war against human nature itself, violating it's most sacred rights of life and liberty". That entire section was stricken from the Declaration.

So now I am overjoyed that we can finally live by the self-evident truth that all men are created equal. But I am most intrigued by this method of nonviolent resistance for it points to a way of revolution without, as you say, wounding, as well as reuniting a community broken by injustice.

(Gentlemen,) "Experience hath shown that even under the best forms of government those entrusted with power have, in time, and by slow operations, perverted it into tyranny. When the Law of the majority ceases to be acknowledged, there government ends, the Law of the strongest takes its place, and life and property are his who can take them."[21]

"Whenever any form of government becomes destructive of life, liberty, and the pursuit of happiness, it is the Right of the People to alter or to abolish it, and to institute new Government."[22]

King: (President Jefferson, in 1945 the country of Vietnam began their Declaration of Independence by quoting yours,) "All men are created equal. They are endowed by their Creator with certain inalienable rights; among these are Life, Liberty, and the pursuit of Happiness."

(Our country ended up going to war with Vietnam. This shows that) "our nation has taken the role of those who make peaceful revolution impossible by refusing to give up the privileges and the pleasures that come from the immense profits of overseas investment.

"I am convinced that if we are to get on the right side of the world revolution, we as a nation must undergo a radical revolution of values. We must rapidly begin to shift from a 'thing-oriented' society to a 'person-oriented' society. When machines and computers, profit motives and property rights are considered more important than people, the giant triplets of racism, extreme materialism, and militarism are incapable of being conquered.

"Our only hope today lies in our ability to recapture the revolutionary spirit and go out into a sometimes hostile world declaring eternal hostility to poverty, racism and militarism. With this powerful commitment we shall boldly challenge the status quo and unjust mores."[23]

Eisenhower: (As for militarism), "if men can develop weapons that are so terrifying as to make the thought of global war include almost a sentence for suicide, you would think that man's intelligence and his comprehension... would include also his ability to find a peaceful solution.

"The hunger for peace is too great, the hour in history too late, for any government to mock men's hopes with mere words and promises and gestures."[24]

"I like to believe that people in the long run are going to do more to promote peace than our governments. Indeed, I think that people want peace so much that one of these days; governments had better get out of the way and let them have it."[25]

Host: Gentlemen, thank you all for your deep insights. It is now time that each of you give a closing statement. First President Jefferson, then Rev. King, and ending with President Eisenhower.

Closing Statements

Jefferson: Rev. King points to a lag where moral and spiritual ends are overwhelmed by material and technological powers. I believe it was the consolidation of religious powers that caused that lag. "For it was but a short time that elapsed after the death of the great reformer of the Jewish religion before his principles were departed from by those who professed to be his special servants, and perverted them into an engine for enslaving mankind: that the purest system of morals ever before preached to man has been adulterated and sophisticated by artificial constructions, into a mere contrivance to filch wealth and power to themselves, ~~that~~ (when) rational men ~~not being~~ (were not) able to swallow their impious heresies, (the religious aristocracy) in order to force ~~them~~ (their heresies) down their throats, ~~they~~ raise the hue and cry of infidelity, while they themselves are the greatest obstacles to the advancement of the real doctrines of Jesus, and do in fact constitute the real Anti-Christ."[26] (Thus the spiritual lag arises from moral intolerance enforced by the abuse of religious power.)

King: "We can no longer afford to worship the God of hate or bow before the altar of retaliation. The oceans of history are made turbulent by the ever-rising tides of hate. History is cluttered with the wreckage of nations and individuals that pursued this self-defeating path of hate. This means that more and more our loyalties must become ecumenical rather than sectional. We must now give an overriding loyalty to mankind as a whole in order to preserve the best in our individual societies. This call for a worldwide fellowship that lifts neighborly concern beyond one's tribe, race, class, and nation is in reality a call for an all-embracing and unconditional love for all men. Love is the key to the solution of the problems of the world."[27]

Eisenhower: "We pray that peoples of all faiths, all races, all nations, may have their great human needs satisfied; that those now denied opportunity shall come to enjoy it to the full; that all who yearn for freedom may experience its spiritual blessings; that those who have freedom will understand, also, its heavy responsibilities; that all who are insensitive to the needs of others will learn charity; that the scourges of poverty, disease and ignorance will be made to disappear from the earth, and that, in the goodness of time, all peoples will come to live together in a peace guaranteed by the binding force of mutual respect and love."[28]

King: Amen.

Host: Thank you gentlemen. And so we, citizens of now, face their diagnosis of dangers for our country, our culture, even our character.

For Eisenhower the danger is the accumulation of power by the collusion between the military, industry and government to such a degree that war becomes suicide; his medicine — we the people, not the government, must free each other from that cross of iron that is war and restrain a government that makes war inevitable. But what if the government will not yield to the people's hunger for peace? Eisenhower warns the government that it better get out of the way and let people have peace.

For Jefferson the danger is the accumulation of power in government and religion; his medicine — a revolution of institutions that keeps pace with our progress of knowledge and protects human rights for everyone, worldwide revolutions to share power and constrain its abuses.

For King the danger is that our consciences are deluded by fear, hate, and extreme materialism into believing that violence is the best way to settle conflicts. His medicine — to save the soul of America we need a revolution of values with a wisdom that we depend on each other, with a justice that rejects profits at the expense of human needs, and with an all embracing and unconditional love for humanity.

And so, citizens of the world, are we to be paralyzed by fear and let these festering dangers threaten the entire world or will we follow Rev. King's lead and use the powerful force of nonviolence, "and recapture the revolutionary spirit and go out into a sometimes hostile world declaring eternal ~~hostility~~ (resistance) to poverty, racism and militarism and boldly challenge the status quo and unjust mores?"

It is our choice — the cross of iron that is war, or peace guaranteed by the binding force of unconditional respect and love.

Thank you, gentlemen

And thank you, audience.

Wally Myers is the President of the Eisenhower Chapter of Veterans For Peace, and Vice-Chair of North Carolina Peace Action. His life's journey to peace has taken him to live with the Hopi Tribe (the peaceful people) and to convert to Buddhism. He has written and performed the role of General Smedley Butler (*War is a Racket*) throughout North Carolina.

An ICBM Launch on World Peace Day

By Ann Wright

You certainly would not know it was World Peace Day on September 21st by actions of the United States.

In addition to the continuing wars in Iraq and Afghanistan, on World Peace Day, in violation of its commitment to disarmament under the Nuclear Non-Proliferation Treaty (NPT), the United States will fire an Intercontinental Ballistic Missile (ICBM) from Vandenberg Air Force Base, California over Hawaii and the Pacific Missile Range tracking facility (PMRF) to crash into the Pacific Ocean near Kwajalein in the Marshall Islands.

The Marshall Islands are the same islands that the United States blew up in the 1950s and 1960s in the nuclear and hydrogen bomb tests from which Marshall Islanders are still suffering from radiation sickness and unable to return to the radioactive islands.

The expansion of the U.S. missile "defense" system is causing dangerous repercussions around the world, making hotspots even hotter — from China and North Korea to Turkey, Israel and Iran.

Pacific Missile Range in Hawaii Expanded for the Aegis Missile Test Complex — Testing to Kill or to Defend?

On Kauai, Hawaii, the Hawaii congressional delegation continues to bring home the bacon, the pork barrel projects that include expansion of the Pacific Missile Range Facility. The latest project is the construction of the Aegis Ashore Missile Defense Test Complex that will provide testing and evaluation of the systems.

U.S. Senator from Hawaii Daniel Inouye said at the groundbreaking ceremony for the new missile test complex on August 29th, "There are people in the world who would harm and kill us. We are not testing to kill, but to defend. ... I pray the product of testing will not be used, but will be a deterrent for those who would harm us."

Construction of the Aegis Missile Defense Test Complex in Hawaii will be completed in 2013. The Aegis Ballistic Missile Defense System is used on 81 naval ships throughout the world with more than 25 additional Aegis-equipped ships planned or under contract. There are six naval Aegis-equipped ships home-ported at Pearl Harbor on Oahu, Hawaii.

Ballistic Missile Defense Systems to be installed in Romania and Poland

The Aegis system is the sea-based component of the Ballistic Missile Defense System under development by the Missile Defense Agency which integrates with submarines, surface ships as well as the U.S. Army and Air Force missiles. The U.S. will install the Ballistic Missile Defense system in Romania in 2015 and in Poland in 2018. The systems that will be sent to Romania and Poland were tested in Hawaii at the Pacific Missile Range Facility.

Jeju Island, South Korea Protests Against The Aegis Missile System And Construction of A Naval Base To Homeport Aegis Destroyers

On Jeju Island, South Korea, citizens have been protesting for four years the construction of a new naval base that will homeport Aegis missile destroyers as a part of the U.S. missile defense system. On September 2, hundreds of mainland South Koreans flew in "peace planes" to join Jeju Island activists in a major confrontation with government forces.

On the same day, more than 1,000 South Korean riot police from the mainland descended upon citizens of all ages who were blockading crews from access to the naval base construction site on Jeju Island. At least 50 protestors were arrested, including villagers, Catholic priests, college students, visiting artists and citizen journalists. Several were wounded and hospitalized.

However, back in Hawaii, not all who live on Kauai agree with the aims of the Aegis program and its effects on other countries. In a Kauai Garden Island newspaper op-ed on September 4, Koohan Paik, a Hawaii citizen activist of Korean heritage observed,

> There happens to be a very strong connection between Jeju's current troubles and business-as-usual on the Garden Isle (Kauai). You see, the primary purpose of Jeju's unwanted base is to port Aegis destroyer warships. And it is right here, at Kauai's Pacific Missile Range Facility, that all product testing takes place for the Aegis missile manufacturers. ... So it is no surprise that the tenacious, democracy-loving Koreans have been protesting again — this time for over four years, non-stop, day and night. They are determined to prevent construction of a huge military base on S. Korea's Jeju Island that will cement over a reef in an area so precious it contains three UNESCO World Heritage Sites.[29]

Turkey Agrees to Host Missile Defense Radar Installations — Data Not to Be Shared With Israel

Halfway around the planet in another hotspot where the U.S. is pushing the missile defense system, on September 2, the same day it denounced UN

Secretary General Ban Ki-Moon's four-person committee's report on the Gaza flotilla and then announced sanctions on Israel for murdering eight Turkish citizens and one American citizen on the 2010 Gaza flotilla, Turkey also revealed that it had reached agreement to host radar installations as part of the American-sponsored NATO "missile defense" program.

Press reports indicate that as part of the deal, the U.S. acceded to a Turkish demand that data from the Turkish-hosted radars not be shared with Israel.

Turkey played the odds that it has increasingly greater value to the United States in the eastern Mediterranean region than does Israel, which is increasingly a strategic and political burden to the United States.

The upcoming United Nations session with its discussion on statehood for Palestine will again put the United States in the miniscule number of nations that will vote against Palestinian initiatives — Israel and those whom the U.S. pays through the Compact of Free Association to vote with it: Micronesia, the Marshall Islands, and Palau.

America's Belligerent Actions On World Peace Day And The Nobel Peace Prize

As America shoves World Peace Day aside with its launch on September 21 of the ICBM missile, it brings to mind President Obama's war speech upon accepting, only eight months into office, a Nobel Prize for Peace for having done little for peace, except to defeat John McCain for the presidency. Obama spoke at length of the necessity of war to make the world a peaceful place.

In this vein, it makes perfect sense to the Obama administration to launch a missile on World Peace Day, a missile for peace, no doubt!!

But it makes NO sense to me and to, I suspect, hundreds of millions of people around the world. I hope on World Peace Day, the citizens of the world will let the Obama administration know of their disgust for this act of intimidation and disrespect for the planet!

Ann Wright, first as a military officer and then as a diplomat, spent 35 years serving the U.S. government. She rose to public prominence in March, 2003, when she became one of only three State Department officials to resign in opposition to the U.S. invasion of Iraq. Since resigning, she has been a persistent, committed anti-war activist, and co-author of *Dissent: Voices of Conscience.*

Jeju Island, South Korea
By Ann Wright

On August 24, 2011, sirens wailed for citizens to come to the main gate of the Naval Base in Kang Jeong Village on Jeju Island, South Korea where the Korean Navy wants to continue construction of a naval base for 18 ships and two submarines in an area that will destroy a pristine shoreline and endanger marine life. Local villagers and activists from the mainland of South Korea have struggled for five years to prevent the construction of the base.

Sirens Signal an Emergency — The Mayor And Four Activists Are Arrested

The siren sounds like a tsunami warning signaling an emergency. And that is what it is — an emergency with five activists arrested, including the mayor of the village of Kang Jeong at a huge construction crane on the base. The crane had been brought onto the naval base several years ago in the middle of the night in the Navy's attempt to escape the wrath of the villagers. It is a huge crane weighing 250 tons and it was brought over a bridge that can hold only 50 tons. The mayor of the village is intent on not allowing the illegal crane to be operated. He wants it dismantled and taken away. The mayor, the peace camp cook, and three activists who came racing to the aid of the mayor were also arrested.

Hearing the emergency siren, 60 people quickly arrived to block the main gate of the base with trucks, cars and their own bodies. Others raced to the back entrance to the base to block it. Many were local farmers who had come directly from their fields of tangerine trees and from hot houses where they grow vegetables. They had jumped on their motor scooters to answer the emergency call, not bothering to change from their farm work clothes and wide brimmed work hats and rubber boots. Text messages were flying explaining the situation and directing people to go to the gates of the base. Tweets were alerting solidarity activists around the world to the emergency. An international peace camp had been held here the previous week and those activists would want to know about the situation.

At the main gate, ten citizens locked chains around their necks and around each other and sat directly in front of a police line that had been placed in front of the gate. One citizen locked a chain around his neck and directly onto a truck that was blocking the entrance to the base.

Crowd Stops Police Car And Surrounds The Police

Four of those arrested had been moved from the naval base to the local jail by the time the entrances were blocked. Only the mayor remained inside the base. After several hours, the crowd spotted a police car attempting to leave the base by another entrance, and inside was the mayor. The crowd chased the police car on foot, caught it and put their bodies in the way so the driver could not move forward. Cars and trucks quickly followed successfully blocking the police car.

About 60 police reinforcements with batons and shields but no weapons pushed their way past the activists and formed a protective ring around the police car. The police appeared to be new recruits who were doing their obligatory government service. They were very young and looked very scared.

Very quickly the citizens encircled the police and the police car and sat down. From time to time, the police would attempt to move the crowd out of the way, but the citizens would stand up and move directly in front of the police shields. Women, old and young alike, were on the front lines refusing to let the police move and pushing back furiously.

Remarkably, the police did not use their batons on the demonstrators. One person told me that the police on the island are very aware of the history of Jeju Island in which over 30,000 persons, many of whom wanted their country unified after World War II, were massacred by the right wing government of Sighman Rhee that considered them communist sympathizers. Any people found farther inland than two miles were considered guerillas and were hunted down in a scorched earth policy by military and right wing youth brought in from the mainland of Korea.

Many of the police who live on the island had relatives that were killed in what is called the April 3 massacre that lasted over 18 months (1947-48). The small island police force does not want to be seen as heavy handed. Because of this attitude, the national government last month heavy-handedly sent 1,500 mainland police to Jeju Island to use water cannons and tear gas against those challenging the construction of the naval base.

The stalemate of citizens encircling and trapping the police lasted for five hours and took on a community event atmosphere. The fiery wife of the mayor stood on the top of a vehicle and urged the crowd to protect her husband, and then dived into the police line from on top of the vehicle! A huge sound system on the top of another van blasted favorite protest songs including one that told the story of the April 3 massacre. The nightly 8 p.m. candlelight vigil was held in the road with candles placed in front of the police line. Friends sat in small groups talking about the next steps in preventing further construction of the naval base.

Activists Chain Themselves To A Van

Another scene was unfolding back at the main gate. As the police rushed from the main gate up the road to protect the police car carrying the mayor, the way was left open for a protest van to move onto the entrance of the bridge just past the main gate, blocking one of the main roads on the island.

Citizens with chains surged to the vehicle and locked themselves onto the undercarriage of the van. A smaller group of police then surrounded the van, but after several hours of watching the group chained to the van, they got tired and sat down along the sides of the bridge.

Police Double-Cross

By midnight a deal had been struck. The mayor and four others would be released after making an appearance at the Seogwipo Police Station/jail. The crowds slowly opened so the police and the police car could leave. Not all the citizens agreed to the deal, thinking that once the mayor left in the police car, their leverage was gone.

And they were right. Fifty citizens slept all the rest of the night on the sidewalk outside the jail waiting for the appearance of the mayor and the other activists — to no avail! The police violated their agreement, and at 2 p.m. all were still in jail.

Another Emergency

In the meantime, another emergency siren blared this morning, calling people to the construction site again. A crane operator was moving some heavy equipment. Citizens raced to the site and lay down in front of the crane where they still are.

Here goes the siren again — another emergency in the lives of the citizens of Kang Jeong to save their lovely land.

Ann Wright, first as a military officer and then as a diplomat, spent 35 years serving the U.S. government. She rose to public prominence in March, 2003, when she became one of only three State Department officials to resign in opposition to the U.S. invasion of Iraq. Since resigning, she has been a persistent, committed anti-war activist, and co-author of *Dissent: Voices of Conscience*.

CIA's Push for Drone War Driven by Internal Needs

By Gareth Porter

When David Petraeus walks into the Central Intelligence Agency Tuesday, he will be taking over an organization whose mission has changed in recent years from gathering and analyzing intelligence to waging military campaigns through drone strikes in Pakistan, as well as in Yemen and Somalia.

But the transformation of the CIA did not simply follow the expansion of the drone war in Pakistan to its present level. CIA Director Michael Hayden lobbied hard for that expansion at a time when drone strikes seemed like a failed experiment.

The reason Hayden pushed for a much bigger drone war, it now appears, is that it had already created a whole bureaucracy in the anticipation of such a war.

During 2010, the CIA "drone war" in Pakistan killed as many as 1,000 people a year, compared with the roughly 2,000 a year officially estimated to have been killed by the SOF "night raids" in Afghanistan, according to a report in the Sep. 1 *Washington Post*.[30]

A CIA official was quoted by the *Post* as saying that the CIA had become "one hell of a killing machine", before quickly revising the phrase to "one hell of an operational tool".

The shift in the CIA mission's has been reflected in the spectacular growth of its Counter-Terrorism Center (CTC) from 300 employees in September

2001 to about 2,000 people today — 10 percent of the agency's entire workforce, according to the Post report. The agency's analytical branch, which had been previously devoted entirely to providing intelligence assessments for policymakers, has been profoundly affected.

More than one-third of the personnel in the agency's analytical branch are now engaged wholly or primarily in providing support to CIA operations, according to senior agency officials cited by the Post. And nearly two-thirds of those are analyzing data used by the CTC drone war staff to make decisions on targeting.

Some of that shift of internal staffing to support of the drone has followed the rise in the number of drone strikes in Pakistan since mid-2008, but the CIA began to lay the institutional basis for a bigger drone campaign well before that.

Crucial to understanding the role of internal dynamics in CIA decisions on the issue is the fact that the drone campaign in Pakistan started off very badly. During the four years from 2004 through 2007, the CIA carried out a total of only 12 drone strikes in Pakistan, all supposedly aimed at identifiable high-value targets of Al-Qaeda and its affiliates.

The George W. Bush administration's policy on use of drones was cautious in large part because the President of Pakistan, Gen. Pervez Musharraf, was considered such a reliable ally that the administration was reluctant to take actions that would risk destabilizing his regime.

Thus relatively tight constraints were imposed on the CIA in choosing targets for drone strikes. They were only to be used against known "high-value" officials of Al-Qaeda and their affiliates in Pakistan, and the CIA had to have evidence that no civilians would be killed as a result of the strike.

Those first 12 strikes killed only three identifiable Al-Qaeda or Pakistani Taliban figures. But despite the prohibition against strikes that would incur "collateral damage", the same strikes killed a total of 121 civilians, as revealed by a thorough analysis of news media reports. A single strike against a madrassa on Oct. 26, 2006, that killed 80 local students accounted for two-thirds of the total of civilian casualties.

Despite that disastrous start, however, the CIA had quickly become deeply committed internally to building a major program around the drone war. In 2005, the agency had created a career track in targeting for the drone program for analysts in the intelligence directorate, the Sept. 2nd *Post* article revealed.

That decision meant that analysts who chose to specialize in targeting for CIA drone operations were promised that they could stay within that specialty and get promotions throughout their careers. Thus the agency had made far-reaching commitments to its own staff in the expectation that the drone war would grow far beyond the three strikes a year and that it would continue indefinitely.

By 2007, the agency realized that, in order to keep those commitments, it had to get the White House to change the rules by relaxing existing restrictions on drone strikes.

That's when Hayden began lobbying President George W. Bush to dispense with the constraints limiting the targeting for drone attacks, according to the account in *New York Times* reporter David Sanger's book *The Inheritance*. Hayden asked for permission to carry out strikes against houses or cars merely on the basis of behavior that matched a "pattern of life" associated with Al-Qaeda or other groups.

In January 2008, Bush took an unidentified first step toward the loosening of the requirements that Hayden sought, but most of the restrictions on drone strikes remained in place. In the first six months of 2008, only four strikes were carried out.

In mid-2008, however, Director of National Intelligence Mike McConnell returned from a May 2008 trip to Pakistan determined to prove that the Pakistani military was covertly supporting Taliban insurgents — especially the Haqqani network — who were gaining momentum in Afghanistan.

A formal assessment by McConnell's staff making that case was produced in June and sent to the White House and other top officials, according to Sanger. That forced Bush, who had been praising Musharraf as an ally against the Taliban, to do something to show that he was being tough on the Pakistani military as well as on the Afghan insurgents who enjoyed safe havens in northwest Pakistan.

Bush wanted the drone strikes to focus primarily on the Afghan Taliban targets rather than Al-Qaeda and its Pakistani Taliban allies. And according to Sanger's account, Bush quickly removed all of the previous requirements for accurate intelligence on specific high-value targets and for assurances against civilian casualties.

Released from the original constraints on the drone program, the CIA immediately increased the level of drone strikes in the second half of 2008 to between four and five per month on average.

As Bob Woodward's account in *Obama Wars* of internal discussions in the early weeks of the Barack Obama White House shows, there were serious doubts from the beginning that it could actually defeat Al- Qaeda.

But Leon Panetta, Obama's new CIA director, was firmly committed to the drone war. He continued to present it to the public as a strategy to destroy Al-Qaeda, even though he knew the CIA was now striking mainly Afghan Taliban and their allies, not Al-Qaeda.

In his first press conference on Feb. 25, 2009, Panetta, in an indirect but obvious reference to the drone strikes, said that the effort to destabilize Al-Qaeda and destroy its leadership "have been successful".

Under Panetta, the rate of drone strikes continued throughout 2009 at the same accelerated pace as in the second half of 2008. And in 2010 the number of strikes more than doubled from 53 in 2009 to 118.

The CIA finally had the major drone campaign it had originally anticipated.

Two years ago, Petraeus appeared to take a somewhat skeptical view of drone strikes in Pakistan. In a secret assessment as CENTCOM commander on May 27, 2009, which was leaked to the *Washington Post*, Petraeus warned that drone strikes were fueling anti-U.S. sentiments in Pakistan.

Now, however, Petraeus's personal view of the drone war may no longer be relevant. The CIA's institutional interests in continuing the drone war may have become so commanding that no director could afford to override those interests on the basis of his own analysis of how the drone strikes affect U.S. interests.

Gareth Porter is an investigative historian and journalist special-izing in U.S. national security policy. The paperback edition of his latest book, *Perils of Dominance: Imbalance of Power and the Road to War in Vietnam*, was published in 2006.

II. JOBS OR WARS

Pitfalls of Military Keynesianism

By Dave Shreve

*"You cannot qualify war in harsher terms than I will. War is cruelty
and you cannot refine it; and those who brought war into our country
deserve all the curses and maledictions a people can pour out."*
—William Tecumseh Sherman, September 1864

When departing President Dwight Eisenhower warned of the "grave
implications" of the "military industrial complex" in his January
17, 1961 valedictory, two ideas appeared paramount. The first stemmed
from Ike's ongoing concern for fiscal soundness and reflected his belief that
an influential and emasculating cadre of newly permanent war contractors
(and a university-based "technological elite" who worked increasingly on
their behalf) threatened federal budget balance and what Ike implied to be
a critical *economic* balance, "between the private and the public economy."
To many of his Republican cohorts, unable to summon the leavening of
Bryce Harlow's or Ralph Williams' speechwriting, this secondary peril
of imbalance was "creeping socialism," the surpassing domestic threat to
which they devoted great political and rhetorical energy.[31] The second of
the key ideas in the outgoing president's address mirrored his belief that
the increasingly outsized budgetary demands of this "complex" threatened
also "the material assets of our grandchildren" and, implicitly, in his eyes,
the nation's ability to foster "human betterment." Here, Ike offered little
novelty, for he was merely repackaging the "debt as a burden on our
grandchildren" mythology, fought and subdued by Alexander Hamilton
in the earliest days of the American republic, but which is also nearly as
old as civilization itself and as resistant to a contradictory reality as any
longstanding fable.

Though Eisenhower had not just imagined the rise of such a "complex," which *was* increasingly powerful and a source of no small number of economic weaknesses, his general economic concern made little sense, betraying his limited knowledge of economic theory and of the sound policy that might flow even from the most superficial command of its most basic precepts. Put another way, Ike's inability to understand Keynesian economic policy transformed his cautionary address into a treatise on problems that did not exist and which were unlikely to emerge, but which also glossed over the real peril of a military industrial complex and the sub-par, clumsily designed political economy that it helped reinforce.

The most critical error was the 34th president's conception of deficit spending and public debt. In what remains a very common and unfortunately compelling misjudgment, Eisenhower simply failed to understand that public debt has to be viewed most generally on two critical dimensions, neither of which resembled anything within his ill-formed conception of sound economic policy.

On the first, it represents the assets demanded by a capitalist economy, as a safe productive outlet for the savings it generates. It is precisely this role — creating assets based on the full faith and credit of an entire nation and its economy — that Hamilton envisioned as the bulwark of the new nation, and which moved him to call the federal debt our "national blessing."

On the second, it is the vehicle by which *essential* redistribution — without which capitalism cannot prosper or survive — can be transmitted sufficiently enough to provide both an economically critical level of public goods and services and a requisite level of aggregate demand. As Keynes demonstrated, a fiscal policy constructed on progressive taxation always did *some* of this essential building of aggregate demand — by taxing at higher rates those who tended to *save* more of their income, and by spending in a way that bestowed the greatest benefit on those who tended to *spend* more

of their income.[32] Regular but varying doses of deficit spending ensured —
along with a regime of low long-term interest rates — that this bolstering
of aggregate demand via fiscal policy redistribution would be sufficient to
deliver full employment (see Figure 1).

The Keynesian Levers

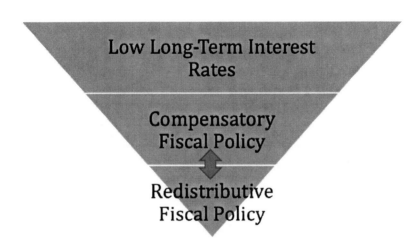

Figure 1. The Keynesian Recipe for Full Employment

What this implies, then, is that the level of federal (or federalist, including
state and local) governmental debt has to be predicated upon economic
activity, which is predicated largely on other dimensions of fiscal and
monetary policy and how it may discourage or exacerbate the economic
inequality generated always by the otherwise *freely* functioning marketplace
for goods and services. If policy exacerbates or leaves untouched natural
levels of inequality, in other words, which tend to rise automatically in a
laissez-faire economy, it will reduce economic activity, increase savings
relative to consumption, and reduce the likelihood that privately generated
assets can be secure or profitable enough to absorb the new higher level

of savings without significant loss. The resulting equation is simple: if the nation desires full employment and opportunity, rising inequality in a laissez-faire regime or rising inequality in a mixed economy with too little redistribution *requires* deficit spending and rising levels of debt. Indeed, because the natural tendency toward inequality is so profound in modern capitalist economies, deficits of some magnitude are almost always required and surpluses can be tolerated only briefly and only at the full employment apex of a fairly long period of steady employment growth. This is why all eleven periods of annual federal budget surplus in the twentieth century, covering a total of thirty-one years, gave way quickly to periods of officially recognized recessions. (see Figure 2)

Surplus Years	Officially Recognized Recessions
1901-03	September 1902-August 1904
1906-07	May 1907- June 1908
1911-12	January 1913- December 1914
1916	August 1918-March 1919
1920-30	May 1923-July 1924
	October 1926-November 1927
	August 1929-March 1933
1947-1949	November 1948-October 1949
1951	July 1953-May 1954
1956-57	August 1957-April 1958
1960	April 1960-February 1961
1969	December 1969-November 1970
1998-2001	March 2001-November 2001

Figure 2. U.S. Budget Surplus Years and Recessions

Those made uneasy by the very idea of indebtedness — like Ike or Virginia's Senator Harry Byrd — could have logically assuaged their anxiety, then, by attending to inequality first and by promoting sufficient indebtedness while policy chipped away at inequality. As it always has, the resulting increase in demand, employment, and revenue would then begin to lessen annual deficits and overall debt precisely when they become less necessary for overall economic balance. To make matters even simpler, most of the heavy lifting in this regard could have been and still can be done simply by imposing graduated income taxes and spending the proceeds on goods and services that modern civilization requires (roads, public safety, education, and health care), goods and services that *everyone* needs in such a civilization, and which employ a lot of not-so-rich citizens to make it all happen. Given the stubborn persistence of discrimination, disability, and dislocation in the real world, direct aid ("welfare" or "transfer payments") is always necessary, too, but if the core business of taxing progressively and spending on required public goods is done fully and consistently enough, such direct aid need not be very large, and the required amount is likely to shrink rather than grow.

Taking a cue from Ike and Harry Byrd, instead, by ignoring inequality and by attempting to reduce debt *only* by limiting its issuance, would only introduce a vicious cycle and make progressively *larger* the amount of debt that corresponds with full employment and widespread prosperity. And though Eisenhower was rebuffed by his own affinity for highway building, by the preservation and occasional expansion of the New Deal at the behest of a still robust Democratic opposition — particularly in housing assistance, agricultural subsidy, and Social Security — and by the lagged effects of the Korean War spending bulge, he did successfully impose debt limitations of this second, counterproductive type. Budget surpluses were engineered in 1956 and 1957, and again in the presidential election year 1960, and recessions followed immediately thereafter in each case, running from August 1957 to April 1958 and from April 1960 to February 1961. While the maintenance of a fairly progressive federal tax structure ensured that the austerity "offset" did less overall damage to the economy than it would have in its absence, in his second term Ike also ignored what Keynes considered the "general" imperative of his *General Theory*, pushing up interest rates instead in a futile attempt to stave off inflation and making it harder still for savings to find sufficiently secure and profitable assets of any type. And since 1951 was also a budget surplus year — followed by all too modest deficit spending in 1952 and 1953, Ike seemed to be setting a troubling pattern, having presided over the first of his administration's three recessions only months into his first term, in this case from July 1953 to May 1954.

Given the way in which Truman administration austerity dovetailed with that of his successor, Eisenhower's contention that the Korean conflict may well have been avoided if Truman had not removed U.S. troops from South Korea in 1948 — to reduce that year's federal budget — remains both ironic and prophetic. When Eisenhower moved aggressively to reduce defense expenditures on his own, from an estimated $526 billion at the beginning of his presidency to $382 billion at the end (in 2011 dollars), he did so largely by introducing what he called the New Look national security strategy — substituting inexpensive covert action and a massive nuclear threat for relatively expensive troops and bases and tanks and artillery. A plausible argument can be made that it was the overarching emphasis on covert action and nuclear brinkmanship inherent to the New Look transformation that trapped the U.S. in Vietnam in the late 1950s, stoking civil war and communist predation and necessitating a fateful choice between compete abandonment or a potentially difficult and protracted hot war response in the 1960s. At the least, Defense Secretary Wilson's blindness to any criticism of this approach — even from the ranks of the military's general officers — made it appear that this fateful dilemma was not emerging to *any* extent, critical or not, and the American people soon became "trapped by success" in Southeast Asia.[33] However idiosyncratic and irrational the diplomacy of that period may have been — driving outcomes that may be regarded also as idiosyncratic — two lessons were felt and could be at least dimly comprehended in retrospect: defense reductions made not in the name of conversion or efficiency but budgetary austerity alone could possibly engender a dangerous power vacuum; and, though much less clearly or powerfully felt, the same austerity, however it may have been generated, was very likely to produce also increased joblessness and recession.

These still very resonant historical lessons, however, are *felt* much more readily than they are understood and are still viewed much too completely through a glass darkly. We like and expect Keynesian results, but we accept Keynesian policy only when it is disguised, clothed in military armor or in the agreeable tailoring of "trickle down" tax cuts. We can get low long term interest rates, in other words, if there is a serious recession or a need to recapitalize banks, but it cannot be introduced, as Keynes urged, in the form of conventional policy and as a critical part of a "general" theory, for times good and bad. We can get some measure of deficit spending, too, but only as a temporary stimulus and, especially in the most recent generation, only when the deficits are generated mostly or completely by tax cuts or by additions to the nation's military budget. When Dick Cheney argued that "deficits don't matter," it was precisely this rationale that substantiated his otherwise odd and somewhat surprising declaration.

Moreover, because deficits generated in this manner automatically weaken the essential redistributive power of deficit spending, they tend to convince casual observers of two counterproductive economic policy myths: that Keynesian deficit spending in general is either completely ineffective or much less effective than it once was; and that the tax cuts or the military spending increases, by which the deficits are now often introduced, were in themselves the principal, even irreplaceable catalysts but simply too small or too temporary to do the requisite economic stimulus. Few ever see through to the essential reality: that deficit spending per se remains a critical tool for economic stimulus, full employment, and even the survival of capitalism, and that the generation of deficits with tax cuts and defense contracts only dilutes their impact and the cogency of a policy constructed around them.

The first lesson of the Eisenhower years, in which defense cuts threaten national security, is also greatly misconstrued. It is typically accepted by some as a story of principal cause and effect, in which cuts of any type equal insecurity. But it is really something else all together, transforming economic and social insecurity abroad and the fateful passions of nationalism and revolution that often coincide with such insecurity, into prolonged conflict, not because of reduced military spending in general but because an emphasis on reduced spending *of all types* fundamentally altered the way in which military spending was undertaken. New military schemes and postures — put into motion by a strange combination of austerity and the false bravado of the strategic bombers — likely had some role in trapping us in a conflict that few expected or estimated accurately, even if defense spending reductions, per se, were not the critical factor.

Fast forward to the Lyndon Johnson administration, and we see the same misunderstanding and policy confusion in its diametrically opposed form. In an administration that understood and embraced Keynesian fiscal and monetary policy, and which fostered the kind of basic redistributive taxation, public investment, and low interest rate policy that can alone deliver the economy we've always been promised, such policy has usually been ignored. Spending for the ugly war in Vietnam garners both far too much credit for the positive economic results that ensued and too much blame for the unraveling of the economy afterward, in the 1970s, when policymakers used Vietnam (too much spending, on "guns and butter") to reject Keynes even while continuing to expect Keynesian results.

We tend to forget, for example, that from 1962 to the end of 1966, military spending declined as a percentage of GNP, from 9.5% to 7.3%. Blinded, perhaps, by our hatred of the war that came into our living rooms at the end of this period and a sense that LBJ *must* have desired it as both an economic crutch and an outlet for his Lone Star ego or cowboy madness, we also forget that he understood better than almost every president before and after him the waste and inefficiency of defense spending. On December 4, 1963, only days into his presidency, President Johnson met with Columbia University professor, Seymour Melman, a well-known scholar of the economics of "conversion," under which military spending would be transferred propitiously into more socially useful and economically beneficial channels.[34] It was an initiative that he hoped to undertake and sustain, even if it required a carefully calibrated politics and no small measure of traveling quietly under the radar. "I'm catching more hell for seeing [civil rights activist James] Farmer and Melman and all that group than I ever caught from anybody," LBJ told Assistant Press secretary Andy Hatcher later that month.[35]

He continued to press the case forcefully, despite the political backlash, especially with friends and allies such as United Auto Workers leader Walter Reuther, with whom he spoke on the same evening that he had complained to Andy Hatcher. "I'm closing up all these archaic bases," Johnson told Reuther, "and I'm stopping the WPA atomic bomb projects, where we're building atomic bombs that we don't need, and I'm going to try and give them for human needs....we've got 150 Russian submarines. We've got 4,000 anti-submarine nuclear weapons, that cost half-a-million apiece. And we're still building them out of our ears. So let's save 25 million [dollars] now, and give it to grandma, inside my poverty project."[36]

To Ambassador Henry Cabot Lodge, early the following year, LBJ issued a lament well known among those who worked with him on a daily basis: "Generals know only two words — spend and bomb."[37] And a year later he scolded the Joint Chiefs at a private White House meeting: "You've done a good job of protecting my two girls for years, but you're the biggest wasters and spenders in the country."[38] Even with escalating Vietnam expenditures as a backdrop, there could be little doubt: President Johnson sought Melman's brand of conversion whenever possible.

We also forget that LBJ never desired the war as a substitute for an economic policy he was somehow too timid or confused or ignorant to bring about. After months of hearing the same message from the president fall increasingly on deaf ears, key Johnson administration economist Walter Heller spoke out in mid-1968: "War in Vietnam — or elsewhere — is not necessary to create jobs and to keep factories humming in America. Nor is it such a drain on the economy that we have to give up our wars on poverty, slums, ignorance, and pollution here at home…wars do generate demand and thus enlarge total spending, income, jobs, profits, and production. But today we can do all of these things in other ways and do them far better."[39]

In effect, Heller was echoing the Keynesian insight he had absorbed as a young economist at the U.S. Department of the Treasury in the 1940s. Writing in 1936, Keynes underscored the same blindness and economic policy timidity that LBJ and Heller tried vainly to abolish. "Pyramid building, earthquakes, even wars may serve to increase wealth," Keynes noted, "if the education of our statesmen on the principles of classical economics stands in the way of anything better."[40] After comparing pyramid building and wars to the absurd example of filling old bottles with banknotes, burying them in "disused coal mines," and then paying citizens to unearth them again, he closed with an implicit challenge: "It would, indeed, be more sensible to build houses and the like; but if there are political and practical difficulties in the way of this, the above would be better than nothing."[41] In retrospect, Keynes may well have been guilty of speaking too indirectly and he may have committed a sin many of his colleagues saw him commit repeatedly throughout his brilliant and illustrious career: assuming that most other people were as sensible as he was, and that they would not misjudge intentionally absurd comparisons designed to underscore plain, unequivocal ideas.

History tells us, however, that policymakers and many citizens have failed utterly to comprehend Keynes's subtle logic and have failed, therefore, to understand his comparison of military spending to "pyramids and earthquakes." Even though very few read Keynes in the original, his ideas have often been transmitted poorly and even more poorly understood in their secondary rendering, and we continue to pretend that wars and defense spending represent optimum fiscal policy, if only because powerful opposition, inertia, and widespread mis-education on fiscal and monetary policy encourage political timidity, an intellectually lazy reading of economic history, and both a geographically and temporally limited outlook. We're likely also victimized by the psychological tendency to misapprehend the very positive outcomes connected to basic progressive economic policy and to conversion — building houses instead of Hummers, as Keynes may have explained it today. On those rare occasions when we have moved in this direction and have met with predictable success, particularly in the 1960s and the 1990s, we have been plagued by the paradox of prosperity; when public policy changes matter a lot, we're seemingly hard-wired to imagine that they matter little, and that our intrinsic talent and our dedicated effort combine to make the principal difference. Precisely when there is "proof in the pudding," in other words, when opportunities to exploit talent *are* magnified, and effort, creativity, and innovation *are* significantly encouraged — *by improved public policy*, there exists also the unique challenge of convincing a resistant citizenry that this public policy transformation is worth knowing and sustaining.

Ignoring or spurning the political challenge of this lesson, we stymie economic opportunity and progress in two distinct ways. First of all, we are simply blinded to the potential of genuine progressive economic policy and of Keynesian economics that goes beyond mere deficit spending. For while the compensatory effect of deficit spending is critical, as is a backdrop of low long term interest rate policy, it all works well or not so well depending upon the way in which fiscal policy choices — for taxing and spending

— produce ample or somewhat less than ample redistribution. When we accede to significant levels of military Keynesianism, where this effect is weak, we reduce the compensatory power of deficit spending and we ensure that we need bigger doses and, simultaneously, that the potential power of such countercyclical spending becomes both less obvious and much more politically circumscribed.

Secondly, especially if the blindness persists for very long, we also introduce unique structural deficiencies that arise out of a heavy reliance on a degraded military Keynesianism. In significant but not readily observed ways, these deficiencies only magnify the corrosive economic (and political) effects tied directly to the sub-optimal compensatory function noted above. There are at least six of these not commonly recognized structural deficiencies.

Low Spin-Off Potential

As suggested already, compared to spending on education, health care, transportation, or public safety, military spending delivers far less bang for the buck and is a poor choice for stimulus dollars, due mostly to the relatively top-heavy distribution of compensation among military contractors and the increasing absence of mid-20th century mass production or consumer market integration within the ranks of these same corporations. In the run-up to the debate on what would become the American Recovery and Redevelopment Act of 2008, for example, this weakness was underscored clearly in an October 2007 study by Robert Pollin and Heidi Garrett-Peltier at the University of Massachusetts-Amherst. Their conclusion was unequivocal: investment in education, transportation, and health care in particular all helped to create many more job opportunities than comparable investment in the nation's military; any economic stimulus legislation ought to focus its investments, then, on the segments of the public sector most likely to spur economic activity and job creation (or preservation).[42]

Taking a somewhat longer view than Pollin and Garrett-Peltier, however, reveals an additional and related problem associated with military contracting, a deficiency that weakens further still the already relatively low multiplier associated with a choice to buy more guns than butter. Unlike World War II and even the Vietnam era, in which most military contractors were also producers of goods and services for civilian markets, today's defense contractor tends to do little else than serve the nation's war machine, limiting the spin-off effects of research and development and the productive capacity and efficiency of the nation's key consumer markets. This is true even in the case of increasing amounts of university research and development, where militarization of contracts has proceeded apace largely in an effort to maintain the funding of some basic and applied research. While swords could once much more easily be beaten into ploughshares, and while the production of swords often even subsidized the production of ploughshares on a significant scale, instilling comparatively larger economic advantages in more markets and for more people in the long run, the defense contracting environment today offers far less of this offsetting advantage. One would expect, therefore, to see a long-run multiplier for investments in national security and defense even lower than that suggested by the important Pollin and Garrett-Peltier analysis.

The Hidden and Unacknowledged Corporate Cost Problem

The nature of these increasingly specialized contracts also tends to produce super-sized profits, keeps more and more affected industries stuck in the "youthful" stage — where monopoly and specialized pricing power reign supreme — and encourages less investment in sustainable business structures built on lower but also much more stable levels of profit. Regarded as permanent features in a political economy that extends steady support to military Keynesianism, these effects damage future economic prospects in two important ways: they encourage and offer a suitable rationalization for expensive top-level compensation that cannot possibly work well in a "normal" economy and which engenders significant economy stifling inequality, and they build in relatively opaque inflationary costs that often spur ill-targeted and destructive interest rate increases, as if production worker costs or excess demand were the source of the inflationary momentum. So locked in are we to the false notion that inflation of this type is an indicator of excess demand and that Federal Reserve control of short-term interest rates is the only useful tool with which to combat it, that the best we can muster as an alternative to a purely reflexive interest rate response to inflation is the so-called "Taylor Rule," which recommends interest rate changes based on inflation *and* the gap between actual and potential output. And even though the prevailing anti-Keynesian or military Keynesian bias has preserved a yawning gap between actual and potential output — keeping Taylor rule monetary policy far enough away from counterproductive and ill-targeted interest rate increases in recent years — this general tendency remains an integral part of our conventional economic policy toolkit, if for no other reason than the way in which defense contractor cost accounting encourages the misapprehension of inflation and the policies that may be used to reduce it. Taken far enough, of course, this is the ancient recipe for stagflation, by which the higher interest rates do two counterproductive things at once: reduce employment by making private investments less profitable and attractive; and increase costs (and the inflation they are designed to control) by ratcheting up the capital costs of the dwindling number of businesses that remain solvent or profitable within such a monetary squeeze. Too remote and opaque to garner much serious attention, this hidden cost problem has shortchanged American productivity and prosperity for decades.

"Gunbelt" Hot and Cold Spots

Such overreliance on a version of Keynesianism that eschews the most universally useful and socially productive economic channels also tends to produce economic hot and cold spots. Though we hear often about the spreading of the wealth of the military contracting regime and the not infrequent efforts to sprinkle these contracts into as many congressional districts as possible, this is limited significantly by sunk costs, by the prevailing power of committee-based appropriation, by the low spin-off potential noted above, and by the ultimately limited political geography of the "gunbelt."[43] While everyone can get a little, perhaps, the nature of military contracting ensures that initial outlays give rise to ongoing outlays and that this weak form of public "investment" automatically introduces wide geographic disparities. What this generates, in turn, is an economic geography marked increasingly by hot and cold real estate markets, by increasing real estate speculation that marks such a landscape, by impaired labor mobility and affordability crises tied to this speculative gap, by a brain drain to increasingly isolated industries and areas, and by increasing educational inequality, geared as that is to localized fiscal policy (property taxes) and the prevailing geographic inequality.[44] And when such geographic disparity leads to interstate battles — to pry loose or defend the advantages of prevailing hotspots — it leads also to a counterproductive "race to the bottom," in which corporate tax cuts function both as popular (but fairly ineffective) recruiting tools and as a brake on educational investment in areas that can least afford to let it fall. Like the hidden and associated corporate cost problem, these problems often accumulate slowly and silently, rendering the hot-cold problems of labor scarcity and labor shortage, of housing affordability and housing market stagnation, and of increasingly prominent educational finance imbalances as seemingly "natural" features of the modern economic landscape. Though they are often created and are greatly encouraged by military Keynesianism, in other words, these problems are seldom connected directly to the scourge of this corrosive economic strategy, spawning mostly vain attempts to combat or ameliorate them with ill-suited or mostly ineffective policy tools.

Military Keynesianism, De-unionization, and Inequality

Banking significantly on defense industries in this way also connects the threat of work stoppage or labor influence to national security, encouraging an already powerful political momentum for de-unionization. Since this exacerbates inequality at the same time that it encourages the unsustainable top-heavy compensation common to such de-unionized sectors and industries, this blunts the overall demand for goods and services, reduces the inducement to invest (in anything but these isolated industries, but also less robustly overall) and magnifies the need for compensatory deficit spending and the issuance of expanded government debt. There is little doubt: as members of an industry marked by hyper-profitability and resilience, defense contractors encourage these counterproductive tendencies in two ways — directly, by pleading on behalf of national security, and indirectly, by standing as a model for other industries and companies that wish to mimic their apparently useful and exemplary labor practices.

Hyper-Financialization of the U.S. Economy

Lastly, by making possible the vast majority of historic venture capital investment — almost always tied in significant measure to military contracts and their supercharged profitability — economic reliance on military contracting has transformed Wall Street *casino* "investment" into a segment of our economy that can much more readily pretend to function as a vehicle for *genuine* investment, that presumably allocates capital efficiently and leads to significant job creation. It seldom does either of these things, but the gloss of venture capitalism, underwritten by the massive shift to military Keynesianism in the post-World War II era, has critically reinforced this myth, transforming the conventional venture capitalist from a creature actually dependent upon socialized investment and insider knowledge of the same into a mythical and heroic figure of bootstrap capitalism always worth emulating. And due to the limited numbers and geographic focus of the projects socialized extensively enough to sustain real long term investment, profitability, or socially useful spin-off, the progressive aping of this behavior only serves to increase the speculative (or even overtly criminal) financialization and volatility of our economy.

"Speculators may do no harm," Keynes noted, "as bubbles on a steady stream of enterprise, but the position is serious when enterprise becomes a bubble on a whirlpool of speculation. When the capital development of a country becomes the by-product of the activities of a casino, it is likely to be ill-done."[45] As Keynes also noted then, "the measure of success attained by Wall Street, regarded as an institution of which the proper social purpose is to direct new investment into the most profitable channels in terms of future yield, cannot be claimed as one of the outstanding triumphs of laissez-faire capitalism."[46] This remains true today, largely due to the way in which military Keynesianism has sustained the century-old mythology of Wall Street and its most visible speculators.

And In the End...

Taken collectively, these structural deficiencies amount to economic handicaps that are as damaging as they are imperceptible. And because they sap the strength of the already bastardized Keynesianism built on the weak reed of the defense industry multiplier, the lingering advantages of Keynesianism itself become attenuated even further, devalued and increasingly misconstrued in political circles, and felt only perversely by most affected citizens. "Making the eagle scream" as John Dos Passos once described it, to compensate partly with ever increasing military expenditure, can postpone some of the reckoning, just as it did in the last days of the Soviet Union, but it cannot stave off the inevitable weakening of the overall economic fabric.

If the only thing that changes then in such a confusing mélange of timid policy choices, tepid economic performance, and an increasingly confused citizenry is to disregard further the basic tenets of Keynesian economics — low long term interest rates, essential fiscal policy redistribution, and compensatory deficit spending — the odds are quite good that performance will go from tepid to calamitous, that more citizens will be more confused than ever before, and that political audacity will emanate only from the poisonous wellspring of unreason and reaction. In the event, the military-industrial complex can say, as one commentator recently described it, "keep paying us or the economy dies," and we might succumb to the extortion, unwilling to see or incapable of understanding the range of preferred alternatives.[47] If we choose to take a closer look, however, to see the modern capitalist economy for what it is, and to begin to understand again how it works and how it falls apart at the seams, we can seize these alternatives and declare, as Dean Baker has asserted, that if our proposed military spending "doesn't make sense in terms of advancing national security, then it doesn't make sense, period."[48]

Dave Shreve is an economic historian, editor, and assistant editor of six volumes in The Presidential Recordings series. He is the author of *American Promise: Kennedy, Johnson, Nixon, and the Forging of the Modern American Economy*. A former history professor at the University of Virginia, he is an expert in 20th century U.S. political history and national, state, and local economic policy. He is a member of the Virginia Organizing Project Tax Reform Committee.

Destructive Economic Impact of Military Spending

By Robert Naiman

Here's how I want to inspire you. I claim that reality turned an important corner in the United States, brightening prospects for people who want to cut the military budget when Congress passed the Budget Control Act. And many people in America who sympathize with us and want to cut the military budget don't know yet that reality just turned this corner, or at least they aren't yet acting like they know it. So this means that we have an opportunity to seize, if we can just tell people about this opportunity, explain it to them, and mobilize them around it.

If you look at polls, when they ask people, what do you think should happen with the federal budget, that would seem to indicate that we have a lot of friends. The majority of Americans, when you ask them, what do you think about cutting Social Security, the percentage who want to do that is miniscule. And then you ask them, what do you think about raising taxes on the rich? And the response is: "Yay!!!!!" And then you ask, what do you think about cutting the military budget? And the response is: "Yay!!!!!" So that's public opinion, according to polls. The question is translating that public opinion into action in Washington. Because if you took a poll of Washington lobbyists, you'd get a different result. So that's the dynamic that we face: public opinion against the lobbyists, and how do we make public opinion win this debate.

As long as I can remember, it's been a Holy Grail of progressives in the United States to try to cut the military budget. And now we have all these new friends. But America doesn't realize that reality just turned this corner with passage of the Budget Control Act. And if you look around — as I do, I assume many of you do — *Huffington Post, Common Dreams, Truthout* — what are left-liberals saying about politics in America right now? There aren't a lot of people talking about cutting the military budget. There isn't a big buzz around this right now. Which is really kind of shocking, when you think that for any group of people like us — as I look around this room, conversations last night — a lot of us have been at this for a while — John Heuer was talking yesterday about the opposition to Reagan's wars in Central America in the 1980s, which many of us were involved in — so there's a group of people, a lot of people around the United States, all of our adult lives, something that we always wanted to do was to cut the military budget.

I remember that as a college student in the early 1980s, just starting to get active in advocacy for social justice, there was a poster which I'm sure many of you have seen some version of, where there's this beautiful picture of children playing on a playground in a schoolyard, and the caption is: "It will be a great day when our schools have all the money they need, and the Air Force has to hold a bake sale to buy a bomber." And this poster I think really encapsulates how a lot of us view the question of the federal budget. So for as long as we can remember, there's this Holy Grail we've been searching for.

And now reality has turned this corner, where Congress is talking about significant cuts to projected military spending over the next ten years. And so you might think, that all these people around the United States, their whole lives they've been looking forward to the possibility of significant cuts to the military budget, that there would be a reaction, a groundswell: "Yay! At long last! Do it now!" But we're not seeing it. And the clock is ticking. Because by Thanksgiving, the Joint Select Committee on Deficit Reduction — the Supercommittee — is supposed to come up with a proposal for $1.2 trillion in reduced government spending over ten years.

And the question of the day is how much of that $1.2 trillion is going to come out of the projected military budget. And hundreds of billions of dollars of cuts in projected military spending are on the table.

So you would think that people like us would be like: "Holy cow! Pour on Washington! Demand it now!" All our lives we've been saying: cut the military budget, cut the military budget. But right now there's a real possibility that hasn't existed before. If you look since World War II, there's been a few times — at the end of Vietnam, there was a drawdown, at the end of the Cold War, there was a drawdown in military spending. Since 2000, military spending has been going up and up and up, now we have a possibility for a drawdown in military spending. You'd think there would be a tea party-like clamor for cuts in military spending. But we're not really seeing that. The only clamor that we're seeing in the press is the clamor on the other side — the clamor of the military contractors, going to Washington this week with their "Second to None" campaign, that's the clamor that's being reported. This situation should be setting us on fire.

It's certainly true that *Citizens United* was a horrible decision and it's certainly true that the disproportionate political power of corporations is a horrible thing — corporations have all this money to spend on campaigns and what amounts to legalized bribery for Members of Congress.

But there's another side to the story, which is that much of what these military contractors are doing is simply First Amendment political activity of talking to Congress, and our people aren't mobilized, at least, not as much as we could be and as we should be.

So this is the context in which I want to talk about the topic of the impact of military spending on our economy: the context is that the Supercommittee is supposed to come up with $1.2 trillion in reduced government debt over ten years by Thanksgiving — an opportunity for hundreds of billions of dollars of that to come from projected military spending. In fact, a trillion dollars in reduced military spending over ten years is on the table. If you look at the way that the first round of the debt agreement is being characterized, it's being characterized as including a reduction of $350 billion in projected military spending over ten years. The Administration claims, and the press is reporting, that the Administration and Congress have already agreed to reduced military spending by $350 billion over ten years from what was previously projected. Now, we don't have that set in stone. There's no guarantee that $350 billion will be cut from projected military spending, a future Congress can do whatever it wants. But that's become a baseline in the debate, that assumption, so that even Republican Members of Congress who oppose further cuts in military spending are using this as a baseline and saying, ok, $350 billion, but no more. We won't tolerate any more than $350 billion.

On the other hand, you know that under the Budget Control Act, if this Supercommittee doesn't come up with $1.2 trillion in reduced government debt over ten years, or if the proposal that they come up with isn't approved by Congress by December, then that will trigger $1.2 trillion in automatic cuts over ten years. And under the Budget Control Act, half of that $1.2 trillion in automatic cuts has to come from the military. So we have a scenario under the Budget Control Act, a scenario in which the Supercommittee doesn't reach a deal, or Congress doesn't approve the deal, where the military budget will be cut by a trillion dollars from the previously projected path over ten years. And that would take us back to what, at an annual level, what military spending was in 2007. So this is not — you remember that Obama spokesman who said, essentially referring to the people in this room, these people want to abolish the Pentagon. So let's be clear. This is not abolishing the Pentagon. But it would be a significant cut from the previous growth path. It would be a real cut. It would be actually reducing spending something like 15% over the period. It would be like the drawdowns after Vietnam and after the end of the Cold War. It would be a real drawdown in military spending. And it would have real consequences, and it would be meaningful, in terms of a positive impact on the domestic economy that would be felt by the majority.

So this is a possibility. Hundreds of billions of dollars, even a trillion. And of course, if you ask me: what is just? What should we aspire to? That's another story. But it's important for Americans to know, it's important for all of us to know, that this is on the table of debate in Washington right now. One trillion dollars of cuts in projected military spending over ten years is on the table. In the same way that a public option in health care was on the table in discussion and debate, a trillion dollars in cuts in military spending is on the table for debate.

This is realistic, this is practical, this is pragmatic, this could happen in the next couple of months. This is a winnable fight, in the next few months. A trillion dollars in cuts to projected military spending over ten years.

Now let me tell you why that would be a meaningful victory for the majority of Americans in terms of the impact of military spending on the economy. In 2007 and 2009, economists from the University of Massachusetts at Amherst did a study of the comparative impact of military spending on the economy. Remember that this was a time when the economy was imploding because of the housing and financial crisis and people were talking about stimulus and how we need to stimulate the economy so it made sense to say, if there's going to be a stimulus package, how should that money be spent?

And the conclusion of that study was that among the ways that stimulus money might be spent, military spending is the least efficient, has the least impact, the least bang for the buck, among ways that the government could spend money. Including, not only construction, health care, education and mass transit, but even tax cuts for personal consumption create more jobs than military spending. Ideally, we progressives would like a new Works Progress Administration, we want green jobs. But even tax cuts to stimulate personal consumption — like is the main plank of the jobs bill that President Obama just announced, extending the payroll tax holiday, so that's tax cuts to stimulate personal consumption — that creates more jobs than military spending. And this is an absolutely essential key point for people to understand.

Of course it's the case that military spending supports employment. Of course it's the case that if you say we're going to build fighter plans, and we're going to contract with Boeing, then some workers in Seattle will have jobs. But every form of government spending creates jobs, and military spending is the least efficient, it's the least bang for the buck.

This is incredibly important now, newly, in the context of the Budget Control Act. Because military Keynesianism has a logic, and that was alluded to in the last presentation. Because while it's true that military spending is the least efficient in creating jobs, it still might make sense if you were under a political constraint where somebody beat you up and handcuffed you and said you're not allowed to do anything else, then it might make sense. And in a sense that has been true historically in the United States, because of the politics, because of the distribution of power, it was as if somebody passed a law that said, you're not allowed to do these other things, you're not allowed to talk about these other things. So in that context, it makes sense to use military spending to stimulate the economy, if you're not allowed to do anything else.

So when people talk about what happened in the 1930s in the United States — you certainly see a lot of analogies today, including the fact that at the beginning, Roosevelt's team came on strong with stimulus, then there was this blowback, about omigod government debt, and then in 1936-37 they pulled back and then there was another recession, as a result of pulling back on the stimulus. And then there was a spike in production as a result not of the U.S. going to war per se but as a result of the U.S. beginning to participate economically in the war, by arming Western Europe. So that story of how World War II pulled the U.S. out of the Depression — it has some truth. The truth is that the politics of the United States — the demands of rich and powerful people against government spending — were an obstruction to the stimulus that was needed, and the demands of supporting the war in Europe allowed getting around that political obstruction.

But now we are in a different position, because of the Budget Control Act. Because now by agreeing, the President and Congress, that there is a goal of $1.2 trillion in cuts over ten years, some of which may come from the military, now everything has been put on the same table. Every form of government spending over the next ten years — with the partial exception of the wars, I'll come to that — has been put on the table. The base Pentagon budget — the non-war budget — is right in the middle of the table right now. Every dollar that isn't cut from military spending in the plan that the Supercommittee presents to Congress is a dollar that's going to come from somewhere else, probably domestic cuts. Maybe cuts to Social Security, maybe cuts in Medicare benefits. So now it's one-for-one. We're not in the situation where you can do military spending, deficit spending and that's the only thing you can do. We're in a situation where everything's been put on the same table, and it's one-for-one. If you can cut a military dollar, that protects a domestic dollar. If you fail to cut a military dollar, that exposes a domestic dollar. So now the fact that military spending is the least efficient means of creating jobs is critical. Because in the University of Massachusetts study, a billion dollars put into the military budget created 8000 jobs. A billion dollars put into domestic spending, in the least efficient of those alternatives, tax cuts for personal consumption, that created 10,000 jobs. So that means that if you move a billion dollars from the domestic budget to the military budget, you destroy 2000 jobs. If you move a billion dollars from the military budget to the domestic budget, you create 2000 jobs. So that means that if you move $200 billion from the military budget to the domestic budget, you create 400,000 jobs.

If, for example, we could end the war in Iraq this year, like we agreed, if we pull all of our troops out of Iraq this year, like we agreed, by December. If we had zero troops in Afghanistan after 2014, like has been announced, all foreign combat troops are supposed to leave Afghanistan by 2014. If we did that, instead of what the Pentagon wants to do, to have 10,000 U.S. troops in Iraq indefinitely, and have 25,000 troops or more in Afghanistan indefinitely. If you compare those two worlds, a low, cautious, conservative, certain to be underestimate of that difference is $200 billion, what we would save by ending the wars just when we agreed. Not today, not tomorrow, but when we already said. End the wars when we already said, save $200 billion against what the Pentagon wants to do. And if we don't do that, and the money comes out of domestic spending instead, 400,000 jobs destroyed.

What's 400,000 jobs? The U.S. labor force is 150 million people. So if you could put an additional 400,000 Americans to work today, that would reduce the measured unemployment rate from what it is today, 9.1%, to 8.8%. That's not solving the unemployment problem but that's a significant move. Compare this to the jobs bill that the President just announced: private economists estimated that if the whole package were approved by Congress, that would reduce the unemployment rate by one percentage point. So this is of the order of magnitude of the impact of the proposal being made in the President's jobs bill.

And that's just the $200 billion. What if we could take $1.2 trillion? What if we could take a trillion dollar cut out of the base Pentagon budget over ten years, and then we got $200 billion out of the war budget over ten years. Then you have six times the impact. So that would be analogous to reducing the measured unemployment rate by 1.8 percentage points. So that would be like the unemployment rate being 7.3%, instead of 9.1%. These are real impacts. This is a real impact that we could have in the United States in this battle that's happening between now and Thanksgiving, that would help put Americans back to work.

So we face, I think, a kind of emergency, those of us who want to cut the military budget. Because we have this historic opportunity, and America doesn't know it. People who are the constituency of this opportunity don't know it. The other side is highly mobilized. They know exactly what's at stake. Stocks of military contractors have fallen on the expectation of military cuts. They are out in force. Our people are not out in force. We need to mobilize our people right now, across the United States, to hammer Congress, like the Tea Party, make their phones ring off the hook, dog them every time they show their face in public, cut the military budget now, make the Supercommittee cut the military budget and end the wars as part of the deal to reduce the U.S. debt.

Robert Naiman is Policy Director at Just Foreign Policy. He edits the Just Foreign Policy daily news summary and writes on U.S. foreign policy at *Huffington Post*. Naiman has worked as a policy analyst and researcher at the Center for Economic and Policy Research and Public Citizen's Global Trade Watch. He has masters degrees in economics and mathematics from the University of Illinois and has studied and worked in the Middle East.

The Military As a Jobs Program

By Ellen Brown

"Every gun that is made, every warship launched, every rocket fired signifies, in the final sense, a theft from those who hunger and are not fed, those who are cold and are not clothed. ... We pay for a single fighter plane with a half million bushels of wheat. We pay for a single destroyer with new homes that could have housed more than 8,000 people."

— *Dwight David Eisenhower*[49]

In a Wall Street Journal editorial on June 8th bemoaning the failure of the Obama stimulus package, Martin Feldstein wrote:

"Experience shows that the most cost-effective form of temporary fiscal stimulus is direct government spending. The most obvious way to achieve that in 2009 was to repair and replace the military equipment used in Iraq and Afghanistan that would otherwise have to be done in the future. But the Obama stimulus had nothing for the Defense Department."[50]

You can't make this stuff up. The most obvious way to stimulate the economy is to replace military equipment? And the Obama stimulus had nothing for the Defense Department? When veterans' benefits and other past military costs are factored in, the military now devours half the U.S. budget.[51] If military spending is such a cost-effective stimulus, why have the trillions poured into it in the last decade left the economy reeling?

The military is the nation's largest and most firmly entrenched entitlement program, one that takes half of every tax dollar. Even if "national security" is considered our number one priority (a dubious choice when the real unemployment rate is over 16%), estimates are that the military budget could be cut in half or more and we would still have the most powerful military machine in the world.[52] Our enemies (if any) are now "terrorists," not countries; and what is needed to contain them (if anything) is local policing, not global warfare. Much of our military hardware is just good for "shock and awe," not needed for any "real and present danger."

Military spending is the very essence of "built-in obsolescence": it turns out products that are designed to blow up. The military is not subject to ordinary market principles but works on a "cost-plus" basis, with producers reimbursed for whatever they have spent plus a guaranteed profit. Gone are the usual competitive restraints that keep capitalist corporations "lean and mean." Private contractors hired by the government on no-bid contracts can be as wasteful and inefficient as they like and still make a tidy profit. Yet legislators looking to slash wasteful "entitlements" persist in overlooking this obvious elephant in the room.

The reason massive military spending is considered the most "obvious" way to produce a fiscal stimulus is simply that it is the only form of direct government spending that gets a pass from the deficit hawks. The economy is desperate to get money flowing through it, and today only the government is in a position to turn on the spigots; but there is a tourniquet on government spending. That is true for everything but the military, the only program on which the government is allowed to spend seemingly without limit, often even without oversight.

Chalmers Johnson estimated in 2004 that as much as 40% of the Pentagon budget is "black," meaning hidden from public scrutiny.[53] The black budget is so top secret that Congress itself is not allowed to peer in and haggle over the price. Democratic control of the military has broken down. The military is being used for purposes that even Congress is not allowed to know, much less vote on. The U.S. is no longer a constitutional republic but is a national security state. Foreign policy is determined behind closed doors by powerful private interests that use our military presence abroad to secure their access to cheap labor, markets and resources. At least, we assume that is what is going on. A declared objective of U.S. military policy is "full spectrum dominance." That could well mean dominance over the American people along with everyone else.

Why is the military's half of the pie sacrosanct? Wasteful and unnecessary military programs get a pass from legislators because the military is also our largest and most secure jobs program, one that has penetrated into the nooks and crannies of Every Town U.S.A. If it were disbanded, the economy would be crippled by soaring unemployment, plant closures, and bankruptcies. Bruce Gagnon, coordinator of the Global Network Against Weapons and Nuclear Power, writes:

"Most politicians understand ... that weapons production is currently the number one industrial export product of the U.S. They know that major industrial job creation is largely coming from the Pentagon. Thus most politicians, from both parties, want to continue to support the military industrial complex gravy train for their communities."[54]

That explains why the country seems to be permanently at war. If we had peace, the war machine would be out of a job. Every year since World War II, the U.S. has been at war somewhere.[55] It has been said that if we didn't have a war to fight, we would have to create one just to keep the war business going. We have a military empire of over 800 bases around the world.

What is to become of them when the lion lies down with the lamb and peace reigns everywhere?

Military Conversion

Fortunately, there is a way to solve these problems without maintaining a perpetual state of war: keep the jobs but convert them to civilian use. Military conversion is a well thought-out program that could provide real economic stimulus and national security for people here and abroad.[56] Existing military bases, laboratories, and production facilities can be converted to civilian uses. Bases can become industrial parks, schools, airports, hospitals, recreation facilities, and so forth. Converted factories can produce consumer and capital goods: machine tools, electric locomotives, farm machinery, oil field equipment, construction machinery for modernizing infrastructure.

It has been done before. According to Lloyd Dumas in *The Socio-Economic Conversion from War to Peace* (1995):

> *At the end of World War II, ... a large fraction of the nation's output had to be moved from military to civilian production. ... Some 30 percent of U.S. output was transferred in one year without the unemployment rate ever rising above 3 percent. This experience made it clear that it is possible to redirect enormous amounts of productive resources from military to civilian activity without intolerable economic disruption.[57]*

In the early 19th century, when we had no major wars to fight, the U.S. military was turned into a civil service that built infrastructure for the nation.

A successful modern example is the United States Army Corps of Engineers (USACE), the world's largest public engineering, design and construction management agency. Its mission is to provide vital public engineering services to strengthen the nation's security, energize the economy, and reduce risks from disasters. Generally associated with dams, canals and flood protection in the United States, USACE is involved in a wide range of public works both here and abroad. The Corps of Engineers provides 24% of U.S. hydropower capacity and is engaged in environmental regulation and ecosystem restoration, among other useful projects.

The late Seymour Melman, a professor at Columbia University, wrote extensively for fifty years on "economic conversion", the ordered transition from military to civilian production by military industries and facilities. He showed that a carefully designed conversion program could create more jobs than the war machine sustains now.[58] The military actually destroys jobs in the civilian economy. The higher profits from cost-plus military manufacturing cause manufacturers to abandon more competitive civilian endeavors; and the permanent war economy takes engineers, capital and resources away from civilian production.

Bruce Gagnon writes:

Across the nation colleges and universities are turning to the Pentagon for greater research funding as Congress and successive administrations have cut back on scientific research and development investment. As this trend worsens we find growing evidence that engineering, computer science, astronomy, mathematics, and other departments are becoming "militarized" in order to maintain funding levels.[59]

This research and production is not easily transferable to civilian use, since it has been designed for tasks that are radically different from civilian needs. And because we have put so many resources into military production, we have fallen behind industrially.

A 2007 study by Robert Pollin and Heidi Garrett-Peltier of the University of Massachusetts found that government investment in education creates twice as many jobs as investment in the military. Spending on personal consumption, health care, education, mass transit, and construction for home weatherization and infrastructure repair all were found to create more jobs per $1 billon in expenditures than military spending does.[60]

Clearly, the half of the budget now going to military pursuits could be better spent. If we are going to double exports in the next five years, as President Obama has pledged, we will need to divert some of the resources poured down the black hole of war to productive civilian industry.

Ellen Brown is an attorney, author, and president of the Public Banking Institute, http://PublicBankingInstitute.org. In *Web of Debt*, her latest of eleven books, she shows how the power to create money has been usurped from the people, and how we can get it back. Her websites are http://webofdebt.com and http://ellen-brown.com.

Civilizing the Military
By Ellen Brown

In a June 15 article in the *New York Times* titled "Our Lefty Military,"
Nicholas Kristof says that we don't need to turn to Sweden to find a
business model that provides universal health care, educational opportunity,
and relative income equality. We have one right here at home, in the United
States military. He writes:

> *This is a rare enclave of single-payer universal health care, and it
> continues with a veterans' health care system that has much lower
> costs than the American system as a whole. Perhaps the most
> impressive achievement of the American military is ... the military
> day care system for working parents.*

> *... Its universities — the military academies — are excellent, and it
> has R.O.T.C. programs at other campuses around the country. Many
> soldiers get medical training, law degrees, or Ph.D.'s while in service,
> sometimes at the country's finest universities.*

> *Granted, it may seem odd to seek a model of compassion in an
> organization whose mission involves killing people. ... But as we as a
> country grope for new directions in a difficult economic environment,
> the tendency has been to move toward a corporatist model that
> sees investments in people as woolly-minded sentimentalism or as
> unaffordable luxuries. That's not the only model out there.*[61]

Kristof quotes retired four-star general Wesley Clark, who called the U.S.
military "the purest application of socialism there is." The late Chalmers
Johnson, president of the Japan Policy Research Institute, wrote in 1989 that

the military/industrial complex was the closest thing in the United States to the state-guided market system of Japan. The government determines the programs and hires private companies to implement them. He called the U.S. military/industrial complex a form of state-sponsored capitalism that has produced one of the most lucrative and successful industries in the country.[62]

The Japanese model differs, however, in that it achieves this result without the pretext of war. The Japanese government caps military spending at a mere 1% of the national budget.

The Japanese Model

The Japanese state-guided system actually had military roots. In its feudal period, the country was run by a military government headed by the shogun and administered by local lords and their samurai, who were living essentially as drones without wars to keep them busy. This shogunate system owned the land. When it was overthrown in the late 19th century, the new Meiji government abolished feudal land ownership and paid the local lords and samurai sums of money in compensation.[63]

The government got the money simply by issuing it. Japan had become the first nation in Asia to found its own independent state bank. The bank issued new fiat money which was used to pay the nobles, and the nobles were then encouraged to deposit their money in the state bank and to put it to work creating new industries. Additional money was created by the government to aid the new industries. No expense was spared in the process of industrialization.

In this way, the Japanese managed to transform their warrior class into the country's industrialists, successfully shifting their focus to the peaceful business of building the country and developing industry. The old feudal

Japanese dynasties became the multinational Japanese corporations we know today — Mitsubishi, Mitsui, Sumitomo, and so forth.

The Japanese economic model that evolved in the twentieth century is what Chalmers Johnson called a "state-guided market system." The state determines the priorities and commissions the work, then enlists private enterprise to carry it out. The model overcame the defects of the communist system, which put ownership and control in the hands of the state.

Japan, China, and other economic competitors get ahead by *not* wasting money on the military. They invest instead in infrastructure and productive industry. Seymour Melman, writing in the 1990s, noted that while the U.S. was busy investing in war, Japan was investing in its infrastructure and productive capital.64 As a result, Japan had achieved six times the rate of growth in productivity of the U.S. economy.

A similar model was followed during Roosevelt's New Deal with the Works Progress Administration (renamed the Work Projects Administration or WPA). The largest and most ambitious federal agency of the New Deal, the WPA employed millions of unskilled workers to carry out public works projects, including the construction of public buildings and roads. It also operated large arts, drama, media, and literacy projects; fed children; and redistributed food, clothing, and housing. Almost every community in the United States had a park, bridge or school constructed by the WPA.

A Model of Sustainability and Self-sufficiency

The Japanese economy has been called "stagnant," but the Japanese are not aiming for growth. They are aiming for sustainability and quality of life; and at least until this latest nuclear disaster, they were achieving it. The money our government is pouring into the military, the Japanese are pouring into health care, education, and pensions for the elderly.

Like the Meiji government — and like our government when it comes to military spending — they get the money essentially just by printing it. The government advances the funds, then balances the books by issuing bonds, creating a federal debt that is never paid down but is just rolled over from year to year.

This is what governments actually *should* do. In today's world of banking and finance, money is debt, and the national debt sustains the national money supply.[65]

But the U.S. is allowed to draw without objection on the largesse of the national credit card only for the military budget, so that is where the government's money goes. We could, like the Japanese, be spending it on health care and other human goods instead. The money would come from the same place the military gets it. As Representative Barney Frank wrote in *The Nation* in February 2009:

> When I am challenged by people — not all of them conservative — who tell me that they agree, for example, that we should enact comprehensive universal healthcare but wonder how to pay for it, my answer is that I do not know immediately where to get the funding but I know whom I should ask. I was in Congress on September 10, 2001, and I know there was no money in the budget at that time for a war in Iraq. So my answer is that I will go to the people who found the money for that war and ask them if they could find some for healthcare.[66]

Ellen Brown is an attorney, author, and president of the Public Banking Institute, http://PublicBankingInstitute.org. In *Web of Debt*, her latest of eleven books, she shows how the power to create money has been usurped from the people, and how we can get it back. Her websites are http://webofdebt.com and http://ellen-brown.com.

We the 99% Demand a Different Budget

By David Swanson

At the time of the MIC-50 conference, I was working on creating an online tool that would allow people to create pie charts illustrating the way they would like the public discretionary budget to be spent and then compare them with a similar illustration of how the government actually spends our money. I found a programmer named Karl Anliot who did a beautiful job, and by the time it was ready for public promotion we were all speaking the language of Occupy Wall Street.

We can fit our demands on a bumper sticker, I wrote in debuting the tool: "Majority Rule" or "People Over Profits" or "Love Not Greed." But we don't want to. Our government is doing everything wrong, and we should be allowed to present the full list of grievances. We can, however, give the world a thousand words' worth in an image, a pie chart to be exact. Our federal budget funds the wrong things. We want it to fund the right things.

Here are pie charts produced by some of us members of the 99%: http://warisacrime.org/showbudgetgallery. Here's where you can make your own: http://warisacrime.org/newuser. You'll have to register and log in, which prevents spam. Then you'll have a chance to fill in the percentage of the federal budget that you'd like devoted to various areas. This budget tool will let you know if your total adds up to 100%. You can do this in 60 seconds, but I recommend giving it some thought and really making this into your vision for future activism.

After you create your own ideal budget pie chart, you can compare it with the actual government budget and with the ideal budgets created by the rest of us. I suspect the biggest gap is going to be between the government and everybody else. You can also go back in and edit your budget. You can link to it. You can facebook it and tweet it.

Below is an image of my ideal federal budget. I might still change it, but I'm pretty certain of the basics here. This is discretionary spending, so Social Security and other mandatory spending are not included. A trust fund into which we pay, trusting that we will be paid back, should never be placed on the chopping block. Discretionary spending, as the name suggests, is spending over which Congress has discretion each year.

The inner pie chart is broad categories, and the outer layer subcategories for spending. The chart is reproduced in black and white here, but can be seen online in color. The yellow-orange area in the lower right is sustainable policies, including job training, mass transit, pollution control, green energy research, etc. The blue areas include education and research. The green slices are elements of friendly foreign relations. The purple is hostile foreign relations, including the military and wars. The raspberry colored sections cover basic governance, and the little black slice on the right goes to big agriculture and transportation. Whether in black and white or color, you can see that I've given a little to everything, even the military.

The other chart reproduced below is an actual government budget, specifically a budget proposed by the Obama White House for 2015. The first thing you'll notice is that the military and wars have swallowed everything else. The rest of the funding areas are all crammed together in teeny little slices over on the right.

The National Priorities Project has produced a very similar pie chart using 2012 numbers[67], but the numbers used here come from the White House's proposed 2015 budget, also used in a survey by the Program for Public Consultation which inspired this budget tool.[68]

104

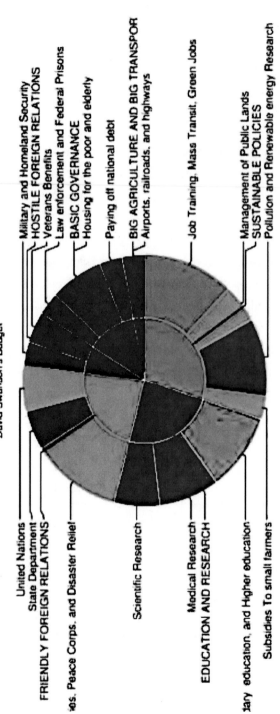

David Swanson's Budget

Military and Homeland Security
HOSTILE FOREIGN RELATIONS
Veterans Benefits
Law enforcement and Federal Prisons
BASIC GOVERNANCE
Housing for the poor and elderly
Paying off national debt
BIG AGRICULTURE AND BIG TRANSPOR
Airports, railroads, and highways

Job Training, Mass Transit, Green Jobs

Management of Public Lands
SUSTAINABLE POLICIES
Pollution and Renewable energy Research

United Nations
State Department
FRIENDLY FOREIGN RELATIONS
ies, Peace Corps, and Disaster Relief

Scientific Research

Medical Research
EDUCATION AND RESEARCH

tary education, and Higher education

Subsidies To small farmers

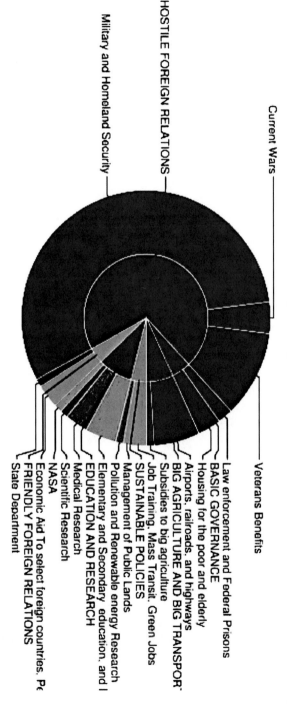

White House Projected Budget for 2015

Current Wars

HOSTILE FOREIGN RELATIONS

Military and Homeland Security

Veterans Benefits

Law enforcement and Federal Prisons
BASIC GOVERNANCE
Housing for the poor and elderly
Airports, railroads, and highways
BIG AGRICULTURE AND BIG TRANSPOR
Subsidies to big agriculture
Job Training, Mass Transit, Green Jobs
SUSTAINABLE POLICIES
Management of Public Lands
Pollution and Renewable energy Research
Elementary and Secondary education, and I
EDUCATION AND RESEARCH
Medical Research
Scientific Research
NASA
Economic Aid To select foreign countries. Po
FRIENDLY FOREIGN RELATIONS
State Department

As much as I sympathize with cries of "jobs not cuts," I wonder if awareness of the state of our budget would lead us to demand that money be moved, that money be cut in one place and added to all the other sectors. Of course it could also be added to by taxing billionaires and corporations. But whatever size the pot, our public funds ought to be distributed fairly, humanely, and sustainably. Perhaps this online tool can help us develop the vision we need moving forward. I recommend using it at conferences and house parties and other events at which you can compare your results with those of your friends and discuss the minor differences between then, as compared with the major chasm between all of our visions and the one being realized by the military industrial complex.

David Swanson is the author of *When the World Outlawed War, War Is A Lie,* and *Daybreak: Undoing the Imperial Presidency and Forming a More Perfect Union.* He blogs at davidswanson.org and warisacrime.org and works for the online activist organizations rootsaction.org and democrats.com.

III. NOTHING IS SAFE

How Private Warmongers and the Military Infiltrated Universities

By Steve Horn and Allen Ruff

A matrix of closely tied university-based strategic studies ventures, the so-called Grand Strategy Programs (GSP), have cropped up on a number of elite campuses around the country, where they function to serve the national security warfare state.

In tandem with allied institutes and think tanks across the country, these programs, centered at Yale University, Duke University, the University of Texas at Austin, Columbia University, Temple University and, until recently, the University of Wisconsin-Madison, illustrate the increasingly influential role of a new breed of warrior academics in the post-9/11 United States. The network marks the ascent and influence of what might be called the "Long War University."

Ostensibly created to train an up-and-coming elite to see a global "big picture," this grand strategy network has brought together scores of foreign policy wonks heavily invested — literally and figuratively — in an unending quest to maintain U.S. global supremacy, a campaign which they increasingly refer to as the Long War.

He Who Pays the Piper ...

The network of grand strategy programs integral to the Long War University came about through the financial backing of Roger Hertog, the multimillionaire financial manager, man of the right and a key patron of the contemporary conservative movement. Hertog is a chairman emeritus of the conservative social policy think tank the Manhattan Institute, and a board member of the right-wing American Enterprise Institute, and the Club for Growth. Hertog additionally served on the executive committee of the influential, neoconservative and pro-Israel Washington Institute for Near East Policy (WINEP), and has been a major financial contributor to Taglit-Birthright Israel.

Respected in various circles as a patron of the arts and culture, of libraries and archives, Hertog was awarded a National Humanities Medal by then-president George W. Bush in November 2007. The ceremonial citation praised him as one, "[whose] wisdom and generosity have rejuvenated institutions that are keepers of American memory."

More recently, Hertog introduced Wisconsin's Gov. Scott Walker at a Manhattan Institute conference on "A New Social Contract: Reforming the Terms of Public Employment in America." Embracing the controversial Republican state executive, Hertog praised him as a figure that would someday be looked upon as someone who "helped save the country."

As a man in the business of shaping intellectual environments, Hertog has been described as "the epitome of the conservative benefactor who bases his politics on conservative intellectualism and moves patiently and strategically to create, support and distribute his ideas." Norman Podhoretz, the former editor of Commentary, said of his longtime friend that, "Roger thinks of philanthropic endeavors as investments. The return he expects is long range."

Hertog has been a staunch advocate of a conservative, results-based "new philanthropy" — the replacement of open-ended funding for endowed university chairs with money for selected projects, made available on a two- or three-year basis. He makes little distinction between the nonprofit and for-profit ventures that he funds, and has spoken of "retail" and "strategic philanthropy" as "leverage" to transform American universities.

The Long War Men at Yale

The Grand Strategy network originally started at Yale University, alma mater for a long line of U.S. strategic planners and intelligence operatives. Its founders were the influential conservative "dean of cold war historians," John Lewis Gaddis, global historian Paul Kennedy and "diplomat-in-residence" Charles Hill, the former State Department careerist forced into retirement for concealing the role of his boss, then-secretary of state George Schultz, during the Reagan-era Iran-Contra scandal.

Yale's GSP became the centerpiece of International Securities Studies (ISS), "a center for teaching and research in grand strategy," founded in 1988. Kennedy was the ISS's first director. It was initially funded, in the main, by the John M. Olin and Smith Richardson Foundations, two major financial backers of numerous conservative and right-wing public and foreign policy causes.

The plans for the Yale GSP evolved out of a series of discussions between Kennedy, Hill, Gaddis and others, including the *New York Times'* Thomas Friedman, in early 1999. Central to their thinking, according to Gaddis, was their shared concern "to deliberately ... train the next generation of world leaders."[69]

According to Gaddis, the original ideas shaping the program's curriculum were drawn from the efforts of an earlier generation of strategic planners, such as Henry Kissinger, and stemmed from his experience as a mid-1970s faculty member at the U.S. Naval War College.

The New Haven program became known as the Brady-Johnson Program in Grand Strategy in 2007, in recognition of a $17.5 million, 15-year endowment. The first, Nicholas Brady, had been U.S. secretary of the Treasury under presidents Ronald Reagan and George H.W. Bush, and was a former director of the Mitre Corporation, the privately contracted manager of federally funded research and development projects for the Department of Defense (DoD) and other agencies.

The other benefactor, Brady's billionaire business associate, Charles B. Johnson, is a part-owner of the San Francisco Giants and an "overseer" of the conservative Hoover Institution on War, Revolution and Peace, among other things.

Both Brady and Johnson sit on the board of directors of Darby Private Equity alongside Milwaukee, Wisconsin's philanthropist and venture capitalist Sheldon Lubar, member of the board of directors of the University of Wisconsin Foundation and supporter of what had been the University of Wisconsin Madison's GSP.

Increasingly well-endowed over time, the Yale GSP continued to acquire new associates, among them an additional "diplomat-at-large," John Negroponte, the former national security adviser, U.S. envoy to the United Nations (UN) and controversial U.S. ambassador to Honduras during the 1980s contra war against Nicaragua.

While the identities of those associated with the Yale program certainly speak volumes, the actual program these people devised is far more revealing, especially since it provided the prototype for future efforts elsewhere.

Aspiring Grand Strategy students are required to write application essays, and the cross-discipline pool of graduate students and undergraduates is carefully vetted. The year-long program comprises a focus on "real world practice" and includes the study of "classics" in strategic thinking, from ancient Chinese general and "The Art of War" author Sun Tzu and Greek historian Thucydides to Prussian military strategist Karl von Clausewitz and Kissinger himself.

In addition to their formal studies, students are required to complete summer projects that have included internships at the European Union's (EU) Institute for Security Studies and the National Security Agency (NSA). Students completing the program have gone on to careers with the U.S. Department of State, the CIA, the Department of Homeland Security (DHS), and the DoD's subcontracted Institute for Defense Analyses (IDA).

The year-long GSP course concludes with a "crisis simulation" session, in which teams of students prepare "emergency rapid response" scenarios as if preparing for a "real time" meeting of the National Security Council (NSC) and the president. Role-playing the president and other administration officials, the presenters are then grilled by program faculty who critique their work.

The simulations and seminars have included numbers of exclusive "outside guests." CIA head David Petraeus, at the time general in command of the U.S. military operations in the Middle East, paid an unpublicized visit to the Yale GSP's students and faculty in March 2010.

Other visitors included the likes of Kissinger and George W. Bush's hard-line ambassador to the UN, John Bolton. Observers from the CIA and cadets from West Point also sat in on the seminars.

In February 2009, U.S. Marine Corps officers met with GSP faculty and students. The representatives from the "Combat Development Command and the Corp Commandant's Strategic Initiatives Group" briefed the Yalies and other invited guests on the Marine's "Vision and Strategy 2025," a planning document describing "how the Marine Corps' role and posture in national defense will change in the future global environment."

Gaddis, in fact, told Yale Alumni Magazine in 2003 that, "We now offer workshops in grand strategy at the war colleges and service academies, recreating a connection with the highest levels of the military. ... And Washington has taken notice." Perhaps most significantly, a core of Gaddis and Kennedy students have gone on to become either directors of Grand Strategy projects and related institutes, or to work as closely connected faculty associates elsewhere.

Such students have included historian Matthew Connelly, head of the Hertog Global Strategy Initiative at Columbia University; William Hitchcock, now at the University of Virginia, who helped create the Grand Strategy Program at Temple University; Mark Lawrence of the University of Texas at Austin; Jeremi Suri, currently at the University of Texas at Austin, who created the now-defunct GSP at the University of Wisconsin-Madison; and Hal Brands, formerly with the IDA and now the American grand strategy assistant professor of public policy at Duke University.

Grand Strategy's Launch

In September 2008, some 20 historians and political scientists from around the country gathered at an unpublicized location, a private club near Yale. The participants, carefully chosen by the university's GSP directors, had been invited to meet with Hertog.

The financial management mogul told those at the Yale meet-up that he was willing to spend as much as $10 million over the coming years to fund scholars interested in inaugurating GSPs at their respective campuses. He requested short, three-page proposals from the professors-on-the-rise detailing how they would use his seed money.

He urged them to think about how to connect their projects with others around the country to leverage their collective impact, and cautioned that he did not necessarily want exact replicas of Yale's venture. The subsequent GSPs and allied programs evolved with his financial assistance.

Long War at Duke

One of the recipients of Hertog "strategic philanthropy" has been the Program in American Grand Strategy at Duke University, headed by Peter D. Feaver, a significant figure in strategic planning circles and an important player within the Long War University. A political scientist with a Harvard PhD, he also is the director of Triangle Institute for Security Studies (TISS), the well-established strategic policy consortium with affiliates at Duke, the University of North Carolina-Chapel Hill and North Carolina State University.

An expert on the relationship between civil society and the military, Feaver served under the Clinton administration from 1993 to 1994 as director for defense policy and arms control on the NSC. He then worked as special adviser for strategic planning and institutional reform on the NSC staff during the Bush years, from June 2005 to July 2007. Feaver is also an affiliate of the Center for a New American Security (CNAS), the increasingly influential liberal hawk think tank presided over by the warrior intellectual John Nagl, the former career military man who helped write the influential Counterinsurgency Field Manual under the command of former general Petraeus.

The homepage for the Duke GSP reads, "American grand strategy is the collection of plans and policies by which the leadership of the United States mobilizes and deploys the country's resources and capabilities, both military and non-military, to achieve its national goals." In fulfillment of its mission, Feaver has brought in a number of national security state notables, among them, in September 2010, then-secretary of defense Robert Gates, who gave a public address on the all-volunteer military in an age of the Long War and also taught a session of Feaver's Grand Strategy class.

The Duke GSP and TISS co-sponsored a talk a year earlier by Brig. Gen. H.R. McMaster on "Counterinsurgency and the War in Afghanistan."

McMaster served in both Iraq wars and worked on the team that designed the Iraq "surge," and, at the time of his talk, directed a key division of the Army's warfare planning center at Ft. Monroe, Virginia. Other guests of the Duke GSP have included Gaddis and Kennedy from Yale; Michael Doran, the Roger Hertog senior fellow at the Brookings Institution's Saban Center; and former Bush administration hawks, Stephen Hadley, John Bolton and Douglas Feith.

The Warriors' Temple

A Hertog Program In Grand Strategy was launched at Temple University in spring 2009, with the assistance of a three-year, $225,000 grant from the Hertog Foundation arranged through two foreign policy historians, the Yale alumnus Hitchcock and Richard Immerman, current director of the university's Center for the Study of Force and Diplomacy (CENFAD).

A CENFAD newsletter stated that Temple had been chosen "as a site for replicating Yale University's 'Grand Strategy' course — a yearlong seminar on military strategy taught by Charles Hill, John Lewis Gaddis, and Paul Kennedy ... ." The same article pointed out that Hertog did not believe in making unrestricted gifts to academe, but rather believed in setting benchmarks to ensure the goals he envisioned. It went on to state, "that CENFAD, its associates, and students will expend every effort to meet this challenge to make sure that the Hertog Seminar in Grand Strategy remains at Temple."

Housed at Temple's History Department, CENFAD was founded in 1993 and "fosters interdisciplinary faculty and student research on the historic and contemporary use of force and diplomacy in a global context."

CENFAD is currently directed by Immerman, best known in scholarly circles for his historical writing on the CIA. Immerman served from 2007 to

2008 as assistant deputy director of national intelligence, analytic integrity and standards, and analytic ombudsman at the office of the director of national intelligence, an oversight position created to ensure the standards and accuracy of national intelligence documents.

Columbia University's Long War

Columbia University's variant of the Hertog-funded strategic studies program, the aforementioned Hertog Global Strategy Initiative had its start in 2010 under the direction of the Yale alumnus and former Gaddis student, the historian Connelly. Varying from the GSPs elsewhere, Columbia's is a summer program only. The first year's session, in 2010, focused on "Nuclear Proliferation and the Future of World Power" and was co-taught by Connelly and University of Texas at Austin's Francis Gavin. The summer 2011 session focused on "The History and Future Pandemic Threats and Global Public Health." The projected session for summer 2012 will focus on "Religious Violence and Apocalyptic Movements."

In many ways, the program clearly resembles that developed by Gaddis at Yale. Students spend the first three weeks of the summer in "total immersion," training in the methods of international history. Eight weeks are then spent conducting independent and team projects, followed by a final week where the students present their research, develop future scenarios and participate in a crisis simulation exercise.

Visitors to Columbia's GSP have included the likes of Kissinger, former Deputy Secretary of State James B. Steinberg (also the former dean of the University of Texas-Austin's Lyndon B. Johnson School of Public Affairs, under whose auspices sits the Robert S. Strauss Center of International Security and Law), and Philip Zelikow, a senior foreign policy official in the Bush administration and former director of the 9/11 Commission.

For their final week's simulation exercise in summer 2010, seminar students were led by Dr. Betty Sue Flowers, a leading expert in "future forecasting" and the guiding force behind Shell Oil's Global Scenarios, a much emulated standard for corporate and government scenario projects including the National Intelligence Council's Global Trends Reports.

The Longhorn Long Warriors

In May 2010, Suri, the man behind the now-defunct GSP at the University of Wisconsin-Madison, announced that he was taking a job offer for a joint appointment at the University of Texas-Austin, including a position at the prestigious Strauss Center. A brief survey of the roster there suggests that Suri's move to Austin was the perfect decision for Madison's former wunderkind and "rising star."

The Center has been home for two other Long War intellectuals with high-level national security state ties. One is Philip Bobbitt, concurrently with the Roger Hertog Program on Law and National Security at the Columbia University Law School and a senior fellow at the Strauss Center. The other is Bobby Ray Inman, who recently became the head of the board of directors of Xe Services (formerly known as Blackwater USA), the transnational private military and security firm. He formerly served two terms as dean of the aforementioned home of the Strauss Center, the Lyndon B. Johnson School of Public Affairs.

Bobbitt, once described by Henry Kissinger as "the outstanding political philosopher of our time," and by London's Independent as the "president's brain," formerly served as the counselor for international law at the State Department during the George H. W. Bush administration, and at the NSC, where he was director for intelligence programs. He also was senior director for critical infrastructure and senior director for strategic planning under President Bill Clinton.

Inman wore multiple hats before joining Xe's board. He was a member of the board of directors of the infamous coal company Massey Energy; deputy director of the CIA; director of the NSA; director of naval intelligence; vice director of the Defense Intelligence Agency; and former director of Wackenhut Corporation, another transnational security firm and mercenary contractor. He had also been slated to become President Bill Clinton's Secretary of Defense before withdrawing his name from nomination in 1994.

In 2006, the Strauss Center served as a key backer, along with Columbia University's American Assembly program, for "The Next Generation Project on U.S. Global Policy and the Future of International Institutions," a multiyear national effort to solicit new ideas from a geographically diverse range of strategic thinkers outside the traditional East Coast corridors of power.

Directed by Gavin, another important figure in Long War University circles, the project issued a 2010 report on "U.S. Global Policy: Challenges to Building a 21st Century Grand Strategy." The report was sponsored by the Strauss Center and CNAS.

Long War University Homecoming

In August, 2010 key members of the Long War grand strategist fraternity gathered for a "Workshop on the Teaching of Grand Strategy" at the Naval War College (NWC) at Newport, Rhode Island. It was only logical that they meet there rather than at some university.

The NWC, with its long history of strategic planning dating back to an earlier age of global naval power, had earlier developed the curriculum that became the model for the grand strategies discipline employed at Yale and subsequently elsewhere. For some attendees, such as Gaddis, who spent part of his early teaching career there, the summer return to Newport must have seemed like a homecoming.

The conclave was designed to bring together "some of the nation's most influential thinkers to explore how they design courses on grand strategy." The meet-up's list of attendees read like an abbreviated "who's who" of warrior academics and national security state intellectuals.

Those in attendance included Gaddis, Hill, and Kennedy, as well as their Yale disciples, Columbia's Connelly, Duke's Hal Brands, and then-UW-Madison's Suri.

Among the others were Middle East expert Michael Doran, a Roger Hertog senior fellow at the Saban Center, former deputy assistant secretary of defense under George W. Bush and fellow at the Council on Foreign Relations.

Also present was Peter Mansoor, the current chair of military history at Ohio State University and a former Army colonel who served as an assistant to then- general Petraeus while he was commander of the U.S. occupation forces in Iraq. Also in the mix was Aaron Friedberg, who served as national security adviser to then-vice president Dick Cheney, and Georgetown's Robert J. Lieber, member of the ultraconservative Committee on the Present Danger.

A follow-up thank-you email from the NWC's lead organizer spoke of his "hope that we will stay connected and assist each other in our common enterprise." The same note addressed to the workshop's participants contained an e-mail address likely belonging to Lewis "Scooter" Libby, senior vice president of the Hudson Institute and a past frequent volunteer at the NWC. As Dick Cheney's former chief of staff, Libby was convicted in connection with the federal investigation into the "PlameGate" affair.

The NWC conclave might best be described as an imperial war hawk's "how-to" teach-in. Geared to instruction on how to teach grand strategy to military men, government officials and university students, its sessions included "'Great Books' on Strategy," "Economics and Grand Strategy," "Strategic Leadership," which explored "the relationship of political and military leadership in strategic decision making" and "Great Power Wars," which discussed how to teach "the strategic significance of the commons — maritime, aerospace, and information."

The closing session looked at "how to stay connected with each other," the "sharing of information about courses," "ways to promote cooperation and break down barriers," and "how to promote courses in the professional military and the universities."

The Long War on Campus

The so-called "Grand Strategy Programs" represent but one small component of a proliferating Long War University complex. The number of university programs connected to the national security state, the imperial foreign policy establishment and military planners is vast; so, too, are the numbers of campus-based think tanks and related institutes — well funded by foundations, individual "philanthropy" or federal spending — in service to empire.

"Grand strategy" is little more than imperial doctrine, a "soft" public relations term for strategic studies, a growing academic discipline with origins in the war ministries of an earlier era's imperial powers.

U.S. warfare doctrine in the post-9/11 era has returned to a focus on counterinsurgency, or COIN, on fighting limited "asymmetric" wars against unconventional enemies defined as "terrorists" or insurgents. Not just low-intensity combat, but an increasingly sophisticated spectrum of intervention — of "nation building" and the "reconstruction" of other societies — is now included in COIN doctrine.

That more robust notion of COIN has come to occupy a central place in the thinking of those semi-warrior intellectuals informing one another and an upcoming generation of their students. Sharing a broad consensus on America's role in the world and imbued with a sense of American "exceptionalism," the Long War intellectuals at the national warfare state universities have joined in preparation for permanent war.

Steve Horn is a researcher and writer at DeSmogBlog. He is also a freelance investigative journalist. Follow him on Twitter at @Steve_Horn1022.

Allen Ruff is a U.S. historian and an independent writer on foreign policy issues. He lives in Madison, Wisconsin.

War Is Not Healthy for Civil Liberties

By Jeff Fogel

War is not healthy for people and other living things and, not surprisingly, it's not good for civil liberties either. The military industrial complex, by definition, is designed to keep us on a war footing either by direct involvement or the constant threat of war. We needn't speculate on the impact of war on civil liberties for we have adequate examples from our own history. Let me share some of them with you.

Alien and Sedition Act

In 1798, the Federalist-controlled Congress made it a crime to criticize the government (seditious libel = "writing, printing, uttering, or publishing of any false, scandalous and malicious writing with the intent of bringing the U.S. government or its officials into contempt or disrepute"). The Federalists claimed that this was necessary in light of heightened tensions and the potential for war between the U.S. and France, but all of those charged and convicted under the act were Republicans. In 1801, Jefferson, a Republican, was elected president. He pardoned those who had been convicted, and the act expired by its own terms.

Civil War Suspension of The Writ of Habeas Corpus

Lincoln, the Great Emancipator, early in the civil war, suspended the writ of *habeas corpus*. Tens of thousands of civilians suspected of being disloyal to the Union cause were detained by the military without charge. *Ex parte Milligan* reached the Supreme Court in 1866, after the war. The Attorney General argued that the legal guarantees set forth in the Bill of Rights were "peace provisions." During wartime, he argued, the federal government can suspend the Bill of Rights and impose martial law. If the government chooses to exercise that option, the commanding military officer becomes "the supreme legislator, supreme judge, and supreme executive."

The Supreme Court wrote:

> *During the late wicked Rebellion, the temper of the times did not allow that calmness in deliberation and discussion so necessary to a correct conclusion of a purely judicial question. Then, considerations of safety were mingled with the exercise of power; and feelings and interests prevailed which are happily terminated. Now that the public safety is assured, this question, as well as all others, can be discussed and decided without passion or the admixture of any element not required to form a legal judgment.*

Red Scare of 1917

Shortly after the Russian revolution there was a "red" scare in this county. We had the Palmer Raids and deportations of "dangerous aliens".

The Espionage Act of 1917 made it a crime to "willfully utter, print, write, or publish any disloyal, profane, scurrilous, or abusive language" about the United States. In 1919 the Supreme Court upheld the conviction of socialist Charles Schenck, who had printed and distributed pamphlets urging opposition to the draft. Justice Oliver Wendell Holmes, wrote for a unanimous court, "When a nation is at war many things that might be said in time of peace are such a hindrance to its effort that their utterance will not be endured so long as men fight."

World War II

Franklin Delano Roosevelt, the icon of America liberalism, signed the declaration that resulted in the internment of Japanese Americans — a outrageous act of racism and deprivation of civil liberties, the right to liberty itself, and this was upheld by the Supreme Court.

In 1971, Congress passed the Anti-Detention Act, 18 U.S.C. § 4001(a), which states that "no person shall be imprisoned or otherwise detained by the United States except pursuant to an Act of Congress." Fred Koramatsu, who had brought the unsuccessful case before the Supreme Court, was eventually awarded the Medal of Honor. Congress apologized and provided for limited reparations for this heinous act.

McCarthy Era

As the cold war set in, so did the McCarthy era. The Smith Act made it a crime to knowingly or willfully advocate, abet, advise, or teach the duty, necessity, desirability, or propriety of overthrowing or destroying any government in the United States by force or violence.

In 1951, the Supreme Court upheld the convictions of Eugene Dennis and 10 other leaders of the Communist Party for conspiring to organize the Party and for advocating the overthrow of the government by force and violence. In 1969, in *Brandenburg v. Ohio*, the Warren Court ruled that the government could not prohibit advocacy even of unlawful conduct "except where such advocacy is directed to inciting or producing imminent lawless action and is likely to incite or produce such action."

In 1967 in *U.S. v. Robel*, the Warren Court struck down the portion of the Internal Security Act that prohibited members of communist-action organizations from working in defense plants. "It would indeed be ironic if, in the name of national defense, we would sanction the subversion of one of those liberties ... which makes the defense of the Nation worthwhile... the phrase 'war power' cannot be invoked as a talismanic incantation to support any exercise of power which can be brought within its ambit. Even the war power does not remove constitutional limitations safeguarding essential liberties."

McCarthyism was not only a series of laws (e.g. making membership in a political party a crime or that membership in certain political parties was a disqualification for union leadership or even holding a drivers license) but a process of fear mongering and intimidation that led to the greatest danger to civil liberties, self-censorship something that lasted well into the following decade.

WAR ON TERROR

Patriot Act, One Dissenting Vote in Senate

The USA Patriot Act, passed virtually without debate or discussion in the weeks following 9/11, authorized the executive to conduct certain searches and seizures (e.g. medical records, educational records, financial records, library and bookstore records) on less than the probable cause standard set forth in the Fourth Amendment, so long as the FBI certifies to a judge that it is engaged in a terrorism investigation. The law even made it a crime to disclose the existence of such a search and seizure order.

The Act also established new crimes such as providing material aid to a terrorist organization.

Warrantless Wiretapping

"The NSA activities are supported by the President's well-recognized inherent constitutional authority as Commander in chief and sole organ for the nation in foreign affairs to conduct warrantless surveillance of enemy forces for intelligence purposes to detect and disrupt armed attacks on the United States."

— U.S. Department of Justice memorandum, January 19, 2006.

In this instance, the president acted in direct contradiction to the Foreign Intelligence Security Act which itself provided a mostly secret mechanism for the government to obtain permission from a hand-chosen court to engage in wiretaps that affected national security.

The president asserted the power to declare even a U.S. citizen an "enemy combatant" and to hold that citizen in military custody indefinitely, without trial or other form of due process. The President continues to assert the power to execute even U.S. citizens abroad without any process except what the national security state chooses and that will be hidden from public scrutiny. The invocation of terror, like the invocation of communism, has skewed the balance in the courts as well.

For example, Bret Barsey was arrested while protesting President Bush outside the Columbia, S.C., airport for violating an unannounced "restrictive zone" surrounding the president who had yet to arrive. Thereafter protesters were required to confine themselves to so-called free speech zones that isolated and marginalized their protest.

United for Peace and Justice (UFPJ) was denied a march down First Avenue near the United Nations in New York City to protest the Iraq War, and this was upheld by the courts, all in the name of protecting us from terrorism. When UFPJ sought the use of the great lawn in Central Park, the traditional location for large demonstrations, the judge while acknowledging that fact and that the First Amendment was still in force, nonetheless responded that this was "a new day."

National conventions of the two major political parties, including the Republican National Convention in Minneapolis in 2008, have involved free speech zones, raids on protesters, and undercover operations to disrupt and discredit (reminiscent of COINTELPRO operations against the Black Panthers).

There is a permanent security state in New York City: a little CIA, headed by the CIA, trained by the CIA, employing bag searches, surveillance cameras, arrests for taking pictures, and infiltration of religious communities.

One of the hallmarks of the constant state of war and one of the gravest threats to democracy itself is secrecy. While the President promised transparency in government, the Justice Department repeatedly argues, and usually with success, that the courts are not open to cases that might reveal "state secrets." And we're not talking about how to make a nuclear weapon, but virtually anything that the intelligence community does (e.g. extraordinary rendition) or that might reveal or harm our relations with other governments. Every law student learns the first leading case in the Supreme Court, *Marbury v. Madison,* which teaches that where there is a right under our system of law, there is a remedy. Yet, in the new paradigm, though the Bill of Rights may be violated, there is no remedy in the courts of the United States. A right without a remedy is no right at all. And look at the efforts of this government to prosecute Julian Assange for helping to reveal the kind of important information that citizens in a supposedly free society need to judge their government (of the people and by the people) and their political leaders.

One other war that should not be ignored and that has fostered its own commercial lobby is the War on Drugs and the prison-industrial complex. This has been one of the greatest threats to civil liberties in the past several decades (one aspect of which was characterized by one justice as the "drug exception" to the 4th amendment). The hidden horror of mass incarceration has followed and the result, in part, has been the development of what one wise observer and law professor has called the "New Jim Crow."

In past wars, as I have noted, civil liberties has been one of the casualties, but often, when the war was over, we recognized either the error of our ways or that curtailment of liberties was no longer necessary. Now we face what our politicians (and some of their friends on courts and in the media) call a "war without end," and we thereby face a threat to our liberties without end. What is encouraging, however, and as is apparent here, is the fact that so many people refuse to be silent. After all, neither liberties nor social justice have been or will be achieved or maintained without organized resistance to repression and the demands of the citizenry for social justice. Peace and liberty will come, at home and abroad, not as the result of the so-called victories of war, but as the result of social justice for all.

Jeff Fogel has been a civil rights/civil liberties lawyer for 42 years. He has been the Executive Director and Legal Director of the ACLU of New Jersey, senior staff attorney for the New York Civil Liberties Union, senior attorney for what is now the Puerto Rican Institute for Civil Rights, and Legal Director of the Center for Constitutional Rights.

How Much Does the Military Spend Saving Souls?

By Chris Rodda

When the average American thinks of military spending on religion, they probably think only of the money spent on chaplains and chapels. And, yes, the Department of Defense (DoD) does spend a hell of a lot of money on these basic religious accommodations to provide our troops with the opportunity to exercise their religion while serving our country. But that's just the tip of the iceberg when it comes to the DoD's funding of religion. Also paid for with taxpayer dollars are a plethora of events, programs, and schemes that violate not only the Constitution, but, in many cases, the regulations on federal government contractors, specifically the regulation prohibiting federal government contractors receiving over $10,000 in contracts a year from discriminating based on religion in their hiring practices.

About a year ago, the Military Religious Freedom Foundation (MRFF) began an investigation into just how much money the DoD spends on promoting religion to military personnel and their families. What prompted this interest in DoD spending on religion was finding out what the DoD was spending on certain individual events and programs, such as the $125 million spent on the Army's C4omprehensive Soldier Fitness program and its controversial "Spiritual Fitness" test, a mandatory test that must be taken by all soldiers.[70] The Army insists that this test is not religious, but the countless complaints from soldiers who have failed this "fitness" test tell a different story. The experience of one group of soldiers who weren't "spiritual" enough for the Army can be read online.[71] But the term "Spiritual Fitness" is not limited to this one test. The military began using this term to describe a variety of initiatives and events towards the end of 2006, and this "code phrase" for promoting religion was heavily in use by all branches of the military by 2007.

Although it was clear from the start of MRFF's investigation that determining the total dollar figure for the DoD's rampant promotion of religion (which is always evangelical and/or fundamentalist Christianity) would be next to impossible, as this would require FOIA requests to every one of over 700 military installations to find out how much each is spending out of various funds at the installation level, one thing we could look at was DoD contracts, so that's where we started. What we've found so far is astounding. Even though this is still an ongoing project, and we'll certainly be finding much more, I thought that given all the current brouhaha over what should be cut from the federal budget, people might be interested to see some examples of how the DoD is spending countless millions of taxpayer dollars every year to Christianize the military.

As mentioned above, what MRFF is looking at does not include chaplains or chapels — not even the excessive spending on extravagant "chapels" like the $30,000,000 mega-church at Fort Hood, or the "Spiritual Fitness" centers being built on many military bases as part of what are called Resiliency Campuses. The examples below are all strictly from DoD contracts, with the funding coming out of the appropriations for things like "Operations and Maintenance" and, somehow, "Research and Development." (Summaries of all contracts referenced below are publicly available at usaspending.gov.)

Evangelical Christian Concerts in Guise of "Spiritual Fitness"

One of the most direct expenditures of money on religious proselytizing, under the guise of "Spiritual Fitness" spending, is the funding of concerts with the top evangelical Christian performers. These concerts are most prevalent on Army posts, although they also occur on installations of other branches of the military. One concert series that stands out, both because soldiers were punished last year for not attending one of the concerts and because of the cost of hiring the musical acts, is the "Commanding Generals' Spiritual Fitness Concert Series" at Fort Eustis and Fort Lee in Virginia. This is not a chapel concert series, but a command sponsored "Spiritual Fitness" program, paid for with DoD contracts.

All of the performers for these Spiritual Fitness concerts so far (this concert series is ongoing) have been evangelical Christian artists. Not only is the music itself overtly Christian, but during the concerts there are light shows of large crosses beamed all over the stage, and the performers typically give their Christian testimony or read Bible verses between songs. Some of these performers have Blanket Purchase Agreements and Indefinite Delivery Contracts good until 2012 or 2013, indicating that this concert series is planned to continue at least through the next two years. The total amount of money awarded so far for this concert series, including the amount remaining on Blanket Purchase Agreements and Indefinite Delivery Contracts, is $678,470. This figure is only for the performers fees, and does not include all the other expenses associated with putting on concerts on the scale of those being held at these Army posts.

The following are the amounts of the contracts awarded to Christian talent agencies and bands for this "Commanding General's Spiritual Fitness Concert Series."

- Street Level Artist Agency: $153,000 spent to date, $22,000 remaining on a $50,000 Blanket Purchase Agreement (good until 2012).
- Gregg Oliver Agency: $46,000 spent to date, $54,000 remaining on a $100,000 Indefinite Delivery Contract (good until 2013).
- James D Griggs: $9,900 to date, $141,100 remaining on a $150,000 Blanket Purchase Agreement (good until 2013).

- Titanium Productions, Inc.: $33,470 spent to date, $100,000 remaining on a $100,000 Blanket Purchase Agreement (good until 2012).
- SonicFlood: $24,000 spent to date, $76,000 remaining on a $100,000 Indefinite Delivery Contract (good until 2012).
- The Samoan Brothers LLC: $20,000 spent.

(For these talent agencies and bands where the "amount spent to date" and "amount remaining" on the Blanket Purchase Agreements and Indefinite Delivery Contracts are not equal, it is because these talent agencies have been awarded more than one contract. For example, Titanium Productions, Inc. had contracts totaling $33,470 that were separate from the $100,000 Blanket Purchase Agreement for future concerts in this concert series.)

Evangelical Christian Facilities for Strong Bonds and Other "Spiritual Fitness" Retreats

According to an Army spokesperson on the Pentagon Channel, the Army's Strong Bonds program receives at least $30 million a year in DoD funding. This program of pre- and post-deployment retreats for soldiers and their families are often evangelical Christian retreats, many held at Christian camps and resorts, with evangelical Christian speakers and entertainers.

A search of DoD contracts for the last few years shows that at least 50 of the locations where Strong Bonds and other Spiritual Fitness retreats are regularly held are evangelical Christian camps, resorts, and conference facilities.

The site regularly used by Fort Sill, for example, is Oakridge Camp and Retreat Center, which has received over $500,000 in DoD contracts and has hosted approximately 60 retreats. Oakridge not only requires its employees to be Christians, but even goes as far as requiring on its employment application that the applicant state their views on issues such as abortion and homosexuality. While a private religious organization is free to impose a religious test on its staff, it is quite a different matter for a DoD contractor to do this. And, in the case of Oakridge, it is not only the facility's staff who must adhere to the its Christian beliefs, but all of its guests as well, including the soldiers attending Fort Sill's Strong Bonds and Spiritual Fitness retreats.

For example, the first paragraph of Oakridge's "Policies and Guidelines" for its guests states: "Oakridge is a private Christian retreat center, not a hotel. Therefore, there may be some guidelines and policies that may not seem 'hotel-like.' This is our purposeful intent. Oakridge does not serve the 'general public,' but only those interested in a Christian camp perspective." Moreover, guest groups must attend an "Oakridge Orientation," and it is stated in the "Policies and Guidelines" that "prayer will be offered for all groups at every meal in Jesus' name."

While Strong Bonds is specifically an Army program, the rampant promotion of evangelical Christianity under the guise of Spiritual Fitness is going on in all branches of the military. As an example from another branch of the military, over $120,000 in DoD contracts have been awarded to the Williamsburg Christian Retreat Center, one of the facilities used by both the Army and the Navy for retreats. Another popular site in Virginia for the Navy's Spiritual Fitness and "Personal Growth" retreats is the Peninsula Baptist Association's Eastover Retreat Center, which has received $75,000 in DoD contracts. For its retreats in Rhode Island, the Navy also uses a Baptist facility, the American Baptist Church's Canonicus Camping and Conference Center, which has received $53,000 in DoD contracts.

In addition to the constitutional issue of these military retreats being evangelical Christian retreats, any of the Christian facilities used for these retreats that receives over $10,000 in DoD contracts is in violation of the prohibition on federal government contractors discriminating based on religion in their hiring practices. They all hire only Christians, and many require in their employment applications that potential employees subscribe to a "statement of faith" and provide their Christian "testimony," detailing when and how they were "saved."

Evangelical Christian Performers for Strong Bonds and Other Events

Even retreats that are not located at religious camps regularly feature evangelical Christian speakers and entertainers. The contract amounts range from a few thousand dollars paid to each of a number of individual "motivational" speakers for single retreats to tens of thousands of dollars for evangelical Christian ministries and performers hired for multiple retreats. For example, Quail Ministries, a Christian music ministry that provides performances "liberally seasoned with songs, stories, and anecdotal Scripturally-based lessons," has received over $84,000 in DoD contracts for performances at about a dozen Strong Bonds retreats.

Unlimited Potential, Inc., a ministry "Serving Christ Through Baseball" by sending evangelical Christian major league baseball players to military events, received over $80,000 in DoD contracts for just two retreats, one Strong Bonds retreat and one Spiritual Fitness retreat. Unlimited Potential has been at many other military bases for various other events that do not show up in DoD contracts, presumably because these appearances were paid for with base funds.

DoD Funded Evangelical Christian Youth Programs

Service members are not the only ones targeted by evangelical Christian programs paid for with DoD contracts. Military children are also heavily targeted, both here in the U.S. and on bases overseas. Evangelizing the children of service members is one of the largest areas of spending.

The biggest ministry contracted by the DoD to target children is Military Community Youth Ministries (MCYM), whose mission statement is "Celebrate life with military teens, Introduce them to the Life-Giver, Jesus Christ, And help them become more like Him." MCYM has received $12,346,333 in DoD contracts since 2000. One of MCYM's tactics? Stalking "unchurched" military children by following their schools buses.

Ranking second is Cadence International, with over $2,671,603 in contracts since 2003. Cadence describes itself as "an evangelical mission agency dedicated to reaching the military communities of the United States and of the world with the Good News of Jesus Christ." Cadence not only targets young service members and military children for conversion to evangelical Christianity, but also actively tries to convert members of foreign militaries in the countries where they operate under DoD contracts.

In addition to military youth ministries like MCYM and Cadence, military children are also targeted by military base Religious Education Directors, also hired with DoD contracts. These ministries and Religious Education Directors employ tactics that can only be described as "stalking" children, with some DoD contracts even requiring that the contractors identify and target the "unchurched" children at non-religious events and activities and get them into chapel programs, and to supply reports naming these children by name.

Conversion by Temptation

As I've been sitting here writing this post, an email came in to MRFF from a soldier who is currently in Advanced Individual Training (AIT), the stage of training between basic training and a soldier's first assignment, where the soldier receives training in the particular job they will be doing. During AIT, soldiers are typically given a few privileges that they didn't have in basic training, but not many.

This soldier's email is a great example of a common strategy that I call "conversion by temptation," where the military ministries and the military itself tempt young soldiers and military children with fun or exciting things to lure them into participating in programs and events where they can be "saved." What young soldier would pass up a vacation at a resort with their spouse that they could never afford on their military salary? That's how the Army's Strong Bonds program gets many soldiers who would never attend a religious retreat to attend evangelical Christian retreats. What teenage kid would pass up a ski trip or week at the beach with the other kids? That's how DoD funded military youth ministries like MCYM lure the teenage kids of our service members.

The email that just came in from the soldier in AIT was about the soldiers in training being granted extra privileges if they attend the programs on his post run by Cadence International. These privileges include being allowed to have pizza and soda on Friday nights if they go to the Christian "Coffee House," even if they haven't reached the stage of training where this is allowed, and being allowed to wear civilian clothes and engage in all sorts of fun activities if they go to Cadence's on-post weekend retreats.

To a non-Christian soldier in AIT, getting the extra privileges and having some fun are worth the price of having to sit through the fundamentalist Christian sermons that go along with these activities, so many of them do it. Others go along simply because they don't want to stand out from the crowd and be singled out as being of the "wrong" religion or not being religious.

Cadence particularly targets soldiers in AIT for a reason — these are the soldiers likely to soon be facing their first deployment. And this ministry, which, as noted above receives DoD contracts for its work, makes no secret of why it has chosen AIT as its mission field. One of the reasons given by Cadence for the success of its "Strategic Ministry" is: "Deployment and possibly deadly combat are ever-present possibilities. They are shaken.

Shaken people are usually more ready to hear about God than those who are at ease, making them more responsive to the gospel." Of course, they must first gain access to these "shaken" soldiers, but that's no problem — the Army helps them out by allowing them to operate on Army posts and granting the soldiers in AIT extra privileges if they attend Cadence's retreats.

For more details on these and other taxpayer funded schemes to Christianize the U.S. military, see "Against All Enemies, Foreign and Domestic," the chapter I wrote for the 2010 book *Attitudes Aren't Free: Thinking Deeply about Diversity in the US Armed Forces,* published by Air University Press, the publishing arm of the Air Force's Air University at Maxwell Air Force Base.

Chris Rodda is the Senior Research Director for the Military Religious Freedom Foundation (MRFF), and the author of *Liars For Jesus: The Religious Right's Alternate Version of American History.*

What War Does to Law

By Benjamin G. Davis[72]

Introduction

Thank you for the opportunity to address the subject of what war does to law. As an initial matter, I draw your attention to two books that I think are relevant for the work of this conference.

First, I draw your attention to the recently published work of a German author of the early to mid 20th century named Hans Fallada and entitled *Every Man Dies Alone*.[73] The fictional account about a couple called the Quangels is based on the true story of a German couple named Otto and Elise Hampel who, after the death of the brother of Elise in the German assault on France during World War II, started a clandestine anti-Nazi effort in Berlin. The couple wrote little postcards calling for the overthrow of Hitler and dropped these postcards surreptitiously in public places around Berlin. Their dissenting effort lasted two years until they were arrested by the Gestapo, were tried, and ultimately executed. At one point in the novel, the husband explains to the wife what he intends to do and the wife takes the view that the form of dissent — writing these little postcards — is a pretty insignificant form of dissent. The husband agrees but also says something to the effect that if they are caught doing this insignificant thing, it was certain they would be killed.

I draw the attention of the conference participants to this book and this exchange because persons may sometimes feel compelled to dissent or do acts of dissent but ultimately not do anything because they feel their small protests are insignificant and meaningless. We may feel overwhelmed by the state and feel powerless to dissent from actions with which we disagree. Yet, it is important that we each in our modest ways make our voices heard, drop our little postcards on the street in the manner of the Hampels. It is the aggregation of those dissenting voices and acts of dissent that with time can have an influence and, at a minimum, provide inspiration for generations afterward confronted with similar situations.

Second, on movements, the best book that I have found is by an Italian sociologist named Francesco Alberoni and entitled *Movement and Institution*.[74] While we are all warned to beware of systematizers, what is refreshing about Alberoni is that he is agnostic about the content of the movements and yet also analyzes movements from the largest transnational ones like capitalism or communism down to the smallest ones such as a couple falling in love, what he describes as a movement of two people. In addition, Alberoni goes further in that he describes the process by which a person changes prior to becoming part of a movement. He discusses the contradictions that arise in a person between what they feel or think inside and what they experience in society. The result is that the person reaches a state Alberoni describes as "depressive overload" when the contradictions become too much. The person then is spurred by these contradictions to react to what is happening in their environment — and that moment of change is what he calls "the nascent state." Once a person reaches that changed state they tend to seek others who are of a similar view — to seek affinity in Alberoni's terms. It is the process of these persons all sharing the "nascent state" through the process of developing affinity that leads to the birth and growth of the movement. Alberoni goes farther in describing the four generic reactions of the institutions (or "everyday life") with result that the movement is ultimately institutionalized, made extinct, repressed, or dissolves in illusion. An example of a person going through depressive overload is Rosa Parks refusing to stand up on the bus. We are all familiar with the events that transpired subsequent to that brave act.

I submit that many of the participants at this conference are experiencing the depressive overload and have felt a need to dissent to current events.

In coming together in this conference, we are each in our nascent state and seeking the affinity with others. Through that process that Alberoni describes, I am comforted in saying that a movement has arisen. Our efforts and learning will reveal in due course to what extent the interaction of this movement with institutions will lead to an outcome and, if so, which of the potential generic outcomes described above. The key for me is that a process is going forward as we each experience the contradictions of today. It is Alberoni's description of this process that gives me comfort for it foreshadows the possibility of possibilities for change — though it does not guarantee that such change can occur. All we each can do is to try to express our vision of what we hope should be changed and work toward that change.

Dropping the postcards in Fallada is a symbolic expression of the process of reaching the nascent state of dissent that is at the heart of Alberoni. I hope these two references assist persons in understanding their current status and in helping to see how a way forward might be developed.

International Law and the American Project since 9/11

"Everything must change so that everything can stay the same."
— *Il Gattopardo, Giuseppe Tomasi di Lampedusa.*

It is important to keep in mind two types of law: international law and domestic law. International law is defined as international agreements (colloquially treaties), customary international law and general principles of law recognized by civilized states.[75] Domestic law is all the law from the Constitution on down inside a state such as the United States. One of the fundamental rules of international law is that a state may not invoke the provisions of its internal law as justification for its failure to perform its international obligations.[76] What this international law rule means is that as long as the United States has an international law obligation, the internal law changes are of no moment or ability to extract the United

States from its obligations. If the United States changes its domestic law or acts in a manner pursuant to that domestic law that is inconsistent with its international legal obligations the United States is in breach of those obligations — the obligations do not disappear just because of the domestic law modification.

Ten years after 9/11, it appears that the fundamental instruments, and therefore the rules and principles of international law, have not changed. None of the international agreements forming the core of international humanitarian law, human rights law, or even Article 51 of the United Nations Charter have been altered since 9/11, nor has customary international law. Even if we look at the complicity of many states in rendition and torture, the approach was clearly not done out of a sense that the law had changed. So, with regard to all of the current concerns such as national security, Guantanamo, civil liberties, human rights and the law of war since 9/11, international law has not changed.

So if international law has not changed, what has changed? Among the changes are the policy, practice and domestic law of the U.S. that were noted in Jeff Fogel's presentation. Further, the security state has expanded in an unprecedented manner at the federal, state and local level, with surveillance being a permanent feature in the lives of Americans. Law enforcement and armed conflict paradigms are traded with and against an ostensibly new self-defense paradigm to provide legal rationales for the use of various types of force in Afghanistan, Pakistan, Iraq, Yemen, Somalia and surely other places around the world.

While it is said that torture is no longer performed, meaningful high-level accountability for torture and cruel, inhumane and degrading treatment has so far been blocked. The detention facilities at Guantanamo Bay have been opened, expanded, announced to be closed, and yet have remained. The U.S. domestic crime of material support for terrorism and material witness statutes have morphed into terrorism fighting tools. History has been reinterpreted as far back as the Seminole Wars and international precedents strained to argue that some domestic law of war crimes (material support for terrorism[77] and conspiracy[78]) are to be applied as if they were international law of war crimes pursuant to congressional definitions in the ersatz justice of the military commissions. Courts have used or expanded doctrines of state secrets and national security at the request of the federal government to block redress to foreigners for excesses alleged to have been committed. Ironically, one can get more evidence about "torture flights" in a garden variety commercial contract dispute in a New York court than through any procedure attempting to redress the consequences of physical and psychological violence.[79]

The architects of these American policies, whether political leaders from the executive or legislature, lawyers, psychologists and many others, blithely walk the streets unimpeded and often times heralded in media and print. Our government works overtime to dissuade foreign or international tribunals from disturbing these architects of the new U.S. and its policies in the world. Taking the country to war in Iraq on false pretenses is bemoaned by some, challenged by others, but nonetheless eventually forgotten.

The Arab Spring reveals state security apparatuses and their roles in aspects of the American-led War on Terror. Books are published in which political leaders sing the praises of their decisions. At the same time, detainees are shifted around, or languish incommunicado. Some have been driven insane by their treatment.

In sum, international law has not changed but the U.S. domestic policy, practice and law has. It is very important for Americans to understand the view from the international plane of the United States' international legal obligations and the view from the domestic plane of the United States legal obligations because any differences between the two sets of obligations highlight a dissonance in the view of the United States between the rest of the world and the internal view promulgated by our government. Being able to see what the rest of the world might understand and compare it with what is being stated in the United States provides an ability to see more clearly what is being undertaken by the United States government and why the reactions of the rest of the world are as they are. In addition to the military commissions decisions discussed above here are a couple of further examples.

First, on the War in Iraq, the broad consensus among the American people that their leaders lied to them has not lead to accountability for those former leaders. Rather, quite interestingly, in the internal discussions the Iraq war is examined as a "model of intervention" (to be compared, for example, to Libya). This vision looks at the War in Iraq through the lens of the Congressional Authorization for Use of Military Force Against Iraq Resolution of 2002 (i.e. from a domestic law perspective). This vision leaves to the side the international law perspective that unleashing an armed conflict without the authorization of the United Nations Security Council nor a basis in Article 51 of the UN Charter was aggressive war, the supreme crime.

Second, on torture, all of the dubious definitions of torture and cruel, inhumane and degrading treatment in the infamous torture memos, the invocation of the state secrets privilege and other national security privileges are pursuant to interpretations on the domestic plane of both domestic law and international law obligations. However, these domestic law permutations do not change the nature of the international law obligations on the United States under the relevant treaty law.

Whether on the War in Iraq, on torture or on the military commission decisions discussed above, being able to view these seminal events of the 9/11 period from both the domestic law and international law perspective allows one to have great clarity as to what the United States government is doing. Where the United States approach diverges substantially from what is considered appropriate as a matter of international law, one begins to see reasons for disquiet and dissent.

Bringing Light to Dark Matters

One of the benefits of being able to appreciate the same actions of the United States from the domestic and international law perspectives is that one can better see the source of one's disquiet. For example, as discussed above, the crime of material support for terrorism was codified in the *Military Commissions Act* of 2006 and 2009 by the United States Congress. Such a crime is alleged to be an international law of war crime. The military commissions addressing cases where a defendant has been charged with that crime have worked hard to find precedents in the United States and abroad for charging persons with that crime as an international law of war crime. Some of the key precedents cited in the United States take us back to the Seminole Wars and military commissions at that time in which executions of defendants were viewed years later as murder. In a sense, the successful "proof" based on alleged precedents derived from what we might term dark moments in our history requires us to confront those moments or bring light to those dark matters.

The fact that what occurs today is supported by those dark matters helps us confront a current reality where we are asked to go back to somber occasions in the American past to provide a basis for difficult actions done ostensibly in the name of the American people today. The fact that we go to those somber arenas should hopefully give us pause and cause some disquiet. It was for this precise reason, I submit, that Judge James Robertson of the United States District Court for Washington, D.C. in his opinion of July 18, 2008, in an earlier stage of the *Hamdan* case harkened back in this enemy combatant case to the Jim Crow era, to a case in which

African-Americans in the South during segregation were abused in an interrogation. By bringing light to dark matters in our history, I believe that Judge Robertson carefully reminded the United States of a time when hysteria led to profoundly unfair processes.[80]

As leaders draw from the darker chapters of American history to find precedents for what they seek to do, we are called in turn to step back and ask why those parts of history were left in the dark. The willingness of leaders to recall these dark chapters demonstrates an almost pathological misapprehension of what the American project is. A city upon a hill cannot wallow in these dark chapters of history.

What is to be done? Those who oppose these dark matters that fill our present and recent past must continue to shed light on what is going on as a form of earnest struggle to reclaim the American project. Americans must continue to insist on accountability for those in past and current administrations who betrayed our fundamental principles and the peremptory norms of international law. Keeping in mind those who died and were wounded on 9/11, we must renew our faith in the best aspects of American history.

But I would go farther in thinking about these dark matters.

A colleague brought to my attention an article concerning the effort to extradite former Acting General Counsel John Rizzo of the Central Intelligence Agency to places such as Pakistan for him to stand trial for murder with regard to persons killed by drone strikes. This article struck a chord with me because John Rizzo played the key role in authorizing drone strikes on individuals in this administration, but also was a key player as detailed in the Department of Justice Office of Professional Responsibility Report released by Attorney General Holder in seeking legal cover/clarity for the CIA persons engaged in the torture under the Bush Administration.

Rizzo also spoke at my law school last year as part of a law review symposium on the Military Commissions in which persons from the floor raised issues about his role in the torture.

The legality of drone strikes has been the subject of much debate as persons have argued whether they should be analyzed under the legal regimes of international humanitarian law, international human rights law, domestic law such as the Authorization for Use of Military Force, or a construct that has sought to be seen as emerging that might be called international self-defense law. The analysis of the torture over the past years has also sought to look for treaty, customary international law, and domestic federal statutes. For example, we have recently been made aware that two criminal cases concerning torture and the CIA are going forward at the suggestion of U.S. Attorney John Durham. Durham was tasked by the Attorney General at the Department of Justice to review 101 cases regarding detainee treatment and the CIA to see if there were any cases where the treatment was outside the boundaries of the legal advice given. Finally, the definition efforts for the crime of aggressive war in the Rome Statute that recently occurred at Kampala are another aspect of trying to articulate rules for criminal responsibility for actions taken by state actors.

I have looked at drone strikes under different lenses of law. I have urged criminal prosecution of high-level civilians and military generals in U.S. domestic courts for torture and cruel inhuman and degrading treatment. I have questioned the legality of the War in Iraq.

It occurred to me over the past couple of days that there is a common thread across these issues of drones, torture, and illegal wars. The unifying thought was that the use of drones, interrogation, and armed conflict each have various legal regimes that shape them and form the universe of what we see as what is legally permissible. The legality of the manner in which state actors operate in these areas are derived from both domestic and international law rules. The powers of any individual official to act are derived from the internal state structure such as the Constitution.

Just like there is the known universe of these rules that apply for these areas, I started to wonder about what is not seen in the universe: when state actors act with malice aforethought or sufficient *mens rea* and *actus reus* to be a crime. It occurred to me that this part of the universe of law might also be viewed as the dark matter in a similar fashion to how the term is used in astrophysics. Dark matter has not been seen but is used as a way to explain certain phenomenon that are inexplicable by what is seen in the known universe.

An example of dark matter would be a drone strike which does not fit within the proper categories of legality. I thought of this type of dark matter when reading a February 13, 2011 *Newsweek* article on the use of drones which states:

> *A look at the bureaucracy behind the operations reveals that it is multilayered and methodical, run by a corps of civil servants who carry out their duties in a professional manner. Still, the fact that Rizzo was involved in "murder," as he sometimes puts it, and that operations are planned in advance in a legalistic fashion, raises questions.*

> *More than a year after leaving the government, Rizzo, a bearded, elegant 63-year-old who wears cuff links and pale yellow ties, discussed his role in the CIA's "lethal operations" with me over Côtes du Rhone and steak in a Washington restaurant. At times, Rizzo sounded cavalier. "It's basically a hit list," he said. Then he pointed a finger at my forehead and pretended to pull a trigger. "The Predator is the weapon of choice, but it could also be someone putting a bullet in your head."[81]*

From the quote, the person tasked with the determination of who would be subject to a strike would sometimes refer to these actions as "murder." For me, it is not possible to dismiss out of hand the use of that type of language about some of the State's action. Such use of the term murder brought up the possibility that some drone strikes might not be legally justified (whatever the legal regime one asserts) and thus would be properly defined by someone with expertise as murder. Such a murder by the state that was not under a legally permissible regime would form, it appeared to me, part of the dark matter of state responsibility without state legality. In that space, one is tasked with finding how the legal superstructure should respond to the illegality. Do the normal tools of immunity etc. still operate in this sphere of dark matter or are the constructs we normally view no longer protective of the State's servitors precisely because they have stepped outside the outer perimeter of what is legally permitted?

A similar view of dark matter can be seen in two phases in thinking about torture. First, those acting outside the confines of the legal advice on torture would be operating in the state's administratively determined legally impermissible space of this dark matter. Next, are those who operate within the confines of legal advice or those who draft legal advice where that advice itself forms part of the dark matter by trying to make legal things that are not. Again, what is the response of the legal superstructure to persons in these two areas of the dark matter?

A further view of dark matter can be seen in the taking of a country to war on false pretenses. While constitutional forms are followed, at a fundamental level, what if the leader has the *mens rea* that causes a war that resembles or is aggressive war? Do the outer perimeters of the leader's Constitutional and Congressional powers protect the leader? Has the leader by so stepping outside of rules moved into a space of dark matter in which the normal protections may no longer be operable? If so, what then should be the approaches to the person who has an official capacity yet who departs from the constraints upon that official capacity through his *mens rea* in doing his acts?

Whether in drones, torture, or illegal wars, the evidence of things not seen suggests that there is dark matter here too that might need to be brought to light to help us more completely understand the universe of the State in which we live. In understanding, maybe we can learn to comprehend the manner in which such departures by leaders into the dark matter can be properly addressed and integrated to complete our sense of what we need to confront in this existence.

A question that John Rizzo asked in the article above that seemed to be directed at law professors is, "How many law professors have signed off on a death warrant?" Such decisions are no doubt terrible in the context of proper state authority, but when said state authority goes after persons who are only perceived as threats, I sense that we are stepping into the dark matter. The question reminded me of a veiled threat made to me at an American Society of International Law meeting when I called out a former CIA person on the importance of criminal prosecution of even paper pushers.

The Deal — Bring Light

We can be made fearful by such aggressive language about bringing death. In fact, at a time when we are led to understand that the surveillance state has been greatly expanded, at a conference like this each of us might wonder whether in fact what we are saying is being monitored.

I assume that everything that I do is being monitored by the surveillance state. So, as I did in the conference, in this brief presentation I speak to those in the surveillance state who are reading my words. It is a strange situation where one is writing to someone one knows is there, they know you are there, yet you both do not know each other.

The assumption that one is being monitored by the surveillance state should not lead one to cower but to rather take the approach of speaking one's mind. If one is free, then one must act free even when what one is doing is monitored. To self-censor in such a setting is to allow the secret of the surveillance state to cause one to cower. It is to betray such important concepts in the American soul as that enshrined in the motto of the State of New Hampshire where I lived for three years as a child: "Live Free or Die." As I have grown older and the fear of the post-9/11 experience has been pushed at me, the need to live free even in the monitored surveillance state of our current times, has never been more important to me.

At the conference, I went so far as to say "Fuck the Surveillance State." I did that as a means of encouraging those in the room to see how far back the boundaries of freedom can be pushed to counteract the oppressive feeling of being watched. Like those postcards described in the Fallada book or maybe as a result of a profound sense of "depressive overload" about many things done in my name and in the name of all Americans, the act of speaking with freedom has become vitally important to me. So law professors like myself and each of us as ordinary citizens must think to renew our vigilance and play the role of bringers of light to help understanding of our state. I think this "deal" of bringing light is the set of cards we have been dealt in this time of surveillance. By bringing light on these dark matters, we push back the shadows and keep hope of a bright future alive. If we do not continue to bring light, then one can imagine increased repression. For me, the dark matter might come to include even worse questions in the future such as, "How many death warrants have you signed for law professors?" A perceived threat by the state from any of us becomes the only measure for the state to react lethally. Such a future would truly be a dark time.

Therefore, one of our central tasks is to bring light to dark matter in various areas of the law and society in an attempt to hold back the state's lethality to assure the space of dissent, dialogue, and human liberty with security. The other central tasks may be to train those around us to in turn do the same when we are gone. The third may be to write things as I have tried to do most imperfectly here, so that the memory of these efforts remains for future generations faced with the same or similar dark matter — like the memory of the Hampels dropping those postcards in the streets of Hitler's Berlin.[82]

We see what war does to law. International law has not changed and is not in crisis. What has changed is American law and, as is seen sadly each day, it is America that is in crisis. But, by our faith and love of our country, we can work to bring our country back to the light.

Benjamin Davis is an Associate Professor at the University of Toledo College of Law. He is the author of numerous publications, with special interests in conflict resolution, command responsibility, international law, and torture.

Thinking Critically About Mass Media

By Robert Jensen

Perhaps the one thing that unites most Americans is their disgust with, and distrust of, journalism: Everyone hates the mass media. Surveys show that less than a third of Americans say that news organizations generally get the facts straight, and the level of trust is dropping.[83] Much of this distrust is expressed as a belief that journalists are not objective and, therefore, have become a vehicle for propaganda.

As is often the case, these critiques are made with no clear definition of "objectivity" or "propaganda." In this essay I will offer some suggestions about definitions, in the hopes not that everyone will come to agreement about journalism, but that disagreements will be more productive.

Objectivity

Like all terms, "objective" and "objectivity" are used in different ways in different contexts. In everyday conversation, if someone is making an argument that seems to be unfairly biased or unnecessarily argumentative, we often counsel that the person to "try to be objective." What we typically mean is that the other person's passion might be impeding their ability to see things clearly. Being objective, in this case, means something like this: Try to understand your preconceived ideas about the subject and recognize how those preconceptions might skew your perspective, even to the point that you may be tempted to fudge the facts or make claims that aren't true. When we ask each other to be objective, we are reminding ourselves to keep an open mind and not make things up just because they bolster our argument.

In that everyday sense of the term, objectivity is a good thing — for me, for you, for journalists, for everyone. Objectivity is just another way of reminding ourselves what good intellectual practice looks like. To be objective, we need not pretend we don't have a point of view, that we aren't passionate about our ideas and commitments. Rather, the reminder to be objective is a corrective if our passion leads us to get sloppy in our critical thinking.

Objectivity also has a more specific meaning in the context of a scientific laboratory. Because science is an enterprise carried out by humans, scientists don't claim to have developed a method that brackets out all subjective decisions. But the scientific method offers a way to generate knowledge that can be rigorously tested and verified. Scientists develop protocols for measuring aspects of the world they wish to study and devising experiments to test hypotheses. These methods are not foolproof, but they have been extremely successful in expanding our understanding of the world.

This scientific sense of objectivity may guide our intellectual practices — we adapt ideas about measurement and experimentation in rough fashion to our everyday life. For example, if we want to know whether a dish we've cooked tasted better with or without hot peppers, we might conduct an ad hoc experiment by preparing the food both ways and asking our dinner guests which they prefer. Journalists do this as well, but not with the kind of rigor that one sees in a laboratory. Scientific objectivity, in the strict sense, isn't possible in journalism.

Neither of those definitions captures what objectivity means in mainstream corporate-commercial journalism in the United States today.[84] Yes, journalists strive to be objective in the everyday sense, and when possible journalists mimic the method of scientists. But "objectivity" in practice in mainstream journalism defines a set of professional practices that are most concerned with who and what is a trustworthy source. This practice of objective journalism favors what are typically called "official sources," which actually undermines the ability of journalists to do their job responsibly.

While journalists move about in the world and sometimes directly observe events they write about, much of journalism is based on other people's accounts of what happens. Journalists get this information through interviewing people or reviewing documents that others have produced. The crucial question for journalists is which people and which written accounts are most authoritative? When there are conflicting accounts of the world, which can be trusted? The research on this subject,[85] and my own experience as a working journalist, points to a simple conclusion: Official sources dominate the mainstream news. An official source, in journalistic practice, is one who is associated with a reputable organization that has some credibility and status in the culture. In the contemporary United States, that means the government and the corporation, and a few other institutions that are seen as producing trustworthy knowledge, such as universities and think tanks. These become the "authorized knowers" on whom journalists rely.

Here's an example of how journalists rely on these sources. After many of the claims made to justify the U.S. invasion of Iraq in 2003 were demonstrated to be false, journalists were challenged to explain their failure to provide a critical and independent evaluation of those claims. One such exchange took place on *The Daily Show*, with Jon Stewart questioning *CNN* anchor Wolf Blitzer. After acknowledging the failure, Blitzer explained that he and other journalists had done the necessary reporting but still were unable to learn the truth:

> *So, I remember going off. I had all the briefings. I went over, got the briefings from the CIA, the Pentagon, spoke to all the members*

of Congress, the intelligence committees, the House side, the Senate side. Everybody said the same thing: There is no doubt there are stockpiles of chemical and biological weapons, and it's only a matter of time before he has a nuclear bomb.[86]

Note the sources that Blitzer includes in his list of "all the briefings" that were important in reporting the story: His sources were all officials from the U.S. government. Those officials don't really constitute "all" of the potential sources, of course; Blitzer is suggesting that they are all the relevant sources. But might there have been others who would provide information and analysis that questioned the U.S. claims about Iraq's weapons programs? What about sources in the anti-war movement in the United States, including former government officials who were warning that the WMD claims were overblown? Or sources in the Middle East who might have first-hand knowledge? Or sources who could speak to past cases where government officials lied about a foreign threat to justify war?[87]

Blitzer's reflexive defense of his reporting is common in mainstream journalism. This reliance on official sources may not always produce good journalism — and sometimes may produce truly reprehensible journalism — but it's easy to understand why the practice continues. Using official sources takes less time; government and corporate officials have large public relations operations that churn out information in a form journalists can easily use. That information is presumed credible, and journalists don't have to defend their reporting techniques to news managers since that's the way it's always been done. This means the news managers can hire fewer reporters, saving on labor costs and increasing profits. And because most journalists think of themselves as working in a profession, in the same kind of position as lawyers, there is a subtle class allegiance at play. When evaluating sources, it's not surprising that journalists favor folks who they view as being similar to them in education, social class, and worldview.

While we shouldn't accept the claim that journalists' professional practices produce objectivity, we also shouldn't assume that the production of news is a totally subjective enterprise open to the whims of individuals. Journalists work within a system, interacting with political actors also working within systems, all responding to the people reading and watching the news. Rather than ask whether any one person in these systems is objective or subjective, we should understand news — like all human knowledge — as the product of an intersubjective process. The relevant questions are about the power each group has to affect the direction, framing, and content of the news. These officials are not only sources for news stories but also news shapers; they play a key role in defining what counts as news.[88] When representative of the wealthy and powerful have a disproportionate influence in that intersubjective process, the news is skewed toward the perspective of the those forces and tends to marginalize dissident voices, which reinforces the ideology of the powerful and helps make it the "common sense" of the culture by virtue of its constant repetition. These conventional reporting practices absorb a particular ideology but do not make it explicit.

One last warning about how words are used: As "objectivity" became increasingly suspect to more and more news consumers, some journalists abandoned the term and began describing their goal as "fairness." While it's healthy for journalists to recognize that naïve notions of objectivity are counterproductive, what's needed is not just a shift in the term but in the underlying practices. If the professional practices that were described by "objectivity" don't change, then relabeling them as "fairness" changes nothing. The problem isn't the label we use to describe the practices, it's the practices themselves.

Critiquing these professional routines is central to any sensible analysis of journalism, just as an evaluation of the practices of other professionals such as lawyers is part of understanding the role of law in society. Assessing journalism also requires that we look at the effects of the corporate-commercial structure of the mainstream news media and the larger ideological framework within which journalists work. Two important critics of the news media have argued that these forces create a journalism that often serves a propaganda function for the powerful.[89] To make sense of that claim, we need to think clearly about what we mean when we label a communication "propaganda".

Propaganda and Persuasion

Much like objectivity, propaganda is a term frequently used and infrequently defined clearly. The term originates in the 17th century as part of the Catholic Counter-Reformation, when the Sacred Congregation for the Propagation of the Faith was charged with spreading doctrine in response to the Protestant challenge. Until World War I, the term was used to mean any attempt to spread information and was not generally seen as a pejorative term. During that war the United States created its first official state propaganda agency to move public opinion toward support for a generally unpopular war, and the term began to acquire a negative connotation. By the end of World War II, the successful — but ugly and destructive — propaganda efforts of the Nazis solidified that association of propaganda with communication strategies designed to undermine people's ability to participate in the honest and open dialogue essential to democracy. Today, to label someone's communication effort as propaganda is understood as criticism.

But because democracy is based on people engaging each to persuade the other to support their proposals, it's not enough to define propaganda as a systematic attempt to convince another to get on board with their political project. How will we distinguish between attempts to persuade that are consistent with good intellectual practice and democracy, and attempts to manipulate people that are inconsistent with good intellectual practice and democracy, what we might call propaganda? The distinction is not as easy to make as we may wish it were.

For example, this is the definition offered in a widely used textbook by two contemporary scholars: "Propaganda is the deliberate, systematic attempt to shape perceptions, manipulate cognitions, and direct behavior to achieve a response that furthers the desired intent of the propagandist."[90] I often give public talks about political subjects. In those speeches, I engage in a deliberate, systematic attempt to affect my audience's perceptions, cognitions, and behaviors. If they don't agree with me, I want them to change their minds. If they do agree with me, I want to solidify their position. In doing this, I don't mention every possibly relevant fact or put forward every interpretation of those facts; I select the evidence and arguments that I think most important. Inevitably, I shape and, in some sense, manipulate. Is that propaganda? Working from that definition, it's hard to tell.

When I pose this question to my students — is there a principled way to distinguish persuasion from propaganda? — some common answers emerge. First, they say, "propaganda is lying," the knowing use of false statements to support a position. Certainly some of what we intuitively understand to be propaganda includes false statements, but much propaganda isn't about claims that are clearly true or false, but about interpretation and impressions. Second, "propaganda uses emotion to manipulate people." Again, that's often the case, but is emotion not part of how we understand the world? If any appeal to emotion to influence people is propaganda, then there would be no role for our emotional reactions in public life, making for a sterile and inhuman public discourse. Third, "propaganda exploits powerful images to override rational thought." But does that mean photography and film are not legitimate ways to present information about the world? If images always override our critical capacities, then we're in real trouble.

I have not found, nor been able to construct, a definition of propaganda that with precision can distinguish propaganda from persuasion; such are the limits of language when dealing with the messiness of human affairs.

But the attempt to clarify these concepts matters, because democracy is based on deliberation that, at least in theory, can produce resolutions of policy disagreements that are acceptable to every individual. In a democratic system we don't hold out for the unrealistic goal of everyone agreeing about everything, but rather that everyone commits to a process that produces a fair resolution based on an honest and transparent process. If propaganda is a useful term to mark the communication techniques that derail that process, then we should struggle to deepen our understanding.

Rather than searching for a legalistic definition, I will offer a list of features of systems that intuitively we think of as healthy persuasion and unhealthy propaganda.

Democratic persuasion involves:
- a serious effort to create background conditions that give each person access to the resources needed to fully participate in discussion; and
- a serious effort to create forums in which access to the discussion is based not on power or money but on a principle of equality; and
- a commitment of all participants to intellectual honesty in presenting arguments and a willingness to respond to the arguments of others.
- Undemocratic propaganda involves deliberate:
- falsification of accounts of the world to support one's interests, and/or
- attempts to ignore or bury accurate accounts of the world that are in conflict with one's interests, and/or
- diversion of discussion away from questions that would produce accounts of the world in conflict with one's interests.

There is one disturbing implication of this framework: It suggests that virtually all commercial advertising and a significant portion of our political discourse is propaganda, or at least at some level propagandistic. From this perspective, the advertising, marketing, and public relations industries would be described collectively as the propaganda industries. When we consider how much our environment is constructed by those industries, we would hesitate to speak glibly about living in a democratic political system and a free society. When journalists become the transmission vehicle for much of this material, we might hesitate to speak glibly about a free press.

What do we say about the state of our political discourse when a presidential campaign can win the advertising industry's "marketer of the year" award, as the Obama campaign did in 2008?[91] What do we say about a democracy in which a president's chief of staff, when asked why the Bush administration waited until after Labor Day to launch its campaign to convince the American public that military action against Iraq was necessary, says, "From a marketing point of view, you don't introduce new products in August."[92]

We are left to ponder the degree to which deception, distortion, and distraction have become not perversions of an otherwise healthy public discourse but the perverse norm of that discourse. That question is disturbing, but rather than undermine our commitment to critical thinking, it should spur us to be more creative, soulful, and courageous.

Robert Jensen teaches at the School of Journalism at the University of Texas at Austin. He has a Ph.D. in media ethics and law, and worked as a journalist for a decade prior to joining academia. He presently teaches courses in media law, ethics, and politics.

Militarism and the Economics of Extinction

By Clare Hanrahan

War is an all-out assault on life. Every living being is in peril. The interrelated systems that sustain life are approaching total collapse from resource depletion, wanton killing and the environmental degradation of centuries of senseless war. The single most egregious and unrelenting source of ecocide is the Pentagon, an agency that consumes nearly 50 percent of each U.S. tax dollar extorted from the workers in the name of national defense.

More than 50 years ago U.S. President Dwight D. Eisenhower warned that "the problem in defense is how far you can go without destroying from within what you are trying to defend from without." We have gone way too far — beyond the limits of law, morality and of sane self interest.

With the Pentagon's practices of obfuscation and denial, it is a daunting task to uncover and document the staggering facts of just how severe — and in some instances irreversible — is the ecological damage brought on by militarism. What is known of the grim statistics is a stunning indictment of the woefully misnamed Department of Defense. How did this happen? What is the extent of the poisoning? Who will clean up the mess? Is it too late to turn this around?

Warfare has never been easy on the earth, yet throughout thousands of years of recorded military history, this living planet has managed to recover and adjust to a succession of trampling armies encroaching with roads, leveling forests, damming rivers, polluting the air, the soil and water, digging entrenchments, bombarding and poisoning the lands, destroying habitat and crops, raping, pillaging and eliminating uncounted species of plants and animals.

The human cost in war has also been high, but in past centuries was limited mostly to combatants. That is no longer the reality. The United Nations Children's Fund (UNICEF) estimated in the 1990s that civilian deaths constituted 90 percent of all deaths in war. In recent decades more children have been killed than soldiers, and more deaths occur after the battlefield is abandoned than during combat.

In almost every U.S. community where the Department of Defense and its corporate military contractors employ millions in the production, maintenance, and storage of "conventional," chemical, and nuclear weapons, the health of the workers and the natural environment is sacrificed. According to a 1989 U.S. General Accounting Office report, the U.S. Military produces more than 400,000 tons of hazardous waste each year. That figure is most certainly a low estimate.

With astounding obedience, *We the People* have been willing to relinquish our lives, our children's lives, our values and the very survival of the earth in the name of national security.

In 1942, the 3,000 residents of five rural Tennessee mountain communities were given just a few weeks' notice to vacate their homes and ancestral farms. Thus was the "secret city" of Oak Ridge established, and the 60,000 acres of Tennessee valleys and ridges expropriated for the war effort. The Manhattan Project was developed to enrich the uranium used for the Hiroshima bomb.

In subsequent decades, and in the name of national security, officials knowingly subjected atomic industry workers, soldiers and nearby residents to deadly doses of radiation at nuclear sites throughout the country. "Some 300,000 people, or half of those who ever worked in the U.S. nuclear weapons complex, are believed to have been affected by exposure to radiation," asserts Michael Renner, of the World Watch Institute writing in the 1997 book *War and Public Health*. Every step of the nuclear bomb-making process involves severe environmental contamination that lingers for generations.

"Of all the different ways in which military operations have an impact on human health and the environment, nuclear weapons production and testing is the most severe and enduring," Renner says. As a result of naval accidents there are at least 50 nuclear warheads and 11 nuclear reactors littering the ocean floor. Some researchers estimate that the radioactive fallout from atmospheric nuclear tests have already caused as many as 86,000 birth defects and 150,000 premature deaths. Two million more cancer deaths may yet ensue from the now-banned above ground explosions.

Despite the horrific consequences of nuclear energy in Oak Ridge today, the Obama administration has approved an additional $7.5 billion for refurbishing the next generation of thermonuclear weapons, assuring a stockpile of death for generations to come.

The unprecedented atomic devastation of Hiroshima and Nagasaki, murdering hundreds of thousands, pales in comparison to the impact of modern weapons of mass destruction. Militarism in this atomic age has developed and used weapons so heinous as to extend the murderous reach to all future generations.

After more than 60 years producing atomic weapons and nuclear energy, the Department of Defense and Department of Energy have accumulated over 500,000 tons of so-called depleted uranium, which they offer free of charge to weapons makers throughout the world.

In Jonesborough, Tennessee, down a quiet country lane in the heart of the Southern Appalachian Mountains, Aerojet Ordnance employs a small workforce to produce weaponized uranium armaments. Bullets are coated with the radioactive waste from enriching U-235 to produce fuel for nuclear reactors and atomic bombs.

According to investigative reporter Bob Nichols, writing in 2010 for the *San Francisco Bay View*, Iraq and virtually all the rest of the Middle East and Central Asia have been continually dosed for almost 20 years with thousands of tons of weaponized ceramic uranium oxide gas, also known as depleted uranium. These bullets, shells and bombs, when exploded, reach temperatures over 3,000 degrees centigrade and become a lethal uranium aerosol that "never stops indiscriminately maiming and killing."

The contamination persists for billions of years, both on the battlefield and at U.S. manufacturing and storage sites. Research has confirmed that uranium oxide (UO) particles, when inhaled, migrate up the olfactory nerve to the brain. They are so small they can even enter the body through the skin, destroying cells in the brains, bones, and testicles or ovaries of anyone contaminated with the radioactive particles — friend, foe or noncombatant.

In addition to the horrific crimes of authorizing, producing, and deploying weaponized uranium, the U.S. military's lethal footprint around the globe includes toxins from heavy metals, dioxins, PCB's, asbestos, mustard, sarin and nerve gas, as well as other chemical and biological weapons. And scattered on battlefields throughout the world are as many as 100 million unexploded antipersonnel land mines. Eighty percent of landmine victims have been noncombatants.

In Viet Nam, from 1962 to 1970, the U.S. military engaged in chemical warfare, dousing the country with 19 million gallons of herbicides, mostly

Agent Orange produced by Monsanto, Dow Chemical and other U.S. manufacturers. The dioxin-rich chemicals contaminated about five million acres of farmland, forest and waters. At least one million Vietnamese people and more than 100,000 Americans and allied troops were poisoned with deadly effects that have continued into the third generation. The human and environmental devastation in Central America during the U.S. proxy wars of the 1980s is yet another horrific chapter in the tragedy of U.S. militarism.

In the United States alone, the Pentagon is responsible for at least 25,000 contaminated properties in all 50 states, according to a 2008 *Washington Post* report. Nine hundred abandoned military bases, weapons manufacturing and testing sites and other military-related industries are listed on the Environmental Protection Agency's list of 1,300 sites most hazardous to human and ecological health, and that is only a portion of the polluted sites. As many as 20 million Americans in 43 states drink water contaminated by cancer-causing perchlorate, a carcinogen found in missile and rocket fuel.

According to a 1991 edition of *Rachel's Hazardous Waste News* (#224), "... the military has exposed thousands (perhaps millions) of innocent Americans to deadly amounts of radioactivity and to a witch's brew of potent chemical toxins, has covered up these facts, has lied to the victims and their families, has lied to the press, has lied to Congress. It is a scandal and an outrage on such a scale that it takes your breath away." In 2011 it is still hard to catch one's breath in the face of this ongoing and intentional assault on the earth.

And of course, it is not just the Pentagon with its lethal global reach, but the insidious corporate/government alliance that Dwight D. Eisenhower warned of over fifty years ago — a crime syndicate that colludes to profit from and deny responsibility for planetary ecocide.

Gaia isn't bound by national borders, nor is this distressed planet protected by the false distinctions militarists make between combat zones and the lands they claim to defend. The militarists and the scientists in their employ have reached into the very heavens to harness the energies of the ionosphere in the service of war.

Dr. Rosalie Bertell, a scientist and Roman Catholic nun confirms that, "U.S. military scientists are working on weather systems as a potential weapon. The methods include the enhancing of storms and the diverting of vapor rivers in the Earth's atmosphere to produce targeted droughts or floods."

The U.S. military practiced this so-called "geophysical warfare" in Viet Nam with Project Skyfire and Project Stormfury. Now the Pentagon is arrogantly pursuing what it calls "full spectrum" U.S. military domination. Dr. Bertell has written of military experiments that may have played a part in earthquakes and unusual weather conditions and even accelerated global warming. Current military projects such as HAARP (High-frequency Active Auroral Research Program) are part of a "growing chain of astonishingly powerful, and potentially interactive, military installations, using varied types of electromagnetic fields or wavelengths, each with a different ability to affect the earth or its atmosphere," according to Dr. Bertell.

Is there no end to the arrogance? We must intervene. We must put a stop to the militarism characterized by Academy of Natural Sciences writer Roland Wall as "a direct and relentless assault on human and natural ecosystems."

The Department of Defense uses 360,000 barrels of oil each day. This amount makes the DoD the single largest oil consumer in the world. According to Sharon E. Burke, the Pentagon's director of operational energy plans and programs, the Defense Logistics Agency delivers more than 170,000 barrels of oil each day to the war theaters, at a cost of $9.6 billion in 2010.

Climate change activists, rightly concerned about the continued use of fossil fuels to power our insatiable energy demands, have taken to the streets of Washington, DC, to call for a halt to the tar sands oil pipeline, other resisters march in the hundreds to the sites of mountain top removal coal mining, or stand in resistance at the nuclear weapons and nuclear power complexes throughout the nation. Arrests, fines, jail and imprisonment is the lot of many who take a bold stand to call an end to the U.S. military industrial choke hold on the planet.

But a strategically disastrous divide persists between activists in the environmental sustainability movements and war resisters who challenge more directly the militarism that is the largest single cause of the Earth's imminent collapse.

Have we blindly accepted the paradigm that war is inevitable, that violence is intrinsic to our nature, and that our security depends on a strong military? It is a lie — repeated again and again — but it is still a lie.

"Challenging the destruction and damage to the environment and the massive exploitation of oil and metal resources for the military-industrial war machine must become paramount in the work for peace," scientist and author H. Patricia Hynes writes in a recent series of articles on the environmental impact of U.S. militarism. Indeed, as the United Nations asserts, "there can be no durable peace if the natural resources that sustain livelihoods and ecosystems are destroyed."

"We don't know how to extricate ourselves from our complicity very surely or very soon," poet and social critic Wendell Berry asserts. "How could we live without the war economy and the holocaust of the fossil fuels?"

We must find the answer to our deadly dilemma and put an end to our complicity in the desecration of the world and destruction of all creation.

"To the offer of more abundant life," Berry writes, "we have chosen to respond with the economics of extinction." We cannot let this be the end.

Further Reading

Wendell Berry, *The Way of Ignorance*, Shoemaker and Hoard, 2005.

Rosalie Bertell, *Planet Earth the Latest Weapon of War — A Critical Study into the Military and the Environment,* The Women's Press, London, 2000.

H. Patricia Hynes, "War and the Tragedy of the Commons," *Truthout. org,* August, 2011.

Barry S. Levy et al., "The Environmental Consequences of War," in Barry S. Levy and Victor W. Sidel, *War and Public Health,* American Public Health Association, 2000.

Michael Renner, "Environmental Health Effects of Weapons Production, Testing, and Maintenance," in Barry S. Levy and Victor W. Sidel, *op cit.*

Barry Sanders, *The Green Zone: The Environmental Costs of Militarism,* AK Press, 2009.

Clare Hanrahan and Coleman Smith have more than half a century of activist experience including war resistance, opposition to nuclear weapons and power development, mountaintop removal, and much more. They are building the New South Network of War Resisters.

Atomic Appalachia and the Militarized Southeast

By Clare Hanrahan, Coleman Smith

A beautiful power point to accompany this article is available at http://warisacrime.org/downloads/waronearth.pptx

Militarism is killing us. It is waging a war on the Earth, and the devastation wrought is far beyond what can be presented here. We are not academics; we're activists and organizers who care deeply about our homeland in the Southern U.S., the region where we live and work, and the most militarized region in the country. We have limited most of our report to the Southeast U.S. and a special place we refer to as Atomic Appalachia. Like Middle Earth in a Tolkien story, Atomic Appalachia is a little known part of our region squeezed in between the Central and Southern Appalachians. It is a region where the impact of militarism is especially evident.

War is an all-out assault on life. Every living being is in peril. The systems that sustain life are approaching total collapse from resource depletion, wanton killing and the environmental degradation of centuries of senseless war. The single most egregious and unrelenting source of ecocide is the Pentagon.

It is not just the Pentagon with its lethal global reach, but the insidious corporate/government alliance — a crime syndicate that colludes to profit from and denies responsibility for planetary ecocide. President Dwight D. Eisenhower, in his prophetic 1961 Farewell Address, warned of the Military Industrial Complex (MIC) whose "total influence — economic, political, even spiritual — is felt in every city, every statehouse, every office of the federal government." [93]

The U.S. government, global corporate, and the military work together to drive U.S. foreign economic policy and to fund and promote war with tax payers' money. Nearly every industry today is connected to the Military Industrial Complex — from weapons manufacturers to infrastructure and logistical support; to university research, think tanks, corporate media, venture capitalists, Big Oil, and private mercenary armies — everyone involved makes big money from war. Many corporations are closely connected to the political establishment. They contribute millions to political campaigns to secure lucrative military contracts.

Essentially, war profiteers sell war to politicians who sell it to the public using the cynical rhetoric of freedom, national security, and pride. One definition of fascism is the conjoining of state interests with corporate interests. Just follow the money and decide for yourself who is, or what is, making the decisions that affect the survival of life on this planet. Capitalism's destructive and polluting reign spans the entire globe — and it is only getting worse. With each day, more and more species are lost to extinction, forests and mountains are reduced to moonscapes, and polar icecaps melt into the sea.

We can remain in subjugation as the world deteriorates around us, or we can take action against the institutions which control our lives and planet. The decision is ours — individually and collectively.

We see no other path but to resist.

"The problem in defense", Eisenhower further warned, "is how far you can go without destroying from within what you are trying to defend from without." We have gone way too far — beyond the limits of law, morality, and of sane self interest. With the Pentagon's practices of obfuscation and denial, it is a daunting task to uncover and document the staggering facts of just how severe — and in some instances irreversible — is the ecological damage brought on by militarism. What is known of the grim statistics is a stunning indictment of the woefully misnamed Department of Defense.

Militarism Defiles the Sacred Earth, Air, Rivers and Springs

The beautiful Nolichucky River drains the Blue Ridge Mountains of western North Carolina and eastern Tennessee and provides drinking water for many Tennessee communities. There are no known sources of enriched uranium in the area other than Nuclear Fuel Services in Erwin, Tenn., manufacturer of fuel for the U.S. Navy's fleet of nuclear-powered submarines and aircraft carriers. NFS is a subsidiary of the Babcock and Wilcox Company. Its work also includes down-blending highly-enriched uranium to a low-enriched form to fuel Tennessee Valley Authority (TVA) nuclear reactors. The plant has a history of serious safety problems.[94]

According to reports of water and soil testing over a three-county area downstream from the plant presented at a Nuclear Regulatory Commission (NRC) meeting in Erwin in 2010, "Most of these samples demonstrate, unequivocally and beyond any reasonable doubt, that there is highly enriched as well as depleted uranium present in the environment." [95]

Another example of the MIC impacts to rivers is the proposed uranium mining in and around Danville, Va., near the Roanoke River, a national treasure which provides drinking water to more than one million people in Virginia Beach, Norfolk, and other communities. As much as 110 million pounds of uranium ore, worth perhaps $10 billion, is located beneath Virginia farmland — "the largest unmined uranium deposit in the nation," [96] Leases are out on as many as 65,000 acres. In 1982 Virginia banned uranium mining. At the time, the price of "yellow cake" raw processed uranium was not cost-competitive. Now it is.

Every Ocean and Sea Bears Hazardous Effect of Militarism

Over 9,000 military, auxiliary, and merchant marine vessels were sunk during World War II. [97] And there is no mitigation plan or risk analysis in place for the looming threats which include unexploded ordinance, leaking oil, hazardous materials, and chemical weapons causing degradation of the marine habitat and coastlines.

A reported eight nuclear submarines have sunk due to fires or explosions, flooding or other accidents. Any removal efforts would be extremely difficult and costly. Their nuclear reactors litter the ocean floor.

During and after WWII, chemical weapons were routinely dumped at sea. According to reporter John Bull, in his 2005 article "The Deadliness Below," the Army dumped at least 64 million pounds of chemical warfare agents in steel containers — as well as a minimum of 400,000 bombs and rockets and 500 tons of radioactive waste — off the country's shores in 26 ocean dump zones created from 1944 to 1970. [98]

16,000 mustard-gas-filled 100-pound bombs were unloaded into deep water in 1944, only five miles from shore in Hawaii. Four railroad cars containing mustard gas bombs and mines were dumped off the coast of South Carolina. A few months later, up to 23 barges with German-produced nerve gas bombs were dumped in the same location. Each barge carried up to 350 tons of bombs.

Even the Heavens Are Polluted

The U.S. Air Force tracks more than 18,000 objects in orbit — bolts, broken satellites, fuel tanks, rocket motors and other junk. [99] Debris from the Feb. 2009 collision of an Iridium Company communications satellite with a Russian military satellite added even more space debris. And NASA's next Mars Science Laboratory Mission, sometime between November 25th and December 15th 2011 will be fueled with 10.6 pounds of plutonium as a heat source while it probes that cold planet. Plutonium-238 "is about 270 times more radioactive than Plutonium-239 per unit of weight," according to Dr. Arjun Makhijani, a nuclear physicist and president the Institute for Energy and Environmental Research.[100] An accident would be catastrophic.

National Defense? or Full-Spectrum Dominance?

Full-spectrum dominance[101] is a military concept whereby a joint military structure achieves control over all elements of the battle space using land, air, maritime and space based assets. Full Spectrum Dominance requires Full Spectrum Resistance. "The south is vital to this plan for the weaponization and nuclearization of space," says Bruce Gagnon, of the Global Network against Weapons and Nuclear Power in Space. This is evident in Huntsville, Alabama, at the Redstone Arsenal, known as the "nerve center for the Army's missile and rocket programs. Redstone is home to the U.S. Army Missile Command, the Army Ordnance Missile and Munitions Center, and NASA's Marshall Space Flight Center.

Following WWII, after 550 families were forcibly displaced to acquire land for the Redstone facility, Nazi scientists were secretly recruited by the Joint Intelligence Objectives Agency (JIOA) as part of "Operation Paperclip."[102] SS officer Werner von Braun and as many as 700 other German scientists were brought to the United States to exploit Germany's expertise with supersonic rockets, nerve gas, jet aircraft, guided missiles, stealth technology, and hardened armor. In 1950, von Braun and his team were transferred to Huntsville, Alabama, his home for the next twenty years. Between 1950 and 1956, von Braun led the Army's rocket development team at Redstone Arsenal.[103]

By 1955 these "ardent Nazis" had been granted citizenship and given prominent positions in the American scientific community. Many had been longtime members of the Nazi party and the Gestapo, had conducted experiments on humans at concentration camps, had used slave labor, and had committed other war crimes. Their Nazi philosophy is deeply embedded within the U.S. Military Industrial Complex.

Rocket Fueled Water

Not only were our democratic, egalitarian values polluted by Nazi ideology, but our land, water, and air are contaminated with the products of rocket science. Ammonium Perchlorate is a combination of nitrogen, hydrogen, chlorine and oxygen. It is an essential component of military explosives, bottle rockets, fireworks, highway flares, automobile airbags and old-fashioned black powder.[104] A 2003 Environmental Working Group analysis[105] of government data, determined that perchlorate had been found in drinking water, groundwater or soil in at least 43 states — more than 4% of public water systems are affected. The most common and most significant perchlorate contamination is from the manufacture, testing, and disposal of solid rocket fuel, explosives, and fireworks. "Perchlorate is an endocrine disrupter, because it can alter hormone levels. Studies show that perchlorate blocks iodine and inhibits iodine uptake in the thyroid gland and disrupts the thyroid's function. … An impairment of thyroid function may impact the fetus or newborn, resulting in changes in behavior, delayed development and decreased learning capability."[106]

A U.S. Food and Drug Administration (FDA) 2008 study found that three quarters of nearly 300 commonly consumed foods and beverages are contaminated with perchlorate, a toxic rocket fuel ingredient. Many two-year-olds exceed the EPA's "safe" dose of perchlorate via food and water contamination.[107]

We Take Care of Our Own?

The U.S. Marine slogan at the Camp Lejeune, North Carolina, base is tragic given the long time and known exposure between 1957 and 1987 of Marines and their families who drank and bathed in contaminated water. Is this how "We take care of our own?"

The contamination included solvents from a nearby, off-base dry cleaning company, from on-base use of chemicals to clean military equipment, and from between 400,000 and 1.1 million gallons of fuel that leaked from underground fuel storage tanks in and around the main family housing units. Military family water wells were polluted for decades with as many as 70 identified toxins at concentrations 240 to 3400 times that permitted by safety standards. With the military's long history of lost documents, poor management, and deceptive lab testing and results, it is unclear the full extent of the contamination.

Bases, Bases — We All Fall Down!

There are an estimated 900-1,000 U.S. military installations around the globe in almost every country. Major bases, such as Ft. Benning, Ga., Ft. Campbell, Ky., Camp Lejeune and Ft. Bragg, N.C., are city size and contain all the pollution associated with urbanized areas in addition to the military toxics and the negative psycho-social impacts on the mental and physical well being of base personnel and surrounding populations. Twenty-nine million Americans — that's about one in every 10 — live within 10 miles of a toxic military site.[108] That is, a site that's already been labeled under the Superfund Program as a top priority for toxic-waste cleanup. There are many, many, more sites that haven't yet been certified. The military maintains that there must be "national sacrifice zones" where weapons and soldiers can be tested for war. The DOD has admitted to "14,401 toxic hot spots in 1,579 bases in the U.S."[109]

An overseas example of U.S. military toxics is the problem at Clark Airfield and Subic Naval Station in the Philippines. After Mt. Pinatubo erupted, the U.S. relocated 20,000 homeless to the abandoned bases where they dug wells and planted crops. Philippine health officials noticed a sudden rise in stillbirths, spontaneous abortions, birth defects, kidney, skin, nervous system disorders, and increased cancers. They learned later of the heavy metals, acids, solvents, and munitions buried on site ...The Philippine's request for U.S. help was met with the response: "Our laws don't allow us to respond to your request."[110]

Military Addiction to Oil

According to Sharon E. Burke, the Pentagon's director of operational energy plans and programs, the Defense Logistics Agency delivers more than 170,000 barrels of oil each day to the war theaters, at a cost of $9.6 billion in 2010.[111] The U.S. military uses enough oil in *one year* to run all U.S. transit systems for the next 14-22 years.

Another comparison is between the average Civilian's use of 1.3 gallons per day and the Deployed Soldier's use of approximately 15 gallons per day. With about 1.4 million active duty personnel, the military population is less than 1/4 of one percent of the U.S. population. The per capita military use of oil at one million barrels a day is a disproportionate ten times that of civilian use.

With occasional, stop-and-go driving, in one year, the average civilian driver produces about 10,000 pounds of greenhouse gasses — mainly carbon. For the same year, military pollution is equal to that of 14.6 million cars driving 24/7 for the entire year.

Military data at best is an informed estimate. Calculating impact is difficult. How much pollution is produced is influenced by the type of fuel used. Ships and tanks can use "bunker fuel" which is 1000 times dirtier than standard diesel. It produces both SO_2 and CO_2, leaving a thicker layer of gasses in the atmosphere, holding in more heat. Aviation fuel impacts the environment at a rate 2.7 times greater than standard fuel because of the extra NO2, SO2, soot, and H2O vapor it produces.

The H2O vapor forms ice crystals in the upper atmosphere and is a better insulator and traps heat better than greenhouse gases. JP8 fuel is high powered/highly toxic jet fuel and is used more and more. It's heavier, evaporates slowly, clinging to skin and clothes much longer than other fuels. Chronic exposure to JP8 fuel impacts liver function, causes emotional dysfunction, abnormal brain function, and shorter attention span, lowers sensorimotor speed, compromises immune systems, and increases cancer. The only precaution the DOD recommends for its personnel handling JP8, is to wear rubber gloves.

The Awful Truth

"...Even if every person, every automobile, and every factory suddenly emitted zero emissions," says environmental writer Barry Sanders, "the Earth would still be heading head first and full speed towards total disaster for one major reason. The military ... produces enough greenhouse gases, by itself, to place the entire globe, with all of its inhabitants large and small, in the most imminent danger of extinction." [112]

President Franklin Roosevelt's New Deal strategy included a deal with conservative Southern Democrats to seed the Jim Crow South with military bases. As the nation mobilized for war abroad, federal defense dollars flooded southern states in the form of military installations and defense contractors.

The Anniston Ordnance Depot (AOD) began construction in 1941 near Anniston, Alabama, as an ammunition storage site in the foothills of the Appalachian Mountains. The maintenance and storage of chemical munitions began in 1963, and Anniston became a storage site for the U.S. stockpile of cold war era chemical-warfare munitions, which included lethal nerve, blood, and blister agents contained in rockets, artillery shells, and aerosol canisters. An astounding 2,254 tons of chemical munitions were stored for decades in trenches, lagoons, landfills and dirt-covered concrete bunkers at the Depot. In the 1970s and 1980s, toxic industrial chemicals stored in unlined pits, were found to be seeping into groundwater.[113]

In 1997, the U.S. signed the Chemical Weapons Convention treaty for the destruction of chemical weapons stockpiles by 2007. This was extended to 2012. The military decided to use on-site incineration of deadly nerve agents without public representation, violating the National Environmental Protection Act. The Anniston incinerator is the first to be located in a populated area. About 75,000 people live within nine miles of the Depot. Because even a small accident could be catastrophic, 35,000 people were provided with gas masks and kits with duct tape and plastic sheeting.

By 2011, after eight years, nearly 97 percent of all of the chemical weapons stored in Anniston since the 1950s had been burned by Army and Westinghouse contract workers who manned three furnaces in the $855 million dollar incinerator.

America's Arsenal: A "Top Polluter"

The Pine Bluff Arsenal in Arkansas is listed in a Department of Defense report as a "top polluter." For more than 60 years, the Arkansas arsenal stored approximately 3,850 tons of chemical weapons at its 3,500 acre site, and released a reported 721,364 pounds of chemicals into the air, water and land. In a 2005 fire over 7,500 canisters of white phosphorus burned. Pine Bluff is the only active site at which white phosphorous-filled weapons are manufactured and loaded. Today the depot manufactures chemical, smoke, riot control, incendiary and pyrotechnic mixes and munitions. Multiple and cumulative exposures to toxics exist here as they do in Alabama.

The percentage of African Americans in Pine Bluff is 341% higher than the national average, and 28% of the residents live below the poverty level — continuing the practice of environmental racism.

In 2010, the arsenal completed disposal of 12% of the U.S. chemical weapons stockpile and "recycled" 6.5 million pounds of "decontaminated" steel chemical weapons tanks as part of "the Army's commitment to protect the environment."[114]

Milan Army Ammunition Plant near Jackson, Tennessee: this WWII relic occupies a 22,540-acre site now operated by American Ordnance Systems, Inc. The plant loads, assembles, packs, reconditions and disposes of munitions, including weaponized uranium ordnance.

Throughout its nearly 60 years of operation, wastewater discharges have contaminated soil, sediment, and ground water with explosive compounds. Plumes of contaminated ground water have migrated into the Memphis Sand aquifer that supplies drinking water for the 9,000 people in the nearby City of Milan.

In a DOD effort to reduce costs, Milan's military mission will change. Hundreds of local jobs will be lost and the arsenal will primarily serve as storage facility for depleted uranium and a disassembly plant for uranium weaponry.

In East Tennessee, the Holston Army Ammunition Plant was constructed as Holston Ordinance Works in 1942 as part of the Manhattan Project. It produces explosives and propellants for the first-strike Trident Nuclear Submarines. A single Trident carries 192 nuclear warheads.

The Atomic Age — The Most Severe and Enduring Impact on Human Health and The Environment

From 1945 to 1992 there were a reported 1,054 U.S. nuclear tests. Most were detonated at the Nevada Test Site. More than 60 nuclear weapons were dropped on the Marshall Islands. Others were detonated in Alaska, Colorado, Mississippi, and New Mexico. According to World Watch Institute, radioactive fallout from atmospheric nuclear tests has caused 86,000 birth defects and 150,000 premature deaths.

Atomic Soldiers and Downwind Civilians Sacrificed Between 1945-1975: U.S. government's human radiation experiments exposed as many as 16,000 civilian U.S. hospital patients, prisoners, disabled children and pregnant women to high doses of radiation without their knowledge or consent.[115]

Over 200,000 "atomic vets" who worked closely with nuclear detonations at the Nevada test site during the 1950s and 1960s were especially vulnerable to radiation fallout.[116]

The National Cancer Institute (NCI), reported that fallout from the 1950's atomic bomb tests irradiated the nation at levels far in excess of what the government has admitted, which could result in 10,000 to 75,000 cases of thyroid cancer among those exposed. There is a 38 year latency for thyroid cancers. The ultimate effect of atomic testing is still unknown.

Mississippi's Own Atomic Bombs

October 22, 1964, Project Salmon: The Department of Energy (DOE) and Atomic Energy Commission detonated a 5.3 kiloton nuclear device underground in south Mississippi, 28 miles southwest of Hattiesburg, reportedly to study seismic wave propagation in the S.E. United States.[117] The nuclear test site was at the Tatum Salt Dome, about 1,000 feet below ground. Most of the resulting radioactive waste solids and sludge were put back into the ground where it remains today. Some of the radioactive liquids were injected into a vein of salty water located about 2,500 feet underground.

A reported 400 residents were evacuated from the area, and paid $10 per adult and $5 per child for their inconvenience. The zone from which citizens were evacuated stretched five miles downwind of ground zero. Two years later, "The Sterling Event" a 380 ton nuclear device was detonated. These were the only nuclear explosions on U.S. soil east of the Rocky Mountain States. The Sterling bomb delivered the same force as 5,000 tons of TNT. The Project Salmon blast was about one-third as powerful as the bomb that destroyed Hiroshima. U.S. government officials erected a large stone monument at the site, with a brass plaque warning future generations not to drill or dig in the vicinity of this test site.

Oak Ridge, Tennessee: Atomic "Secret City"

The Y-12 National Security Complex is the nation's primary storehouse for weapons-grade uranium and the key producer of uranium parts used in every nuclear weapon in the U.S. arsenal. Oak Ridge is part of the national thermonuclear assembly line which includes the Los Alamos National Labs in New Mexico and a facility in Kansas City, Mo. which produces all non-nuclear components.

When a uranium-fueled atomic bomb devastated Hiroshima on August 6, 1945, it was powered by the output of Oak Ridge's Y-12 and K-25 plants. Three days later, when a plutonium-fueled bomb struck Nagasaki, the destruction was wrought by Hanford, Washington's plutonium.

The DOE's Oak Ridge reservation is a toxic tapestry of some of the worst, longest-lasting poisons known. Oak Ridge has the "highest risk profile" of any DOE cleanup site with at least 711 contaminated sites identified leaking toxic solvents, lubricants, chemicals and metals like uranium, lead, mercury, strontium, thorium and tritium, into the groundwater.

The bomb plant used tons of mercury in lithium enrichment. Huge quantities of this toxic metal pollute the soil, groundwater, creeks, the Clinch River and downstream reservoirs. Mercury poisoning causes disabilities from leukemia to attention deficit disorder.

Over 300,000 people or half of those who ever worked in the U.S. nuclear weapons complex, have been affected by exposure to radiation.

Life Extension or Generations of Genocide?

According to the Oak Ridge Environmental Peace Alliance, the United States has 1,500 nuclear weapons on hair-trigger alert.

Yet, in 2011, President Obama approved $7.5 billion for a new thermonuclear weapons uranium processing facility in Oak Ridge able to produce 80 thermonuclear "secondaries" every year, assuring a stockpile of death for generations to come. The secondary forms the "hydrogen" part of a thermonuclear bomb. Secondaries contain plutonium and uranium, and lithium salt which supply the hydrogen fuel.

This so-called "life extension" of the U.S. nuclear stockpile comes from a President who received the Nobel Peace Prize for his part in negotiating a nuclear arms reduction "understanding" with Dmitriy A. Medvedev, President of the Russian Federation.

Building the Y-12 Uranium Processing Facility will disrupt or destroy eight wetlands areas in Oak Ridge and add to the toxic load of that Tennessee mountain community.

U.S. Soldiers and Sailors Used as "Lab Rats"

During the 1960s and early 1970s, the Department of Defense conducted 46 tests known as Project 112 and Project SHAD using nerve agents, chemical and biological agents on uninformed and unwilling military personnel. These tests, such as, 'Autumn Gold', 'Copperhead', 'Project Shad', and other un-named tests aboard U.S. Navy vessels, may have, in effect, 'Murdered' hundreds — perhaps thousands — of active duty U.S. Military personnel, and then lied to them and refused them treatment for over 40 years.[118]

32 Broken Arrows: Nuclear Weapons Accidents (1950-2000)

A B-47 carrying two nuclear capsules on a nonstop flight from MacDill Air Force Base near Tampa in 1956 to an overseas base failed to make contact with a tanker over the Mediterranean for a second refueling. No trace was ever found of the plane or the nuclear cargo.

Two years later, a B-47 collided with an F-86 in a simulated combat mission off the Georgia coast, near Savannah in 1958. A nuclear weapon on board was jettisoned over water and the plane later landed safely. Searches failed to locate the weapon.

Near Seymour Johnson Air Force Base around Goldsboro, North Carolina, a B-52 on airborne alert in 1961 was damaged during a mid-air refueling. The crew initiated a parachute release of two nuclear weapons. One landed safely with some damage. The second fell free; breaking apart and burrowing deep into a swamp in eastern North Carolina. Defense Secretary Robert McNamara acknowledged the danger: "The bombs' arming mechanism had six or seven steps to go through to detonate, and it went through all but one..." Officials assessed the possibility of a detonation, abandoned the recovery effort, purchased the land, and fenced off the site.

Atoms for Peace

In a 1953 speech before the United Nations General Assembly, President Eisenhower stated that he hoped "to find the way by which the inventiveness of man shall be consecrated to his life." The "Atoms for Peace" program represented Eisenhower›s belief that nuclear power could be used for peace, rather than destruction. The program developed into the International Atomic Energy Agency that seeks to promote the peaceful use of nuclear energy, and to inhibit its use for any military purpose, including nuclear weapons.

But Ike was not right this time. As Ann Harris, a TVA whistleblower, told the Nuclear Regulatory Commission at a public hearing, "Atoms for peace and atoms for war have a marriage made in hell."

The Evil Twins: Nuclear Weapons and Nuclear Power

Most of the potential energy produced by a nuclear power plant has already been used to construct it, and most of the remaining power is lost to inefficiency in long-distance transmission and end use. All that is really produced is a lot of radioactive waste, a lot of money for a few, and weapons grade plutonium. A typical 1000 megawatt reactor produces about 5,000 tons of plutonium a year, enough for 40 nuclear bombs.

- Uranium enrichment is needed for both nuclear power and nuclear weapons production. When uranium is enriched up to 5% U-235, it is reactor-grade. When enriched to around 90% U-235, it is weapons-grade or highly-enriched uranium (HEU).
- Reprocessing irradiated nuclear fuel results in large inventories of plutonium which feeds nuclear weapons proliferation.

Al Gore said, "During my eight years in the White House, every nuclear weapons issue we dealt with was connected to a nuclear reactor program."

Nuclear Power: Dirty, Dangerous and Expensive

The USA has over 70,000 tons of nuclear waste — deadly for tens of thousands of years — with no place for permanent storage. The 104 USA nuclear reactors add 2,000 tons each year of high level radioactive waste. Ninety-five percent of high-level radioactive waste comes from irradiated fuel in the core of nuclear power reactors. Each 1,000 megawatt nuclear power plant produces about 30 metric tons of high-level radioactive waste. According to the Nuclear Information and Resource Service, "All six of the nation's licensed nuclear waste dumps have or are leaking."

South Carolina: Barnwell's Radioactive Waste Dump

For 35 years Barnwell, South Carolina, was the only low-level radioactive waste dump east of the Rockies. Radioactive waste is stored in steel drums, encased in concrete vaults and buried.

In the sense that *Depleted* Uranium is not so depleted, that it is just not efficient enough for reactor fuel, "*Low Level*" is a misleading and inaccurate label. Workers can still be seriously irradiated by the contents of this lower and medium level RAD Waste.

RAD Waste: Move it? Where — Yucca Mt., NV? or Sandy Mush, NC?

After the proposed waste burial site at Yucca Mountain was cancelled, attention has turned again to the continental base granite in the Appalachians of the eastern United States.

It would take 9,600 rail and 1,100 heavy-haul highway shipments over 20 years, to move the first 70,000 tons of nuclear waste to the Savannah River site for reprocessing, to retrieve the weapons grade plutonium. This would bring 240,000 times the measurable radioactivity already buried at Barnwell. If reprocessed in South Carolina, the nearest likely location for a permanent repository of the highly radioactive waste is in Western North Carolina, a 20-minute drive from Asheville.

North Carolina: Asheville the Nuclear Crossroads

Three fatal flaws of Nuclear Waste:

- Inadequate Emergency Response
- Risk of Terrorism and Sabotage
- Radiation Exposure from Routine Shipments

The transport of 10,000 loads of high level nuclear waste would come right through Asheville, North Carolina. This is a powerful motivator for its inhabitants to educate themselves, organize, and prepare resistance to the real possibility of this radioactive poison transport. The new measure of radioactivity is:

One Truckload = Four Barnwells
One Railcar = Sixteen Barnwells

South Carolina: Savannah River Site — Most Contaminated in the World

Since the 310 square mile Savannah River Site (SRS) began operations in 1951 to manufacture tritium and weapons grade plutonium for the U.S. nuclear weapons program, SRS has generated over 140 million gallons of liquid radioactive waste. The SC counties around the SRC have the highest cancer mortality rate in the state due to exposure to ionizing radiation. SRS has dumped 104 million gallons of this liquid waste into the air via evaporation processes.

The current SRS mission involves waste management and vitrification, special nuclear material (SNM) storage, research and development, and technology transfer. SRS also recycles tritium from the weapons stockpile. SRS is currently gearing up to reprocess RAD waste primarily from commercial reactors to recapture weapons grade plutonium. Its name has undergone a metamorphosis from SRS to the Global Nuclear Energy Partnership to a reincarnation as the U.S. Energy Freedom Center. Since the nuclear industry considers reprocessing to be recycling, these jobs are listed as "Green".

Educate, Organize, Agitate, Activate

There is a rising number of activists, as well as everyday citizens, in Atomic Appalachia, who are confronting the nuclear weapons and power complex. One place where citizen action has been strong is TVA's Watts Bar Nuclear Reactor and Tritium Production Plant in East Tennessee. Beyond the health, safety, and economic issues already stated, the production of Tritium is of concern:

- Tritium is the radioactive isotope of hydrogen produced in nuclear reactors or high-energy accelerators.
- Tritium production for nuclear weapons violates international non-proliferation treaties.
- Tritium production is essential for maintaining the U.S. nuclear weapons stockpile.
- Tritium boosts explosive power of nuclear weapons.
- Tritium produced at Watts Bar reactor is shipped in casks for separation at the Tritium Extraction Facility, Savannah River Site.

All production facilities release tritium into the environment. Tritium primarily enters the body when people swallow tritiated water; Tritium also can be inhaled as a gas in the air, and absorbed through the skin. As with all ionizing radiation, exposure to tritium increases the risk of developing cancer.

The South as Sacrifice Zone?

Mississippi, the Carolinas, Tennessee, Georgia and Alabama are cheap-labor "right to work" states. These are the economies that were devastated during the Civil War, and came back only after the United States began mobilizing for WWII.[119] According to Dr. Robert D. Bullard, writing in his book *Dumping In Dixie: Race, Class, and Environmental Quality*, "Environmental risks were offered as unavoidable trade-offs for jobs and a broadened tax base in economically depressed communities."

Mississippi: Grand Gulf Nuclear Station

This nuclear reactor is located near Port Gibson, Mississippi, 25 miles south of Vicksburg, on the east bank of the Mississippi River. In 1983-1984, the first two years in which the existing Grand Gulf reactor operated, significant rises were observed in local rates of infant deaths (+35.3%) and fetal deaths (+57.8%). Local infant mortality remained elevated for the next two decades. These changes are consistent with the large declines in local infant death rates observed near closed nuclear reactors in the first two full years after shutdown.[120] After the 2011 floods, plant workers at the Grand Gulf nuclear station pumped water containing radioactive tritium into the Mississippi River for days before they discovered the toxic release and shut off the pumps. As radioactive water, tritium can cross the placenta, posing some risk of birth defects and early pregnancy failures.

Dumping and Burning in Tennessee

Tennessee is the only state that allows commercial burning of radioactive waste, licensing six incinerators. For at least 20 years, and without any public disclosure, Tennessee and the DOE's "Bulk Survey for Release Program" (BSFR) have allowed radioactive waste to be dumped into five state landfills. Five million pounds was dumped in Tennessee landfills in 2007 alone. The source of the waste is considered "proprietary" information.

Radioactive waste transport and burning runs a high risk of releasing low levels of radiation which increases the risk of lung cancer, leukemia, and other disease. Energy Solutions, Inc. in Oak Ridge will be incinerating 1,000 tons of German radioactive waste, and has applied to import 20,000 tons of Italian nuclear waste for processing, including burning, melting and compaction. Increased incineration at Energy solutions, Inc. is predicted to increase the downwind cancer risk within a two-hour radius from one in every 10,000-100,000 to one in every 70. There's no safe level. Even a little bit increases a person's risk. Seventy-five percent of U.S. "low-level" radioactive waste — 41 million pounds per year — comes to Tennessee.

Memphis, Tennessee: U.S. Army Defense Depot

The environmental crisis in this South Memphis African American neighborhood is an example of a national pattern of environmental racism. Serious illnesses and cancers in the community are linked to contamination from the WWII-era Defense Depot. Some children have contracted cancer and experienced other serious health problems.

In 1995 Doris Bradshaw founded Defense Depot Memphis Tennessee Concerned Citizens Committee to educate and mobilize her neighbors about the contamination in drainage ditches and from food grown in areas near these ditches; from contaminated groundwater; and from mustard gas destroyed and disposed at the Depot in 1946, as well as other chemical agents disposed at nearby Dunn Field.

"The way they have treated people of color throughout the U.S. is the way they are treating countries of color throughout the world," Doris Bradshaw asserts. Family members and neighbors have been sickened and died from cancers directly caused by exposure to the now closed Depot's toxins. Estimates range from 187 to 289 different compounds including arsenic, cadmium, chromium, lead, mercury, trichloro-ethylene, carbon tetrachloride, pesticides, dioxin, chlorodane, PCBs and discarded mustard gas bombs pollute the South Memphis African-American neighborhood.

Round and Round and Round We Go

"The State of Tennessee is licensing processors that can make the determination of "free release" radioactive materials and wastes for reuse, recycling or regular landfills," according to a 2007 Nuclear Information and Resource Service report.[121] DOE is allowing radioactivity generated by its own activities to go to unregulated disposal, recycling and reuse, the report warns. Manmade radioactivity could be getting into everyday consumer products, including construction supplies and equipment, playgrounds, furniture, toys, and personal items, without warning, notification or consent.

Studsvik Memphis: Nuclear Waste Processing

The Swedish company Studsvik, formerly RACE, processes radioactive waste from hospitals, laboratories and nuclear power plants. African American employees were exclusively assigned the most hazardous work — to cut apart a damaged and highly-radioactive reactor. Workers' dosimeters were manipulated by management to mask the actual exposure levels African-American workers received. The company agreed to pay $650,000 to settle a race discrimination lawsuit charging it with exposing African-American workers to higher radiation levels than white workers, according to a report by the Institute for Southern Studies.[122] "Every single federal agency that regulates radiation exposure (the EPA, the DOE, the DOD, the NRC, and HHSD) admits today that even the smallest doses poses a risk of cancer," says John LaForge of the group Nukewatch.

Erwin, Tennessee: Nuclear Fuel Services

The 65 acre, privately owned NFS, about 120 miles north of Knoxville is the largest employer in Unicoi County. It has a history of fines and enforcement actions by the Nuclear Regulatory Commission (NRC). "National security" concerns kept the public in the dark about a March 2006 spill of highly enriched uranium that could have caused a deadly, uncontrolled nuclear reaction. Local authorities were not informed of the spill. NFS supplies nuclear fuel to the U. S. Navy Trident Submarine fleet and converts weapons-grade uranium into commercial reactor fuel.

Kings Bay, Georgia: Trident II Nuclear Submarine

Fueled from uranium enriched in Tennessee, Trident II submarines are an offensive, first-strike weapons platform, with an explosive force 1,536 times greater than the Hiroshima bomb. There is no other weapon system in the U.S. arsenal with the operational risks of a Trident submarine. No other weapon has as much explosive material, in the form of solid rocket propellant, and the number of nuclear warheads tightly packed in a confined vessel.

The sound at Saint Mary's Georgia, near Kings Bay must be dredged several times a year to accommodate the mammoth sub which is as tall as a five-story building and nearly two football fields in length. The dredging impacts aquatic life in the sound, disrupting feeding behavior. The extremely low frequency (ELF) radio waves used to communicate with deeply submerged Trident submarines harm marine life, causing internal bleeding and ear-drum hemorrhaging in sea turtles, dolphins, whales and other sea creatures.

Military sonar is so powerful it can rupture the lungs, brains and ears of marine mammals, permanently deafening fish, and disable divers a hundred miles away. Mass marine mammal strandings worldwide are being linked to powerful naval sonar. The unwise and immoral use of these and other technologies is beginning to plague us with the scale of its destruction.

Florida: Radioactive Baby Teeth Study

The Baby Teeth study specifically measured levels of radioactive Strontium-90 (Sr-90), a known carcinogen released by nuclear facilities. The chemical structure of Sr90 is so similar to that of calcium that the body gets fooled and deposits Sr-90 in the bones and teeth, where it remains, continually emitting cancer-causing radiation. During pregnancy, Sr-90 is transferred from the mother to the fetus and ends up in the baby's teeth and bones. To determine where radioactivity was absorbed from the environment, we need to know where the mother lived during pregnancy and where the baby was born. In Florida, the highest levels of radioactive Strontium-90 were found in the six S.E. Florida counties closest to the Turkey Point and St. Lucie nuclear reactors. Strontium in baby teeth increased 37% from mid-1980s to mid 1990s.

Virginia: North Anna Nuclear Generating Station 2011

The September 2011, a 5.8-magnitude earthquake in the Piedmont region of Virginia shifted 25 massive concrete containers holding high-level nuclear waste. The nuclear plant is 12 miles from the epicenter in Louisa County. The water used to cool steam from the reactors is pumped back into the lake at high temperatures, a kind of thermal pollution that can harm flora and fauna in violation of federal law. It's easier to pay a fine than fix the problem.

Currently, "spent" fuel assemblies are stored at the Surry and North Anna nuclear power plants. Rods are kept in pools of water for 5-10 years to keep this thermally hot, radioactive waste from melting. They are eventually transferred to "dry casks" for storage outdoors on a concrete pad. Storage at nuclear power plants was expected to be a short-term solution, but a long-term storage facility has not been opened yet. Rather than build new pools to accommodate the waste at North Anna and Surry, Virginia Power obtained the first Federal approval to use dry storage technology and opened the first dry cask storage facility in the nation at Surry, followed by one at North Anna. It was these dry cask storage units which shifted during the earthquake.

Genocide for Generation After Generation After …

Just down the road from the Nuclear Fuel Services complex in Erwin, Tennessee, is Jonesborough's Aerojet Ordnance Tenn., Inc. which produces uranium weapons coated with the radioactive waste from fuel production for nuclear reactors and atomic bombs. Hundreds of tons of exploded uranium weapons create genetic damage for generations. Generally referred to as "Depleted Uranium" or DU weapons, this material may only be slightly less enriched than is usable as reactor fuel and still packs a powerful dose of radiation when released to the environment.

These bullets, shells and bombs, when exploded, reach temperatures over 3,000 degrees centigrade and become a lethal uranium aerosol that never stops indiscriminately maiming and killing. The contamination persists for billions of years, both on the battlefield and at U.S. manufacturing and storage sites. Research has confirmed that uranium oxide (UO) particles, when inhaled, migrate up the olfactory nerve to the brain. They are so small they can even enter the body through the skin destroying cells in the brains, bones, and testicles or ovaries of anyone contaminated with the radioactive particles.

The Department of Defense and Department of Energy have accumulated over 500,000 tons of so-called depleted uranium, which it offers free of charge to weapons makers throughout the world. This provides a convenient pathway for disposal of an otherwise costly waste problem. Uranium workers have significant mortality risks from cancer and non-cancerous diseases. Some workers involved in making DU have received very large radiation doses. In some instances workers have been knowingly put at risk without their knowledge.

Weaponized Uranium Warfare

- Gulf War I: 315 - 350 tons of uranium weapons.
- Gulf War II: Estimated DU use 5 times Gulf War I.
- The U.S. has sold DU weapons to 29 countries.

A minimum of 500 to 600 tons of DU dust now litter Afghanistan. Several times more are spread across Iraq. So-called "depleted uranium" has a half life of 4.5 billion years. The U.S. is spreading this eternal devastation in direct violation of the Geneva Convention which prohibits intergenerational impact from weapons. The unprecedented atomic devastation of Hiroshima and Nagasaki, murdering hundreds of thousands, pales in comparison to the impact of modern weapons of mass destruction.

According to Arthur N. Bernklau, executive director of Veterans for Constitutional Law, "Out of the 580,400 soldiers who served in the first Gulf War, 11,000 are now dead! By the year 2000, there were 325,000 on Permanent Medical Disability."[123] This astounding number of 'Disabled Vets' means that a decade later, 56% of those soldiers who served have some form of permanent medical problems, or what we euphemistically call Gulf War Syndrome. Hundreds of tons of radioactive dust is spread across the world's battlefields. The numbers of American troops to be sickened by DU from Gulf War II will be staggering. As they gradually sicken and suffer a slow burn to their graves, the Pentagon will, as it did after Gulf War I, deny that their misery and death is a result of their tour in Iraq.

American War Christianity: An American Religious Jihad?
— A Pollution of the Spiritual and Religious Environment

Chuck Fager, Director of Quaker House in Fayetteville, NC, near Fort Bragg, has written about what he calls "American War Christianity," where "American churches, many actively and others passively, have become tools of militarism's influence over large segments of the citizenry."

Early evidence of American War Christianity appears with Vietnam era active duty military and discharged vets proselytizing within evangelical circles emphasizing a strict obedience and non-questioning of scripture to "spread the faith." Their Jesus is the Prince of War, not Peace, and their gospel message is not to love your enemies, but to hate and kill them, including civilians and children.

American War Christianity can be found around the country, but it has deep roots in Southern White Protestant churches. This conviction holds that the United States is God's chosen instrument to bear the sword against evildoers, and thereby advance the gospel wherever we decide it needs to be forcibly planted. According to Fager, American War Christianity is a key "center of gravity" of U.S. militarism. An active form involves loud pronouncements of wrath on America's designated enemies — "the Commies, those Muslim terrorists, those illegals." A near cult-like fervor glorifies in the righteous violence of our armed forces.

The passive form is seen in thousands of churches, and takes the quieter form of "going along" with whatever the military has been sent to do. Adherents talk primarily of inner peace or peace in the family or church. But this peace slides off when a uniform goes on and it stops at the U.S. border. This ideology blends with the militarization of our society, our borders and our school-aged children.

Loss of Freedoms / Political and Cultural Pollution

The undoing of our democracy is so severe, says Vincent Warren of the Center for Constitutional Rights, that without concerted and deliberate action, the principles and values which defined us before 9/11 may never be regained.[124] After September 11, 2001, G.W. Bush shredded the U.S. Constitution, trampled on the Bill of Rights, discarded the Geneva Conventions, disregarded UN statutes and publicly embraced torture as legal. The Obama Administration has done little to reverse course. Homeland Security has become a growth industry. There is a continuation of extraordinary rendition flights to outsource torture to other countries. "Illegal immigrants" are propagandized as a national security threat to rationalize the militarization of borders and construction of a barrier fence costing $16 to $21 million per mile. The privatization of our public commons and designation of "Free Speech Zones" to control protest and dissent is a frequent occurrence.

There is a resurgence of COINTELPRO-type FBI surveillance, raids, and harassment of anti-war and international solidarity activists with "material support of terrorism" charges, often accompanied by grand jury subpoenas to silence and compromise the movement. From Red Scare to Green Scare, all environmental activists are now labeled as Eco-Terrorists. Many activists now carry "Know Your Rights" cards to be ready if questioned by police, and standard reference materials in activist trainings include the Center for Constitutional Rights' pamphlet *When an Agent Knocks*.

With astounding obedience, *We the People* have been willing to relinquish our lives, our children's lives, our values and the very survival of the earth in the name of national security and pride. The Military Industrial Complex has drawn into its deadly grip more and more of the institutions that once were the bulwarks of democracy. It is *We the People* who must soon, and very soon, find ways to reclaim our power and act together to halt the destruction of the earth.

> *"I do not ask that you put bands upon the tyrant to topple him over, but simply that you support him no longer; then you will behold him, like a great colossus whose pedestal has been pulled away, fall of his own weight."*
>
>   — *The Politics of Obedience: The Discourse of Voluntary Servitude,*
>   by Etienne de la Boetie, 16th century French Philosopher.

Clare Hanrahan and Coleman Smith have more than half a century of activist experience including war resistance, opposition to nuclear weapons and power development, mountaintop removal, and much more. They are building the New South Network of War Resisters.

The Extra Casualties of War

By Mia Austin Scoggins

In the major American wars since World War II, by official figures the United States has lost at least 101,000 soldiers killed, and 296,000 troops wounded. Here's the breakdown:

- In Korea, 38,000 dead, 103,000 wounded.
- In Vietnam, 58,000 dead, 153,000 wounded.
- In Desert Storm, 294 killed, 458 wounded.
- In Iraq, 4457 uniformed dead.
- In Afghanistan, 1594 killed.
- To date, 650,000 Iraq / Afghanistan veterans treated in VA facilities.[125]

There were several smaller wars that we'll have to skip over here due to space constraints. But the above numbers represent substantial losses, and we grieve for all of them. Yet they are not the whole story of the U.S. cost of the wars that are the ultimate product of what is called the Military Industrial Complex. In fact, they're just the start. There are tens of thousands — no, many hundreds of thousands more U.S. "extra casualties" of these wars and of the Military Industrial Complex that has made them. It is these extra U.S. casualties that we want to talk about today.

President Eisenhower noted, in his 1961 Farewell Address:

> *Now this conjunction of an immense military establishment and a large arms industry is new in the American experience. The total influence — economic, political, even spiritual — is felt in every city, every statehouse, every office of the Federal government ... we must*

*guard against the acquisition of unwarranted influence, whether
sought or unsought, by the military industrial complex. ...*

Even as the departing president named it, the MIC was becoming well-entrenched, and its impact and influence has since become pervasive, and apparently permanent. One of the "grave implications" of its ascendance, we contend, is a double-edged one: that its wars produce a high level of "Extra Casualties" — lives damaged and destroyed by its wars that dwarf the official casualty numbers — accompanied at the same time by a low level of public awareness of the true extent of the MIC's domestic human and financial cost.

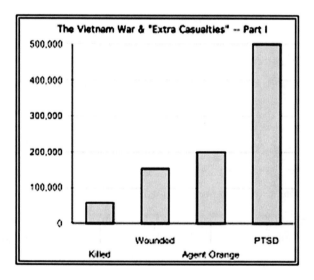

The Vietnam War, August 4, 1964, to January 27, 1973, was (at the time) both our longest and the most unpopular war in U.S. history. The financial cost of the war, to the United States, was $150 billion.

Beginning in 1961, pesticide and herbicide spraying were commonly used to defoliate plant life and to destroy food sources. Tens of millions of gallons of the herbicide "Agent Orange," whose major toxic component was Dioxin, were sprayed across the countryside. More than 200,000 soldiers were exposed to it. A half-century later, the "sprayed and betrayed" troops have suffered illnesses, often fatal, related, they assert, to that exposure. Their children and grandchildren have higher rates of birth defects. Their, and their families', struggle for recognition, treatment, and compensation for Agent-Orange related conditions, continues.

And in Vietnam, the deaths, birth defects and other deformities the spraying has caused among the civilian population runs into the hundreds of thousands, and its effects continue, almost two generations after August 10, 1961.[126] In 2010, the VA estimated that 200,000 or more Vietnam veterans were still afflicted by the aftereffects of Agent Orange.[127]

In 1980, the DSM III (*Diagnostic and Statistical Manual of Mental Disorders*), identified and added to its roster of combat-related mental trauma, "Post Traumatic Stress Disorder", or PTSD. Another major study showed that 15% of Vietnam veterans, almost half a million, had been diagnosed with PTSD by 1988. A later analysis put the figure at over 50% or over a million.[128] "Soldier's Heart," "Shell Shock," "War Neurosis," "Battle Trauma," "Post Traumatic Stress Disorder," … war's deadly doppelganger hitched a ride on the first war wagon and has never gotten off.

Jonathan Shay, author of *Achilles in Vietnam*, rightly noted that the war-induced trauma now identified as PTSD, "is a legitimate war wound, and the veterans who suffer its injury carry the burdens of sacrifice for the rest of us as surely as the amputees, the burned, the blind, and the paralyzed carry them."[129] PTSD can cause severe psychiatric symptoms, including mood disorders, depression, dangerous or aggressive behaviors, substance abuse, and alcoholism. As many of us know, PTSD takes prisoner not only the individuals who suffer it, but the people, and the society at large, who interact with them. Nearly 40 years after the 1973 cease-fire, many veterans are "Still In Saigon". These "Extra Casualties", and those who love them, are lifelong "prisoners of war".

Given this complex set of problems, it was predictable that numerous studies would point to much higher rates of suicide among these veterans than the general population. Indeed, although exact statistics are not available, it seems very likely that many more Vietnam veterans have died by their own hand since the war than the 58,000 who were killed in combat.[130] As one veteran describes it:

> *"Sometimes, my head starts to replay some of my experiences in Nam. Regardless of what I'd like to think about, it comes creeping in. … It's old friends, the ambush, the screams, their faces, tears. When I walk down the street, I get real uncomfortable with people behind me that I can't see. When I sit, I feel most comfortable in the corner of a room, with walls on both sides of me. Loud noses irritate me and sudden movement or noise will make me jump."*

PTSD is about more than just bad dreams or paranoia; it has actual physical consequences. In 2007, Dr. Joseph A. Boscarino, a Vietnam veteran and senior scientist at the New York Academy of Medicine, presented research linking PTSD and auto immune disease among Vietnam-era veterans to the development of auto-immune disorders such as lupus and psoriasis.[131] There is strong correlation demonstrated between PTSD and long-term physical health problems. These include heart disease, rheumatoid arthritis, heart failure, asthma, liver, and peripheral arterial disease.

Altogether, Agent Orange, PTSD and suicide add at least another 800,000 "Extra Casualties" to the toll of the Vietnam war. Along that dead-end road, there are many who experience homelessness. The North Carolina Coalition to End Homelessness conducts a yearly Point-In-Time Count of the state's homeless population. On the night of January 27, 2010, 12,157 people experiencing homelessness were counted. Nine percent (1,054) of the people counted were veterans.[132] Further, among the more than 100,000 veterans who are homeless on any given night, credible estimates are that 60% served in Vietnam or before.[133] In addition, rates of alcohol and drug abuse are also higher, as are rates of divorce and family abuse. Moreover, a 2004 survey found that of the 140,000 veterans serving time in federal or state prisons, fully half were of the Vietnam generation.[134]

It doesn't stop there. For almost all of these troubled veterans, there is a family, which serves as a "force multiplier" to increase the number of "extra casualties" of the war machine. Out of Desert Storm there have been at least 300,000 troops who are struggling with Gulf War Syndrome. That's an amazing number for a war whose official U.S. casualty list, for both dead and wounded, is only about 750 total. In 2008, the Gulf War Research Advisory Committee reported that wartime toxins, not stress, caused profound physical illness in almost 300,000 veterans of the Gulf War.[135] And to these 300,000 soldiers, there again must be added many hundred thousand more family members.

Since 2001's declaration of "War on Terror," over two million service members have been to the wars and returned. Nearly 50% of returning troops will be eligible for some level of disability compensation. Economist and Nobel Laureate, Joseph E. Stiglitz, estimates that future disability payments and health care costs will total S600-$900 billion.[136]

Caregivers of veterans with service-related illness or injuries can be beggared by the "cost of war" in a myriad of ways. The National Alliance for Caregiving and the United Health Foundation report that 96% of veterans' care-givers are women. The youngest veterans requiring care served in Iraq or Afghanistan. Approximately one quarter of these youngest veterans are being cared for by their parents. Caregivers can become highly stressed, isolated, and financially pressed. How do we put a monetary value on the loss of the life that was to be, for the ill or injured veteran? And what is the price, in quality of life, for the veteran, for the caregiver, for the family, for society? How to enter "incalculable" on the balance sheet of the cost of war?

Veterans with disabling mental problems, and those seriously wounded who need help with the activities of daily living, are a particular challenge. In the current wars, modern medical care is keeping alive many soldier with very serious, disabling wounds, soldiers who would have died from similar wounds in Vietnam. Many such survivors, however, require extensive and ongoing care, often for life.

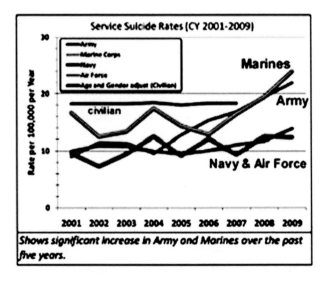

Dr. Ronald J. Glasser, an Army surgeon during the Vietnam war, and author of *Wounded: Vietnam to Iraq*, warned, in 2005, that, "The real 'body count' of this war is not only our dead, but our wounded. The real risk to our troops is no longer the numbers of dead but the numbers ending up on orthopedic wards and neurosurgical units. Ultimately … the most enduring images of the Iraq war will be the sight of legless and addled beggars on our street corners holding cardboard signs that read: 'Iraq Vet. Hungry and Homeless. Please Help.'"[137]

Even when returning troops are physically able, the after-effects of multiple deployments can be more than challenging for families; they can also be deadly. In North Carolina, near Quaker House, Fort Bragg and Camp Lejeune have seen a sad series of shocking, highly-publicized domestic violence cases in the years of the "War On Terror." As for instance the in summer of 2002, when there were seven domestic murders and suicides involving Afghanistan veterans and their spouses. Or in 2007-2008, when four servicewomen were murdered by their male GI spouses or boyfriends. Numerous other isolated homicide cases have occurred with less outside notice. And these two military posts are by no means exceptional.

In 2004, a North Carolina child protection group analyzed 16 years of records involving the murder of children by parents or step-parents. The rates of such homicides were steady across the state's 100 counties, with two exceptions: in Onslow and Cumberland counties, the child homicide rates were consistently *twice as high.* Onslow County is home to Camp Lejeune; Cumberland County hosts Fort Bragg.[138]

Events in North Carolina are a microcosm of what is happening across the United States. Brown University's Eisenhower Research Project on "The Costs of War" notes that more than 2 million children have been affected by one (or both) parents' (often multiple) deployments. As many as 1/2 million of those children may have become clinically depressed. Nationally, rates of child abuse have been three times higher in homes from which a parent is deployed. Partner abuse rates are up 177% in Army families since 2003.[139]

Then there is the matter of suicide. It is well-known that in 2009 and 2010, many more GIs killed themselves than were killed in combat. At Fort Campbell in Kentucky, there was a soldier suicide per week for the first four months of 2010. The protracted wars have provoked a spike in suicides among older veterans as well, in a kind of collective flashback. The Veterans

Administration reported in 2010 that eighteen veterans were committing suicide every day, and its suicide prevention hotline was fielding an average of 10,000 calls per month.[140] Veterans for Common Sense released new suicide-related statistics in September, as part of National Suicide Prevention Week. VCS Executive Director, Paul Sullivan, cited troubling statistics from the VA's crisis hotline. As of July 31, 2011, the VA's crisis line had received 259,000 calls from veterans, and 6,030 calls from active duty service members. There were 16,855 "rescues" of veterans and service members.[141]

Still, as the war in Afghanistan enters its 10th year, and the war in Iraq enters its 21st year, the suicide epidemic is a sad legacy of those wars. Untreated PTSD is a serious issue for veterans, service members, and their families. Repeated deployments, lengthy waits to see doctors, and discrimination against those seeking health care, increase the "Extra Casualty" count. As of this month, September, 2011, some 850,000 veterans are waiting an average of five months for a disability claim decision from VA. Another 250,000 veterans are waiting an average of four more years for a claim decision appeal. 10,000 new Iraq and Afghanistan war veterans seek VA medical care each month.[142]

There is the issue of crime: at Fort Carson in Colorado, a ring of combat-hardened soldiers formed a deadly gang, murdering, raping and robbing dozens of victims.[143] Joint Base Lewis-McChord, in Washington state, was named by independent news source *Stars and Stripes* as the most troubled in the military, thanks to an "incredible" number of incidents rooted in PTSD, says Joseph Carter, a former Army sergeant. Incidents include a sergeant murdering his wife after returning home from his third deployment in Iraq. Another soldier was convicted of waterboarding his three-year-old daughter because she did not know her ABC's. The Afghan Kill Team, which perpetrated a three-month spree of wanton killing and violence against innocent Afghan civilians, was also from Lewis-McChord.

We must speak of rape. We can't pass by the plague of sexual assault. According to Col. Ann Wright, U.S. Army (Ret.), "One in three women are raped or sexually assaulted during their military careers." Col. Wright warns of an "epidemic" of sexual assault by members of, upon members of, the military. "The military is a predatory organization," said Col. Wright. She notes that only eight per cent of the military sexual assault cases are brought to trial. Men are vulnerable to rape and assault, as well. In 2007, 10 per cent of rapes reported by the Army, were of men.[144] In December, 2010, the Service Women's Action Network and the ACLU filed a lawsuit with the U.S. District Court in New Haven, Connecticut, against the Department of Defense and VA for their failure to respond to FOIA requests seeking government records documenting incidents of rape, sexual assault, and sexual harassment in the military. Military Sexual Trauma (MST) is particularly widespread among servicewomen. Many find the return to civilian life a struggle, after suffering sexual assault while serving. Forty percent of homeless women veterans have been sexually assaulted while serving in the armed forces.

Beginning with Vietnam, we've seen that another million veterans not on the official casualty list have suffered long-term, often fatal wounds, damage that has extended to family members as well. Out of Desert Storm there have been at least 300,000 troops who are struggling with Gulf War Syndrome. And in our current wars, the number of "extra casualties" resulting from PTSD, TBI, suicides and other violence is rapidly approaching half a million more, plus families, with no end yet insight to this inhumane "surge." This tally adds not less than 1,500,000 to the grim roster, plus probably as many family members to the toll.

The financial impact of injuries on this scale is in the trillions of dollars. On September 29, 2010, Nobel Laureate Joseph Stiglitz, Ph.D., and Harvard economist Linda Bilmes testified before the House Committee on Veterans' Affairs. The hearing was held to discuss the "true cost of war". When their book, *The Three Trillion Dollar War: The True Cost of the Iraq War,* was published in 2008, many argued that Stiglitz and Bilmes had overestimated the cost of the war in Iraq. Two years later, the economists revised their estimated cost of the war to between $4 and $6 trillion. Today, in 2011, Dr. Stiglitz and Ms. Bilmes estimate that "social costs" to veterans of Iraq/Afghanistan will be higher than their 2008 estimate of between $295 and $400 billion. These costs include physical illness and injury, mental trauma and debility, homelessness, unemployment, poverty, domestic violence, divorce, substance abuse, the burden of caregiving, or just a diminished quality of life.

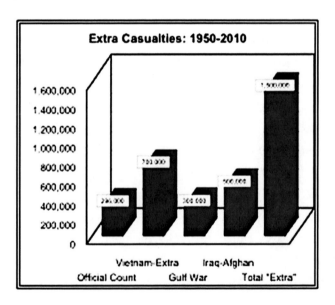

These social costs are not included in the federal budget. The social costs are borne by the veterans, by their families, and by society. For veterans and their dependents, and for our nation, these are among the hidden costs of war. For years, for lifetimes, for generations, these "unfunded liabilities" are America's latest "Extra Casualties" of war. The experiences, issues, and conditions which predispose a veteran to a slipping-down life seldom exist singly. Instead, the Military Industrial Complex manifests in a malignant symbiosis of cause and effect, to further maim and destroy.

This is the Cost of War come marching home.

In his January 17, 1961 Farewell Address, President Eisenhower warned, "In the councils of government, we must guard against the acquisition of unwarranted influence, whether sought or unsought, by the military-industrial complex." At that time, Ike's prescience made his caveat a cautionary tale. In 2011, the tally of "Extra Casualties" across fifty years, renders his warning a manifesto.

Mia Austin Scoggins works with veterans, especially those experiencing homelessness and other trauma. She is Vice President in Charge of Communications for (Eisenhower) Chapter 157, Veterans for Peace, and is Media Coordinator for North Carolina Peace Action.

IV.
NON-COOPERATION
WITH EVIL

Crazy Horse Back on the War Path

By Bruce Gagnon

Well hello everyone. I'm glad to be here. I'm glad that this conference is happening. It is certainly an important time. I live in Bath, Maine. It has a manifestation of the military industrial complex at a shipyard called Bath Iron Works where they build Navy Aegis destroyers.

The Global Network Against Weapons and Nuclear Power in Space was created in 1992. At that time, I was working for the Florida Coalition for Peace and Justice, working on space issues, and we realized the militarization of space was moving forward quickly and that we needed to do more to internationalize knowledge and resistance against it. In Colorado Springs, Colorado, was the only other group in the country that was working on space issues too, a group called Citizens for Peace in Space, because the U.S. Space Command was headquartered at that time there before moving to Offutt Air Force Base in Omaha, Nebraska. So together we created the Global Network in 1992 and today there are about 150 affiliated groups all over the world that are a part of it.

I want to talk to you today about Wasichu. Wasichu is a Lakota word; Lakota are often called the Sioux Indians out in the Dakotas. When they first met the white man, their first contact they had was with a white man who, in the middle of the winter, came into one of their tepees and stole all their food. In this particular tepee, they had stored the fat for the really worst part of the winter when they would run out of everything else and they were just living on fat. Wasichu means the one who steals the fat, the greedy person. Today, in the modern Indian movement, they use the word Wasichu to mean corporations that steal from the people, that steal from the land and that steal the resources, and so this is what I want to talk to you about today, the Wasichu.

I want to tell you a story from South Dakota set in the years of 1877 to 1881, soon after gold had been discovered in the Black Hills that the Lakota people called the Paha Sapa, the heart of the universe. Their sacred lands had been promised to them by treaty for as long as the grass grew green. But gold was discovered there and the military/U.S. Army, people like General Custer, were sent there to clear a military highway from the east into the Black Hills so that the prospectors could go in and get the gold — clear out the Indians, clear out the people. Most all of the clans had been brought onto the reservation by 1877, with the exception of two — Crazy Horse and Sitting Bull. Finally, even Crazy Horse in 1877 was brought onto the reservation as his people were starving to death. The whites coming into the Black Hills had pretty much gotten rid of all of the buffalo. The buffalo had been decimated in the years before by buffalo hunters killing them from the trains, just killing legions of buffalo, taking the hides and leaving the meat to rot on the plains. The native people saw the insanity of the white man during this time.

Crazy Horse decided to go on the reservation, and the deal that he made with the Army was that he would give up his guns and his horses, virtually their entire way of life. He was brought into a tepee on the reservation with essentially nothing and the people were promised provisions by the federal government. As it turned out the blankets they were given were very thin and were laden with smallpox virus. The flour had bugs in it; the meat and bacon were rotten. The contractors who delivered these supplies were cheating the people and pocketing the profits. Crazy Horse's people were even starving there on the reservation.

In 1881, Sitting Bull finally came on the reservation for the same reason, but a problem resulted. The problem was that the military industrial complex that existed at that time had been making big money off the Civil

War and then from the expansion of the Indian wars out onto the Great Plains and into Texas where the Army was wiping out the Comanches. As these Indian wars were brought to a close, these weapons corporations were seeing a drying up of their funding, and so they created a public relations campaign across the country. They had artists do renderings, and stories were written about Crazy Horse back on the warpath, raping women, killing children, marauding against the white settlers that were coming out west. These stories were planted in all the major newspapers across America, "Crazy Horse — Back on the Warpath." The American people rose up in indignation, and Congress swung into action and re-appropriated more money to fight Crazy Horse out in South Dakota. In fact, he was sitting in his tepee on the reservation.

The military industrial complex has an MO. When I was a kid I wanted to be an FBI agent. I wanted to fight organized crime, and so I thought I'd get a head start on everybody else. I subscribed to an FBI correspondence course. I learned about fingerprinting, and I learned about FBI definitions like MO (modus operandi). Every criminal has an MO. This military industrial complex that we are talking about today, which has been in existence essentially since the first Indian wars on this continent in the northeast of the United States, this military industrial complex is a criminal syndicate in operation across our country. In more recent times we saw it manifest itself with the Gulf of Tonkin Resolution in Vietnam and the lies about weapons of mass destruction in Iraq in 2003. The story today is that we know that Al-Qaeda is down to about 100 people, the Pentagon acknowledges, in Afghanistan and Pakistan, but still, the military industrial complex creates justifications to continue that war. And now China is being set up as the next boogieman as the American people are being made to fear the rising Red Army.

In each case, when this military industrial complex moves into gear, what we see next is destroyed societies and cultures. We witness new weapons systems tested and produced. Go back to the Indian wars and you see the repeating rifles and the Gatling guns created, the buffalo destroyed by new high-powered, long-distance rifles. The Persian Gulf War that began in the early 90's was called the first space war because for the first time space technology was used to coordinate and direct an entire war. The Pentagon bragged that before the war even started with Saddam Hussein the Space Command had pre-identified all of his military targets by space satellites, even to the point that they knew where his military communication cables were under the desert floor, they could see them from space. In the first two to three days of the war, the Pentagon bombed 95% of those military targets — the Persian Gulf War lasted for months, and so after the first couple of days the U.S. played cat and mouse with Saddam's remaining military capability. The Pentagon used that time to test out many new weapon systems, and used so many cruise missiles that in Titusville, Florida, at the McDonnell Douglas plant they were working three shifts a day, 24 hours a day to resupply the cruise missiles at a million dollars apiece.

The Pentagon used depleted uranium in Iraq and uses drones today in Afghanistan and Pakistan. As part of this new China scare we have been hearing about cyber warfare. The idea is that you can use computers to invade another country by first essentially crawling inside of their computer so that you can shut down their air defense systems before you attack them and they have no ability to defend themselves. All of these kinds of new systems created, not out of necessity, but out of desire for profit and control.

A few years ago, during the Bush administration, I was watching one of my favorite TV programs, C-Span, and I saw a startling program. They introduced the speaker at a military conference as Donald Rumsfeld's strategy guy. His name was Thomas Barnett, who at that time was an instructor at the Naval War College in Rhode Island. He wrote a book called the Pentagon's New Map. First, I want to say something about the audience. It was a huge auditorium. High-level military brass from all the services was present, and in the introduction they said high-level CIA people were there as well. Barnett was there to lay out for the highest levels of the military the new Pentagon military strategy.

Barnett essentially said this: Because of corporate globalization of the world's economy, every different country is going to have a different role in the future, a different job. We're not going to make things in America anymore. We're not going to have jobs in America because it's cheaper for the corporations to go overseas, maximize profits internationally, to build cars and clothes and shoes, refrigerators, computers, everything else. Our role under corporate globalization will be security export. Thus it's no coincidence that today in America the number one industrial export product of our nation is weapons, and when weapons are your number one industrial export product, what is your global marketing strategy for that product line?

Barnett went on to say that there would essentially be two military services in the future. Because of space technology, the old distinction between Army, Navy, Air Force and Marines, he said, is being rubbed out. One he called "leviathan" whose job would be to go in, shock and awe, do a complete destruction of a particular country, and the other service will be "systems administration," sys-ad he called it. He said these troops would never come home. After we've gone in with leviathan, completely destroyed a country, systems administration will go in and run the country. Yes, they'll set up a puppet government, of course, like Libya or in Afghanistan, but systems administration will run the country and will never come home. In fact, just about two years ago I read that Lockheed Martin had gotten a huge contract from the Pentagon to begin training the new generation of systems administration warriors.

Barnett went on to say that young people in America, the angry, young men who are whiling away their time because they have no jobs would be perfect for leviathan because they're angry, they're connected to computer games, they'll be good at doing things like flying drones, and he basically described the militarization of our culture. Last year I saw a manifestation of this. I heard a rumor that Sears had a new line of kids' clothes, and I went to see it with a friend because I really had to check this out, and what I discovered when I walked into the kids' section of Sears was a complete display of military uniforms turned into kids clothing. The message to the younger generation is this is all you're going to be. This is your future in America, either flipping hamburgers or coming into the military.

The other thing that Barnett talked about which is very important is the Pentagon's new map. He said there is part of the world today that is not submitting to the authority of corporate globalization. He called it the non-integrating gap, and he clearly identified it. He named the Middle East, where, of course, we are in Iraq today with our permanent military bases and these people won't be coming home. Central Asia where we are today in Afghanistan, again, we're not coming home from there. Africa where he said we will be fighting 20 years from now for their oil, well even sooner than that as NATO, our lap dog, has invaded Libya which sits on the largest supply of oil on the African continent. Finally, Barnett said parts of Latin America are included in this non-integrating gap, places like Venezuela where Hugo Chavez is not playing ball with corporate globalization. Barnett maintained our job in America, under security export, will be to go into the non-integrating gap, and secure it to the benefit of corporate globalization. Barnett said America would not do international treaties anymore because they will just stand in our way. Barnett also told this big audience, "Adolph Hitler never had to ask permission to invade another country and neither will we." This arrogance is why we are having endless war today.

Because of diminishing resources around the world, the corporations have determined that they are going to control the oil, the natural gas, the water, the other minerals in places like resource-rich Africa, and it will be our job to go in there and to secure those places. In fact, the more unemployment we have the better because then more young people will have to enter the "economic draft" to go fight endless war to benefit the multinational corporations. So it is no coincidence today that Virginia receives more Pentagon contracts, more Pentagon dollars than any other state in the nation. Virginia is followed by California at #2, Texas at #3, Connecticut at #4 and Massachusetts at #5. Social progress is being defunded and Congress is funding "security export" under the watchful eye of military industrial complex lobbyists.

You might remember that right before George W. Bush left office there was a lot of talk about his deployment of so-called "missile defense" systems in the Czech Republic and in Poland. It was causing quite a bit of stir, and soon after Obama came into office, many people were very excited because Obama said he was not going to go forward with those deployments. Some people called me and said "Bruce, you said Obama wasn't going to be any good, but look, he just canceled Bush's missile defense deployment," and I responded, "Well, you've gotta follow the other hand of the magician."

I have come to call Obama the magician because what you get on the one hand is not necessarily what you get on the other. Soon after this Obama went to Prague in the Czech Republic. You might remember that it was in Prague where he made a disarmament speech saying we're going to get rid of nuclear weapons. Obama next came forward with a new missile defense plan calling for increased deployment of Aegis destroyers, made where I live in Bath, Maine. These Navy warships outfitted with missile defense systems are being deployed surrounding Russia and China. Just this past week, Romania signed a deal with Hillary Clinton to put missile defense interceptors on ground-based launchers in Romania. Turkey recently signed a deal with the U.S. to put missile defense radar systems into their country. Poland has already agreed to put Patriot (Pac-3), the third generation of Patriot missile defense interceptors, in their country just 35 km from the Russian border. The Obama administration has lately been sending these Aegis destroyers outfitted with missile defense interceptors into the Black Sea, the Mediterranean Sea and angering the Russians. The Russians are now saying, "The START II treaty that we signed with you is now in jeopardy because if you continue with these missile defense deployments, Mr. Obama, we're going to pull out of that treaty."

Now what is it about these missile defense systems on the Navy Aegis destroyers that Obama likes so much? Well, right before the 2008 election, a dear old friend in Maine, a guy by the name of Herschel Sternlieb, a Jewish man, asked me "Bruce, you ever heard of the Crown family?" and I said no. He said, "They are from Chicago, the Crown family. Go home and google it." So I did, and I discovered that the Crown family at the time of the 2008 election was the majority stockholders in the General Dynamics Corporation that owns Bath Iron Works in Maine. It was the Crown family in Chicago that "discovered" Obama early on, promoted him within the national Jewish constituency, helped get him elected to the U.S. Senate and then helped create his presidential campaign. As it turns out, Obama received more funding from the military industrial complex in the 2008 election than even the war hawk, John McCain, did. This was reported in *Aviation Week and Space Technology* magazine. To me it's thus no mystery or coincidence that Obama has said he is going to cancel the Bush version of missile defense deployments and in its place go with the version made by General Dynamics Corporation as the preferred option to surround Russia. Now why Russia? It doesn't make sense. Why restart the Cold War? Well, is it possible that a key part of the answer is because Russia has the world's largest supply of natural gas and also significant supplies of oil? Have we not yet learned that it is official U.S. military strategy to surround and control any part of the world that has significant fossil fuel resources?

At the same time, these Aegis destroyers, outfitted with missile defense systems, are also being deployed by the Obama administration to surround China. Today, they are being ported in Japan, in South Korea, and in Australia. Throughout the Asia-Pacific region, the U.S. Pentagon is, in fact, doubling its military presence. Last night, Ann Wright talked about little Jeju Island, an island just south of the Korean mainland. It now has a Navy base being built there. I called the South Korean Embassy in Washington to say stop building this Navy base, we support the Gangjeong villagers who have been living in this village for 400 years, growing food, fishing, their entire way of life is being disrupted. When I, and others, called the embassy, we were told don't call us, call your own government. They're twisting our arm, forcing us to build this base. Why does the U.S. want a Navy base on the south side of Jeju Island? Because, as you look at a map, you see that this is a strategic location in the Yellow Sea. It is essentially the front gate, if you'll think of it that way, of the entryway into their country for China as they import 80% of their oil on ships.

The Pentagon strategy appears to be that while we might not be able to compete with China economically, if we control their access to resources, we will hold the key to their economic engine. In 2001 an article ran in the *Washington Post* called "For Pentagon, Asia Moving to the Forefront" and the article reported that the U.S. was going to double its military presence in the region, it was going to manage China. So imagine China seeing all this with their couple of military satellites up there in space looking down at this massive U.S. militarization in the region. Expanding bases in Guam, putting PAC-3/Patriot missile defense systems even in Taiwan. It's kind of the Cuban Missile Crisis in reverse. So China is now responding, increasing its own military spending, increasing the size of its Navy and, again, as Ann said last night, the Pentagon says, "Oh my God, look at China, look what they're doing." What if the reverse was to happen? What if China was putting Navy ships off the east and west coast of the United States? What if China had military bases in Canada and Mexico? We would be freaking out. We would be going "ballistic."

Princeton Professor Aaron Friedberg, a former close advisor to Dick Cheney, argued in a *New York Times* column on September 4th that American taxpayers must put up with whatever is needed to keep the Chinese under control. "Strength deters aggression," argued Friedberg. "This will cost money," he said. These missile defense systems, what I call the shield of first-strike warfare, are now being used to encircle Russia and China. This is how it works. In a computer war-game run by the U.S. Space Command, reported annually in aerospace industry publications, set in the year 2016, the Pentagon launches the first-strike preemptive attack from space using the new weapons system called the military space plane, now under development to replace the recently retired shuttle. The military space plane, carrying either nuclear or conventional weapons, flies down from orbit, drops a devastating attack on China, and goes back up into space.

China does admittedly have 20 nuclear missiles capable of hitting the west coast of the United States today, and in that first-strike attack by the military space plane, and other weapons systems by the U.S., the Space Command tries to take out China's nukes but are not successful at hitting every one of them. China then fires their remaining retaliatory capability, and it is at that point, after the U.S. sword has been thrust into China's nuclear forces, the U.S. missile defense systems come into play. Their job is to shield, to take out the remaining Chinese nuclear forces to successfully complete the first-strike attack. And so this is the military capability that today is being developed under the name of "missile defense," and is also what is being war-gamed at the U.S. Space Command.

China and Russia obviously are aware of what is going on, they are certainly aware that they are being targeted by the U.S. for the preparation of a first-strike attack and, indeed, massive money is needed to pull this off. The Pentagon and the aerospace industry have long been saying that Star Wars, the weaponization of space — moving the arms race into the heavens — will be the largest industrial project in the history of the planet Earth.

Now where will that money come from? In an editorial in *Space News* just a few years ago they wrote: We have a responsibility as an industry to come up with a funding source and we have. We're now sending our lobbyists to Washington to secure that funding source. It's the entitlement programs. Yes, the entitlement programs that we've been talking about this weekend, which officially are Social Security, Medicare, Medicaid and what's left of the welfare program after Bill Clinton got through with it. These are the programs that the military industrial complex has identified for defunding in order to pay for endless war.

Earlier today there was some mention of the new Super Committee in Congress, what I call the Congressional coup d'etat, where 12 members of the House and Senate have been given the power of God. The Congressional Super Committee, that will be given these extraordinary powers to cut the federal budget, will be co-chaired by Senator Patty Murray, Democrat from Washington. She is often called "Boeing's Senator." There are huge conflicts of interest between these committee members, these 12 people, and the military industrial complex. The *Boston Globe* reported just a few weeks ago that "The six Republicans and six Democrats represent states where the biggest military contractors — Lockheed Martin, General Dynamics, Raytheon, and Boeing Co. — build missiles, aircraft jet fighters and tanks while employing tens of thousands of workers." The *Globe* tried to make the case that it would be a "Doomsday" if this new Super Committee allowed major cuts in military spending. Senator Murray, the Democrat, got $276,200 in campaign donations from these aerospace corporations since 2007, more than any other committee member. Second place goes to Senator Max Baucus, the Democrat from Montana at $139,100, and third place went to the Republican, Dave Camp from Michigan who got $130,800, and the fourth spot was Skull and Bones member, Senator John Kerry, Democrat for Massachusetts, at $73,500. You remember that election don't you? When Skull and Bones ran against Skull and Bones. When it was George W. Bush against John Kerry. You remember that, right? So three out of the top four Super Committee recipients of weapons contractor's cash are Democrats. It's a bad situation, coup d'etat, coup d'etat.

But I like to remind people there's always an Achilles heel. There always is. Every giant has an Achilles heel. Every person has an Achilles heel. Every politician has an Achilles heel and every plan for endless war has an Achilles heel. And in this case, the Achilles heel is called the big green or what the Indians called the green frog skin. The native people said that when the white man came to this continent they noticed he was blinded, they saw a spiritual disconnection between the white man and the Earth, and this is why the white man was destroying his own nest, because he was blinded by his love for the green frog skin. Today, friends, we can no longer afford guns and butter. We now have two freight trains heading for a collision course. One freight train is called social progress, and the other freight train is called endless war. One of them is going to win out. Which will it be? Will it be a return to feudalism, a corporate brand of feudalism, or will we have true democracy and social progress in our time?

We do have a problem today. It's called climate change, and we need every available hand on deck to deal with it. We need every available dollar of our resources available to help us put a small chink in the coming reality of climate change. A study has been done by UMass-Amherst and they found that one billion dollars of military spending creates 8,500 jobs. You take that same billion dollars and you put it into home weatherization, something we really need in Maine where we have the oldest housing stock in the nation, and you get 12,804 jobs. Or if you put it into building mass transit you get 19,795 jobs. Everywhere I go I like to ask people, "Which would you rather have with your tax dollars, 8,500 jobs for endless war or 19,795 jobs building railcars to get us out of our gas-guzzling cars so we don't have to go to war for oil?" I have yet to find anyone in two years of asking this question tell me they want to keep blowing money down the rat hole of Pentagon spending. We must call for the conversion of the military industrial complex.

Fundamentally, as we do our peace work, each and every one of us have got to begin to integrate this jobs issue into our work. We have to talk about jobs everywhere we go. We have to talk about jobs when we talk about war. We have to talk about jobs when we talk to people about peace. We should talk about jobs every time we open our mouths, every time we stand on a street corner with our outdated signs that say "No blood for oil" and "War is not the answer." It's time for us to update our signs and talk about endless war and Bring Our War $$ Home. If we do that we might find that the American people, who in poll after poll are saying that the collapsing economy is their biggest worry, might start listening to us. If we create an alternative sustainable vision of the future, and put it out there as part of our peace work, we might find that the American people just might start paying attention to what we have to say once again.

Bruce Gagnon is co-founder and coordinator of the Global Network Against Weapons and Nuclear Power in Space, and has worked on space issues for more than 20 years. His articles made Project Censored's list of the most censored stories in both 1999 and 2005.

Whistleblowing, and How to Get More of It

Karen Kwiatkowski

To my way of thinking, there are two well-known Generals in our 20th century history who had something important to say about whistleblowing. The second one is Dwight D. Eisenhower who helped coin the language we use to describe the massive interoperable complex of the federal military, our public educational institutions, our corporate manufacturers of a wide variety of goods and services, and the United States Congress. It's mentioned in the title of this conference, and we believe it to be about 50 years old.

But the first General I think of when I think of truth telling and whistleblowing is General Smedley Butler who wrote in the early 1930's that "War is a Racket." Many of you here may have heard of Smedley Butler, and many of you may have read his short essay that described how the federal military in the late 1800s and early 1900s, at the direction of Presidents and Congressmen, moved globally to support the interests of American corporations, banking establishments, and even that of certain politically important families of the day. It was called war, sometimes occupation, and at times, it was publicly accepted as imperialism, the strange imperialism of a Republic, a shining city on the hill seeking to share its vision of liberty and self-government at the point of a gun. Butler starts out his famous essay by noting that,

> *A racket is best described, I believe, as something that is not what it seems to the majority of the people. Only a small "inside" group knows what it is about. It is conducted for the benefit of the very few, at the expense of the very many. Out of war a few people make huge fortunes.*

It has always been so, and it has never mattered if the warring entities were republics or democracies, kingdoms or dictatorships. Smedley Butler was a whistleblower of sorts — and yet it is important to remember that he had served the U.S. Marines for 33 years, reaching the rank of Major General, retiring, and then entered into national politics, sucking hind teat in a Pennsylvania Senate Republican Primary race, a race he lost against a former Republican Secretary of Labor and eugenicist.

Certainly, Butler's honest reflection of the reality of his own service led him to the conclusions he is known for — and indeed, for most people today — we ONLY know of Smedley Butler because he wrote *War is a Racket*. In a sense, all of his work for the military machine of his day is largely forgotten or irrelevant today. But his condemnation of political war — and his understanding that all war is political — lives on and inspires us.

It is also important to recognize that General Eisenhower did not write his famous words urging an "alert and knowledgeable citizenry … so that liberty and security may prosper together" as a serving soldier. Nor did he write these words as a campaign speech. He did not speak those words during his Presidency. He warned us and urged us to be alert and knowledgeable only as he was stepping down from eight years in office, ready to hand over the leadership of the country to a young President at the apogee of the Cold War, amidst global worry about war, about the falsely reported strength and skill of the Soviet Union, and a heavily contested presidential election.

These two famous men, in different ways, are whistleblowers, and they urged us to attempt to truly know what was actually being done in our name on battlefields around the planet, and to know who really stood to benefit from these wars themselves, and for the constant preparation for war. Both understood the "racket" because they worked for that racket, and both had been keys parts of its health and vitality. Smedley Butler and Dwight Eisenhower were the guardians of its secrets for decades.

These two are role models for all whistleblowers — men we honor today for telling the truth, shining a light on the future, even as we may certainly criticize them for not doing enough to secure the rule of law, to uphold the Constitution, and even turn the ship of state around.

These two gentlemen told us that the modern United States had an institutional orientation towards war as a mission, not of defense, but simply as a very important mission of an increasingly corporate state. They could speak publicly on this topic when they did only because both had become, no longer political actors, but rather, political afterthoughts. They were, to paraphrase Emma Goldman's famous quip, allowed to speak because it wouldn't, and couldn't change anything.

Our modern whistleblowers also come from deep within the corporate state, from the day to day workings of the executive departments of defense, homeland security and intelligence, and from inside the interrelated offices of congressmen and the front offices, boardrooms, factories and laboratories of major defense, security, and even pharmaceutical industries. They are either anonymous — in order to keep their jobs but through anonymity they lose credibility, or else they are publically recognized as witnesses and truth tellers, ready to be marginalized by state and political media, and ultimately fired from their positions.

There is a pattern here. It's not new, and it is something that we the people of this country need to recognize. Those who tell the truth about the waste, fraud, misdeeds, and agendas of the political military industrial complex are enemies of the state. They are not welcomed by the state as part of some effort to clean up the state's act, or to be utilized by the state to help the taxpayer understand what it is we pay for and why it is important. Instead, truth tellers, men and women of honor, witnesses and whistleblowers are instantly, without prevarication, enemies of the state.

The more famous stories we do know. Daniel Ellsberg was harassed and attacked, caricatured by the state as a criminal, not a hero. The many witnesses against the U.S. military regarding Agent Orange, and years later, the vaccinations and experimental drugs that are part and parcel of what would become known as Gulf War Syndrome, which today has killed more U.S. citizens than the Vietnam War, all of these men and women were treated as enemies of the state. Those who would tell the truth about the propaganda, and original intent, on the way to the wars in and continuing occupations of both Afghanistan and Iraq, are all made to be enemies of the state. Think about Bunny Greenhouse observing in pre-Iraq invasion contracting, and Sibel Edmonds in the months before 9-11. Fired, stifled, harassed, treated badly by our own government for simply telling the truth. And those who would bear witness to mistreatment and unlawful acts of war and interrogation by the United States here and around the world, are, you guessed it, enemies of the American state.

When I started thinking about this talk today, I wanted to see if there were things we can do to create those alert and knowledgeable citizens that Ike advocated we become. Can we actually raise up aware, thoughtful, honest and courageous people? If we did that, why would those people ever wish to work for a federal state engaged in the prosecution of non-defensive war? And, if those people don't get inside the bureaucratic state, or work inside the military industrial establishment, how credible would they be as whistleblowers, should it come to that?

Clearly, there are inconsistencies here. Wise small-R republicans of all political persuasions, devout Christians, and our most alert and knowledgeable citizens may not wish to serve the machine of state. They might be more interested in liberty and productivity, in peace and prosperity, than the racket of state and corporate military actions, occupations, and regime changes. Eisenhower glimpsed the problem when he suggested in his farewell speech that we should be able to see "both liberty and security prosper together." In fact, as Ben Franklin observed in 1775, "They who can give up essential liberty to obtain a little temporary safety, deserve neither liberty nor safety." 150 years later, the irreverent editor out of Baltimore, H.L. Mencken, explained the more fundamental problem, as follows:

> *What the common man longs for in this world, before and above all his other longings, is the simplest and most ignominious sort of peace: the peace of a trusty in a well-managed penitentiary. He is willing to sacrifice everything else to it. He puts it above his dignity and he puts it above his pride. Above all, he puts it above his liberty.*

If we want peace in our lives, to live the life of the relative privilege of the trustee in a well-managed penitentiary, then we will indeed sacrifice our dignity, our pride, and our liberty. We will bite our tongue, close our eyes, and take orders. For a republic to survive the inevitable pressures of democratic demands for global relevance and proud flag-waving parades, for corporatism, crony capitalism, and empire, we must have the kinds of citizens that are not Mencken's "common man." Our citizens must instead be uncommon men and women.

What I have learned from my own experience in telling the truth from within the military industrial complex when it is politically unpopular, is that our whistleblowers are indeed uncommon men and women. For every truth-teller who feels they must speak honestly and openly to preserve their dignity, their pride, and their liberty, there are one thousand, maybe ten thousand, even one hundred thousand men and women who want nothing more than to be able to pay their mortgage, get along with their employer, and keep their head down, and serve their time in the well-managed penitentiary.

So what can we do, those of us who care about rule of law, about the Constitution, the dreams of our forefathers, and the future of our grandchildren in this so-called Republic?

First of all, we must distinguish between the state we have in this country, the federal government in particular, and the government of our imagination. Too many people believe, as Eisenhower may have, that if we are only alert and informed, it will be enough. It will not.

The institutions of the federal government that conduct war in our name are mostly unelected, and the elected parties are indeed enslaved to a system that demonizes them for every peaceful statement that they might make. If you think I am making this up, then you haven't watched Ron Paul in the past four years in a presidential primary debate. In a country where our largest exports are military related, and the bulk of federal discretionary spending is either defensive or offensive in nature, every Congressman is a indentured servant, and the President not much more than a trustee himself.

The varied institutions of the federal government are, as a whole, not friendly to alert and informed citizens. It isn't who's in charge in Washington — it is that Washington D.C. exists today as a terminal cancer on the rest of the country. To believe otherwise, and to attempt to deal with Washington with anything other than great caution, is folly, in this day and age.

Secondly, while we can't change Washington, we can change ourselves, and those people whose lives are touched by ours. We cannot change their politics, their minds, or their emotional wiring. But we can encourage all of the people we know, to become more alert and better informed. Beyond that, we can encourage them not to become angry as they become more alert and better informed, but rather to use that energy of their awakening to live more freely. To live more bravely, more boldly, and more honestly. For some of these people, it will mean quitting their jobs in the military industrial political establishment, for others it will mean doing those jobs more enthusiastically, more boldly, more honestly. Living honestly naturally creates more whistleblowers, more truth tellers, more fearlessness.

Thirdly, we must consider the power of not just a minority, but the amazing power of even just one person. Our modern history of whistleblowing is a story of a lone voice struggling against the crowd. It is our shared and common understanding of the power of the devil's advocate and the single dissenting "Nay." The majority in a bureaucracy is often wrong, and the majority in a whole country can indeed be wrong, and in many ways it can be persistently wrong. When we embrace ideas of democracy as a means of getting better government, we must understand that it isn't impossible for the entire herd to run off the cliff, or an entire nation to go off the rails, for a Republic to become an empire with the loud blessing of a vast majority of its republican citizens.

If we can lose our awe of, and our fear of, government, and embrace real concepts of human liberty, we will stop seeking change through either force or through majority rule.

If we can build up the stores of dignity, personal pride, and a sense of liberty in all of the people around us, it won't matter if they share our politics or not. These people will love truth, they will love freedom, and they will be brave as they discover both.

If we can quietly stand with a minority, and even alone, for the cause of truth, we make a difference. We can demonstrate to our fellow citizens that standing up for truth is not really that difficult as we have been told, and it's not always as dangerous as the majority seems to believe it is.

I often find that I am dismayed at the directions of government in this country, and I am often dismayed at the general directions of the political culture in this country. But it may be that as the American empire contracts, somewhat reluctantly, we will see a new era of American liberty. While it won't be easy to achieve, it is worth giving up our fear and standing strong with a bold and honest minority.

I hope my words here today have helped some of you, and that they inspire more truth tellers, while sharing my gratitude for those who have gone before us. I have not spoken about my own personal experiences in observing and speaking out about the neoconservatives who beat the war drum in the 80s, the 90s, in 2002 and 2003, and every year since then. I'd like to answer any questions you may have about that or any other topic now. Thank you!

Karen Kwiatkowski is a retired U.S. Air Force Lieutenant Colonel and former Pentagon desk officer who also served in a variety of roles for the National Security Agency. She came to fame for openly and publicly denouncing political influence on the course of military intelligence leading up to the invasion of Iraq in 2003. She is running as a Republican in Virginia's 6th District Republican primary.

Leading With Integrity

By Bunny Greenhouse

My name is Bunnatine Greenhouse; I am the former Civilian Procurement Executive and Chief of Contracting for the United States Army Corps of Engineers and in that position I was responsible for awarding and managing over $23 billion in government contracts each year. I was hired as the Procurement Executive for the Corps in 1997 as an SES (Senior Executive Service) with the protocol of a 1-star general, and with a TALL ORDER: to revolutionize contracting in the Corps and rid the Army Corps of Engineers of the casual and clubby contracting practices that were the hallmark of an entrenched "good old boys" power structure — a power structure that stemmed hundreds of years.

I would like to thank Mr. John Heuer, Ms. Barbara Stanley and Mr. David Swanson and the entire MIC AT 50 Committee for allowing me the opportunity to share my story about standing for what is right even when it had tremendous adverse personal and professional consequences. Know that I do not regret the decisions that I made or the course that they set me on. Know also that I am a person deeply committed to ensuring that integrity and accountability in government procurement is paramount. My goal today is to quickly bring you my story from three perspectives: one, my work as a civil servant; two, what makes me "me"; and three, to challenge you to take your responsibility in helping to move civil servants and members of the military who are committed to truth and protection of the public trust up from second-class citizenry. I shall begin with some of the "woes" of civil leadership.

My Work As A Civil Servant

When I took my oath of office as a Civil Servant Senior Procurement

Executive, the first African American Female SES in the Corps, I pledged to conduct the government's business of contracting with the highest degree of integrity, impartially, above reproach, and with preferential treatment toward none, and following this oath and my belief in honesty, integrity, personal responsibility, and accountability led me to be branded as a whistleblower on the notorious "no bid" five year contract with the Halliburton subsidiary, Kellogg Brown and Root.

Due to past problems in contracting, Congress had enacted laws requiring contracting officers to ensure that small, minority, and women owned businesses were able to compete on the same playing field with large businesses. That level playing field must exist with the largest contracting efforts; even during compelling emergencies and contingency operations.

I was a civil servant. When I took responsibility of being the civilian head of contracting for the Army Corps of Engineers, federal law demanded that I would conduct business with the highest degree of integrity. Apparently, I did something the Army did not expect. I took my oath of office seriously and refused to bend the rules for the well connected and powerful. I didn't do anything special. I did my job with the courage and fortitude to stand up for what is ethical, regardless of the consequences. I did my job so that when I went home I could look myself in the mirror and know that I did the right things for the right reasons. Today, there must be a greater focus in our government on accountability and the realities of leadership and ethics.

In my experiences in contracting, I have seen many tragedies that are the direct result of a lack of integrity, lack of transparency, and a lack of accountability. I resolved that I would not stoop to these kinds of practices. My only concern was for the best interest of the public trust for which I had been given a small charge to protect.

After my best qualified selection as the Procurement Executive for the Corps, I was shocked to learn that improper contracting practices were the norm with the corps. In my charge by LTG Joe Ballard, the then Commander of the Army Corps of Engineers, I quickly turned to my courage and determination for the strength to revolutionize the contracting process by bringing fairness and integrity to the process. I was to "right-size" every large effort to make sure effective competition prevailed for the best value of the government and all stakeholders in the process; I was to make sure that all impediments were removed that would inhibit competition. Not only was this my job, but my duty to the nation.

However, a white male dominated military thought it was absurd that a black woman would hold them accountable to the rules. I encountered hostility, blatantly tied to my race and gender, but I did all I could do to create a system of checks and balances that would make it increasingly difficult for the inappropriate and clubby contracting practices to continue.

The Commanders of the Corps could not tolerate that my checks and balances hindered their ability to broker those clubby contracting deals. Congress passed the Defense Acquisition Workforce Improvement Act (DAWIA), which these commanders found difficult to follow. DAWIA mandated that professional contracting officers were in control of the contracting process. This contradicted the previous policy of military commanders being the Contracting Officers and in control of both requirements operations and Contracting, while the professional Contracting Officers served only as Administrative Clerks. My heart bled at an early Offsite in 1997, when a Contracting Officer stated, "We feel like we are in the kitchen cleaning up after all of the mess is made, but we are never invited to the table."

Under my tenure, civilian contracting professionals became capable and ready to independently and successfully support the business side of any and all operations. However, many were still prevented from doing so because of the intimidation and interference by their Military Commanders.

Regardless, Change was happening in the Corps under my leadership! The change was hard-fought and difficult but it was happening. Even though I was faced with a hostile environment, I continued to conduct my job with integrity.

My annual performance reviews written by the Deputy Commander and Commander of the Corps who brought me in to reform contracting by changing the system, spoke the truth of my work ethic. These evaluations observed that — and I quote: "ethics are above reproach"; "Unquestionable loyalty, integrity, and dedication to mission; Not Timid— has the fortitude to tell it as it is; Courage in Convictions, Candor, sage judgment and Passions, Always Evident"; "Unsurpassed as a contracting and acquisition expert and Professional Advisor. … Has no equal when it comes to technical, acquisition strategy and business cases analyses."

I do not say these things to trump my own horn. I say these things so that you understand that I know what it is like to work with people higher up than you requiring that unethical practices should be followed. It is easier to say nothing and go along with the crowd. However, if enough people rise to do the right thing, change can happen. Your work ethics will not go unnoticed and the people willing to tell the truth see the examples that you have set.

I was removed as the Procurement Executive after holding that position for eight years, not for impropriety but for being unwilling to continue the improper practices of clubby contracting, without compliance to the Law.

I was never asked to defend my actions or inactions in managing the contracting process; all contracting commitments at the end of each of my eight fiscal years were successfully completed on time; and most importantly, I professionalized and developed a contracting workforce, second to none. Let there be no mistake, I was removed from my office and demoted out of the Senior Executive Service and Contracting because I did my job too well!

After the change of the Chief of Engineers I was hired under, my skill set of complying with the laws and regulations was no longer wanted by the Army Corps Command. I was considered too powerful and viewed by commanders as an obstacle standing in their way, by refusing to return to the "good old days" when contracts were awarded based primarily on relationships.

Things came to a head with the ramp-up to the Iraq war when I questioned the actions that would lead to the improper award of billions of dollars of no-bid, no-compete contracts to Halliburton subsidiary KBR. This type of no-bid, unfairly awarded contract often opens the floodgates to corruption and lack of the best value for our soldiers and government.

The no-bid contracts awarded to Halliburton were immorally exclusionary and contrary to contracting guidelines at every level, and they undermined the level playing field that I had strived to create. In fact, the favored treatment toward Halliburton represented the most blatant contract abuse I witnessed during the course of my career.

I could not remain silent. I raised my concerns with my command structure; I raised my concerns directly to representatives of the Secretary of Defense and the Secretary of the Army. When my efforts reached a dead end, I did the only thing left for me to do: I hand-wrote a comment next to my signature on the original copies of critical procurement documents associated with the award of a five year Compelling Emergency, $7 billion no-bid, no compete Restore Iraqi Oil contract to Halliburton. My handwritten comments challenged the duration of the award. That I had the audacity to document by hand-writing my concerns directly onto the Halliburton procurement documents was the last straw — I had to be removed.

The Army initially attempted to remove me on October 5, 2004. However, I had the great fortune of being represented by Mr. Michael Kohn, General Counsel to the National Whistleblower Center. With his help, I was able to stop the system from grinding me down. The then Acting Secretary of the Army was forced to send a letter to Mr. Kohn stating that I could not be removed until the Department of Defense, Office of the Inspector General, could investigate my allegations and (I quote) "a sufficient record is available to address the specific matters." However, to this day, the DOD IG never contacted me and no investigation of my concerns was ever undertaken.

In June of 2005, I was asked to appear before the Democratic Policy Committee to discuss the no-bid Halliburton contracts and I agreed to do so. The Acting General Counsel of the U.S. Army Corps of Engineers visited me to inform me, in no uncertain terms, that to appear before the committee would not be in my best interest. I ignored this threat to my professional career; appeared before that congressional committee and stated that the contract abuse related to Halliburton was the worst abuse I witnessed during the course of my professional career. I was thereafter swiftly removed from the Senior Executive Service.

I was removed from a position in which I had been described as having work ethics, "second to none" and recognized as the most knowledgeable and critical thinking contracting professional ever within the Army Corps. I was first replaced by a civilian SES who was not a contracting careerist and had not served a day as a contracting officer and had to receive a waiver for the experience and training requirements of the DAWIA law, and she retired and then the head of civilian contracting became an Army Colonel, who lacked the full complement of training and experience necessary to competently do the job.

My removal from office caused a chilling effect throughout the contracting community and the SES corps. I took great pride in the fact that my past accomplishments were viewed with enthusiasm within the federal contracting community. Unfortunately, my removal clarified to the federal contracting community that those who battle contract abuse will not be thanked, but fired. In fact, it sent a chilling effect to anyone who works to stand for what is right and promotes ethical practices. Because I would not take their initial offer to retire immediately with the SES Status, the Army Corps set me as an example to show that people who desire to do the right thing and report corruption would suffer greatly. My response was: SO BE IT!

In my transition from the SES, I was directed to report to the Army Corps' Civil Works Engineering and Construction Division where I was supposed to function as a "program manager" with no approved duties other than to support the colonel who had replaced me as the Chief Contracting Officer. Hurricane Katrina had struck New Orleans. The response to the Katrina disaster was one of the largest contracting civil works efforts the Army Corps had ever faced; despite my credentials and work experience, I was excluded from the Katrina management meetings that were held in my new office area, behind closed doors.

I was born and raised in Louisiana and am a member of the Louisiana Hall of Fame for Women in Government, and I can assure you that it pained me greatly that I was not permitted to assist with the Katrina disaster.

After my demotion, I experienced isolation; I received repeatedly inappropriately down-graded performance reviews; my top secret clearance was withdrawn; others took credit for my work; no training opportunities were identified since I had no engineering and construction mission responsibilities, being in an "overhire" unauthorized and unfunded position, but most importantly, I had been prevented from returning to the contracting career field and to the SES.

However, there was some solace, In July, 2006; I was honored with the Cliff Robertson's Sentinel Award that bears the inscription: "For Choosing Truth Over Self." Also, in December, 2005, I received the Joe A. Callaway Award for Civic Courage, as a Whistleblower in the Nation's Service, with a partial citation which states: "Bunny Greenhouse defies pressure to go along to get along, choosing to protect the public trust at high personal cost. Her integrity and unwavering adherence to principle stand as a beacon to all public servants and represent the best in our democracy."

What Makes Me "ME"!

Again, what are the values that I am not willing to Compromise? Integrity, Honesty, Personal Responsibility, and Accountability, Not turning my head and denying Misconduct. My Work Ethics.

What kept me positive in the midst of the storms? I refused to look at the dynamics of the storms of life. I struggled to see the rainbows and I believe that "big storms bring gigantic rainbows." I also believe that "It's not the mountain in your path that holds you back, but the pebbles in your shoe." I always focus on managing the pebbles as I move ahead from day to day!

But most of all, I was just "Bunny Greenhouse", an ordinary person. I find it humbling to be honored and celebrated for simply doing my job; during a job I was privileged to do as a civil servant, but it is gravely disappointing to be punished for having the courage to do the job strictly to the best of my ability; for the best interest of our government! However, it is alright with me since I know that it has been for some bigger purpose than Bunny Greenhouse.

My actions as a "whistleblower" were in congruence with my ethics, civic, moral, and religious values and I shall never compromise my belief that integrity in government is not an option, it is an obligation".

The fact is that "speaking truth to power," destroyed my career and caused me great personal hardship. But my duty was clear to me. Regardless of any personal risk, a patriotic American must stand up for what is right.

What You Can Do

My charge now and to you is to urge Congress and the Obama administration to demand accountability for the type of arrogance I experienced. The federal government must pass an effective whistleblower law; much better laws are needed to protect federal workers who are committed to protecting the public trust at all costs; the government must commit to removing the lack of accountability among the persons who engage in misconduct; and must find that balance between civil and military leadership so that civilians are not prevented from executing their duties to protect the public trust, but will be permanently removed from second-class citizenry.

The federal workforce should not be gagged when improprieties are hurting our economic welfare. There is a "No Fear" law, so why is there no protection against retaliation in the workplace? Why is it always the whistle-blower who ends up in court?

The good news from my perspective:
- Public Support was tremendous; emails and letters voicing their

support of my actions had a major impact on the government. Remember United we Must Stand and United We Shall Make a Difference!

- There have been some sweeping legal reforms that will bring a halt to the gross abuses I brought to the conscience of our government. The Army has publicly decided not to give anymore "sweetheart contracts" to Halliburton —Wow!

- My portrait is now being painted for Robert Shetterly's collection, called "Americans Who Tell the Truth," where he travels to schools and libraries to speak to students about civics and government.

- I appeared in the Rachel Maddow Documentary September 1st and 2nd on the Decade After 9/11 and the Wars.

- I am appearing in a French Documentary on September 26th on the Decade After 9/11, also.

- A CEO of a large company in California wrote to seek my interest in being nominated for the recently vacated Special Inspector General for Afghanistan Reconstruction (SIGAR).

Former contracting officers who were forced out of government are writing to me about their disappointment of "being replaced by privateers, highlighting the outsourcing and the change from federal bureaucrats following the law to politicos demanding that their favorite companies get the bids vs. competition."

For more details on my struggle, and whistleblowing in general, a great resource is the National Whistleblower Center, which provides an educational website at whistleblowers.org.

For more information on this organization, I have provided some contact information for your conference attendees.

Thank You.

Bunnatine (Bunny) H. Greenhouse is a former procurement executive and chief contracting officer for the U.S. Army Corps of Engineers. In 2005 she revealed waste and fraud in secret no-bid contracts for Halliburton in Iraq. She was demoted and marginalized in retribution. In 2011 a U.S. District Court awarded her $970,000 in restitution.

A Soldier's Roadmap to a Peaceful Future

An Interview of Paul Chappell by Leslee Goodman

Paul K. Chappell was born in 1980 and raised in Alabama, the son of a half-black and half-white father and his Korean bride. Paul's father was a soldier in the Korean and Vietnam wars, joining the Army while it was still segregated. He returned from battle a deeply troubled and violent man. Despite this legacy, Paul chose to pursue a military career and was accepted to West Point. A member of West Point's bicentennial class of 2002, the terrorist attacks occurred during his senior year. He was in a class on national security on the morning of Sept. 11, when another professor walked into the room, told Paul's professor to turn on the television, and together in silence Paul and his classmates watched the second plane hit and the towers collapse.

Although West Point is less than an hour from New York City, classes went on as usual, but Paul says, "The atmosphere was changed. We knew we would be going to war."

During the next several years, Paul saw his friends and comrades deploy to Afghanistan and Iraq, as the United States struggled to fight an expanding war on terrorism. To protect its citizens from the threats it perceived, the U.S. government relied upon a foreign policy of military might. Paul himself served a tour of duty in Iraq, but slowly his beliefs about the strategy his country was pursuing began to change. In 2008, while still an active duty officer, his first published book was released — *Will War Ever End? A Soldier's Vision of Peace for the 21st Century.* Two years later came his second published book, *The End of War: How Waging Peace Can Save Humanity, Our Planet, and Our Future.* Both books have won acclaim from luminaries such as Archbishop Desmond Tutu and awards including Peacemaker of the Year from the Independent Publisher Book Awards.

Paul is now the Peace Leadership Director at the Nuclear Age Peace Foundation and speaks to colleges, high schools, churches, veterans groups, and activist organizations throughout the country as a soldier of peace. He thinks there is a better way to protect America and the world in the 21st century than our past policies. His website is willwareverend.com.

What do you think of our response to the attacks on 9/11?

From a strategic, economic, and security perspective, our response to the attacks on September 11th has created many more problems than it has solved. For example, invading the Greater Middle East violated the most basic principles of military strategy. According to Sun Tzu, who wrote *The Art of War,* one of the worst things a leader can do in war is become angry. Sun Tzu knew that when people are enraged, they cannot think clearly and will make self-destructive decisions. This is why one of the best things a leader can do in war is make his opponent angry, because when leaders — whether military or civilian — become angry they lose concern for consequences, and they become reckless and careless. An angry and reckless opponent is much easier to lure into a trap than a calm and rational opponent.

We must keep in mind that by invading the Greater Middle East, we fell right into Osama bin Laden's trap. He wanted to make us so angry that we would make a catastrophic strategic error, and the attacks on September 11th generated so much rage that it prevented many people from thinking clearly. After September 11th, I have a difficult time imagining any American saying, "Let's do exactly what Osama bin Laden wants us to do." Yet by invading Afghanistan and Iraq, we did exactly what he wanted us to do. We fell right into his trap.

Abdul Bari Atawan, a Western journalist who interviewed Osama bin Laden in 1996, said:

> *It seems Osama bin Laden had a long-term strategy. He told me personally that he can't go and fight the Americans and their country. But if he manages to provoke them and bring them to the Middle East and to their Muslim worlds, where he can find them or fight them on his own turf, he will actually teach them a lesson. …*
>
> *He told me, again, that [while President Clinton was in office] he expected the Americans to send troops to Somalia and he sent his people to that country to wait for them in order to fight them. They managed actually to shoot down an American helicopter where 19 soldiers were killed and regretted that the Clinton Administration decided to pull out their troops from Somalia and run away. He was so saddened by this. He thought they would stay there so he could fight them there. But for his bad luck, according to his definition, they left, and he was planning another provocation in order to drag them to Muslim soil.*

But why did bin Laden want us to invade the Middle East?

Prior to the September 11th attacks and the U.S. invasion of two Muslim countries — Afghanistan and Iraq — many people in the Middle East thought Osama bin Laden was crazy. But he knew that if we invaded the Middle East and committed ourselves to a long-term war, he could mobilize many people in the region against us and increase recruitment for terrorism. Imagine if a foreign army invaded the U.S. tomorrow. Americans would go berserk, because most people don't like armed foreign soldiers on their land. Osama bin Laden knew that if we invaded a Muslim country, people could be mobilized to fight what would be perceived as a foreign occupation. And just look at the results. Because of our military presence in the Middle East, Osama bin Laden went from being a terrorist that many people had never heard of to one of the most famous people in the world with a growing number of sympathizers and supporters. Now Osama bin Laden is seen by many marginalized Muslims as a martyr who died for his cause, and the amount of Al Qaeda, Al Qaeda imitators, Al Qaeda sympathizers, and insurgents throughout the Middle East and Africa who want to kill Americans is significantly higher today than it was ten years ago.

Another important lesson from basic military strategy is that it is extremely dangerous to underestimate your opponent. When people said, "If Osama bin Laden wants a fight, let's give it to him!" they not only underestimated Osama bin Laden but the dangerous situation our country was in after September 11th. Of all the negative things we could say about Osama bin Laden — his cruelty, lack of compassion, fanaticism — one thing we could not say is that he was stupid. After all, he had a track record of beating superpowers in the Greater Middle East. He helped beat the Soviets in Afghanistan, and he knew we lost in Vietnam. The Vietnam War was a situation where we won every battle but lost the war.

Osama bin Laden could never have won a decisive battle against us, but he could defeat us in Afghanistan the same way he beat the Soviets, by bankrupting our country. In a November 2004 videotape, Osama bin Laden said, "We, along with the mujahedeen, bled Russia for ten years, until it went bankrupt and was forced to withdraw in defeat. ... So we are continuing this policy in bleeding America to the point of bankruptcy." He also boasted that Al Qaeda had only spent $500,000 on the September 11th attacks. But after only a couple of years, he said America had spent "according to the lowest estimate, $500 billion ... meaning that every dollar of Al Qaeda defeated a million dollars [of America]." He also said, "As for the size of the economic deficit, it has reached record astronomical numbers." In 2004 when he made these statements, many Americans probably couldn't imagine our country going bankrupt. But when we look at how our economy and society in 2011 are being strangled by the debt crisis, high level of unemployment, big budget cuts, and ongoing recession, we realize that Osama bin Laden's plan to damage our economy by increasing our war spending beyond what we can afford is working.

Of all the talk about the soaring national debt and growing economic crisis, few people are discussing the trillions of dollars we are spending on war, which could be better used to help the American people. How much longer can we afford to have a large military and contractor presence in Afghanistan and Iraq? Instead of being defeated in a decisive battle, we are slowly being bled to death economically. The tenth anniversary of September 11th is upon us, and compare our economy 10 years ago to what it is today. Our economy today is in terrible shape due to many factors, but one major factor rarely being discussed is vast war spending. In his Cross of Iron Speech, General Dwight Eisenhower said that over a long period of time a war economy is equivalent to crucifixion, because it slowly bleeds a country's economy, resources, and wellbeing to death.

Of course, the Soviet Union collapsed due to many reasons, but in front of the 27th congress of the Soviet Union's Communist Party in February 1986, Mikhail Gorbachev referred to the war in Afghanistan as "our bleeding wound." The war in Afghanistan accelerated the collapse of the Soviet Union by wasting large amounts of money the Soviets desperately needed, and the war also used up a great deal of time, energy, resources, and brainpower that the Soviets could have invested toward solving their other problems.

I — along with many Americans — would understand the need for a high military budget if it were actually making us and the rest of the world safer, but it is actually doing the opposite. It is threatening our security along with our economy, and it is causing us to become more entangled in Osama bin Laden's trap. But during this critical time in American history we have an amazing opportunity to implement a new and more effective security strategy that would not only reduce the military budget, but would also better support our troops and truly promote peace and freedom around the world. Osama bin Laden wanted us to stay in Afghanistan until our government ran out of money and the American people suffered enormous economic hardship, but instead of allowing such a catastrophe to happen, this new and more effective security strategy is something that I don't think Osama bin Laden ever expected us to do.

When Osama bin Laden was killed recently, we must keep in mind that although he did not want to die, he preferred being killed to being captured. He would much rather have been a martyr who died in a blaze of glory than a prisoner in a tiny cell. So by killing him instead of capturing him, we gave him what he wanted yet again. I am against doing what Osama bin Laden wanted us to do. I am against letting his strategy bankrupt and destroy our economy. I am against falling into cleverly-laid traps that endanger the security and wellbeing of our country. I think we certainly have to fight terrorism, but there is a more effective way to combat terrorism that is not only better for our economy, but better for American and global security, along with peace and freedom around the world.

What is this new and more effective security strategy, and what should our response to terrorism have been?

West Point gave me an excellent education, but one thing I wish West Point would have taught me — which is crucial information that every American citizen who cares about his or her country should know — is that if we want to truly understand how to protect America in the 21st century, we must realize how the hypocrisy of American politicians is undermining both American and global security in the 21st century. Eisenhower, the first president to identify Middle Eastern unrest as a threat to the United States, realized that the reason many people in the Middle East hate us is because we suppress freedom there. We support dictatorships. We prevent democratic progress, which is the opposite of what we say we're doing.

America has some of the most incredible ideals in the world, such as freedom, democracy, justice, and opportunity. But the world for the most part isn't angry at our ideals. The world for the most part is angry that we don't live up to our ideals. When Wael Ghonim, who helped lead the peaceful protests in Egypt, was asked in a *60 Minutes* interview how he felt when President Obama spoke in support of the peaceful protestors in Egypt who were challenging their dictator, Ghonim replied, "It was good that he [President Obama] supports the revolution. That's a good stand, but we don't really need him. I wrote a Tweet. I wrote 'Dear western governments, you have been supporting the regime that was oppressing us for 30 years. Please don't get involved now. We don't need you.'"

After the attacks on September 11th, American politicians said, "They hate us because we're free," but during the past year people all over the Middle East have been protesting because they want their freedom. Protests have been occurring throughout the Middle East against dictatorships we support, such as those in Bahrain, Saudi Arabia, Egypt, and Tunisia, and other dictatorships that are not closely allied with us. The bottom line is that many people in the Middle East are fed up with living under oppression and tyranny, just as our Founding Fathers were fed up, Susan B. Anthony and the many women in the women's rights movement were fed up, and Martin Luther King, Jr. and the many African Americans in the civil rights movement were fed up. It is a myth that the majority of people in the Middle East are a bunch of freedom-hating terrorists who want to kill us because they hate our way of life.

We have actually been supporting dictatorships in the Middle East for decades, such as the Shah of Iran, Saddam Hussein, and the government in Pakistan. Our politicians preach about freedom, democracy, and liberty, while they support dictatorships. They talk about the importance of liberating the oppressed women in Afghanistan, while they are closely allied with the Saudi Arabian government — which is as oppressive toward women as the Taliban. This makes us look like hypocrites, and it causes people in the Middle East to question our true intentions. Are we really in Iraq to support democracy, or are we more concerned with oil?

Politicians are often stereotyped as being dishonest, deceptive, two-faced, and self-serving. Of course, there are honest politicians who work hard to maintain their integrity, but deception is a large part of the political game, and we all know it. So I think it is odd when Americans — who have no problem seeing politicians as dishonest, deceptive, two-faced, and self-serving — are surprised when their government lies to them. Who do they think is running our government? Politicians. Is it any surprise that our government lies to us?

One of the most undemocratic things I have ever heard — which I hear often — is that the American President is the leader of the free world. If we understand what the ideal of democracy truly means, we realize that the people are supposed to lead, and the president is supposed to be the administrator of the people's will. Although we live in a representative democracy instead of a direct democracy, we still have methods to pressure our politicians to do what we want. Susan B. Anthony, Martin Luther King, Jr., and many other patriotic Americans have applied this pressure in order to create positive change. There are many politicians who mean well and want to do the right thing, and the American people can use their power as citizens to pressure the political system into creating positive change.

So several of the key components in a new and more effective strategy for fighting terrorism are to use our power as American citizens to stop the hypocrisy of our politicians and end the injustice of our foreign policy; and to prioritize American democratic ideals such as liberty and justice above the desires of the privileged few who profit from war at the expense of the many, which Smedley Butler — a Marine General who was twice awarded the Medal of Honor — explained in his book *War is a Racket*. Another component in a new and more effective American security strategy is to wage peace instead of waging war. The purpose of the American military is to protect the American people, and one of the best ways to protect the American people in the 21st century is to help people around the world. The cover of the July 2011 issue of *Military Officer* magazine featured an article titled "Waging Peace: America's fighting forces are working to build peace and stability through assistance and relief." According to the article, in 2009 U.S. military units conducted 154 humanitarian projects in 61 countries. These efforts focused on medical, dental, and veterinary needs as well as construction projects. Imagine if around the world the U.S. had the following reputation — when a humanitarian crisis or natural disaster happens the Americans come, help, and leave. This would not only help us win hearts and minds around the world, but it would combat the poverty and hopelessness that provide fertile soil for terrorism to grow.

Having hundreds of military bases around the world — as we do now — is not only economically unsustainable, but it makes people question our intentions and become suspicious when we provide humanitarian aid and disaster relief. They wonder if we are really there to help them or if our true intentions are to put a military base in their country. To understand why having military bases all over the world endangers American security, we must remember that we supported Osama bin Laden during the 1980s, but he turned against us when we put military bases in Saudi Arabia — where Islamic holy land is located. How would Americans feel if a foreign country put a military base on our soil? How would we react? As I mentioned earlier, we would go berserk. Brian Fishman, who teaches at the Combating Terrorism Center at West Point, said in an interview on *Bill Moyers Journal*, "It's not good enough to leave 20 or 30 thousand troops in Iraq… those 20 or 30 thousand Americans are going to remain a sticking point and a propaganda tool for Al Qaeda around the world."

In addition to stopping the hypocrisy of our politicians, ending the injustice of our foreign policy, and having the U.S. military wage peace instead of waging war, we must understand that Al Qaeda has more in common with a criminal enterprise like the Mafia than with a monolithic government like the Soviet Union or Nazi Germany. Al Qaeda is a transnational criminal network, and you cannot defeat a transnational criminal network by invading and occupying a country. September 11th was planned from Hamburg, Germany, and a person can plan a terrorist attack from San Francisco. A person can plan a terrorist attack from a Western country and even the United States, and waging war in a Muslim country to combat terrorism creates a high number of civilian casualties that exacerbates terrorism.

For example, in a *60 Minutes* interview, Marine lieutenant colonel Christian Cabaniss said that if you kill a thousand Taliban and two civilians, it's a loss. It turns the local population against you, and this is why the U.S. military is trying to minimize civilian casualties. But since World War II, the majority of people killed in war have been civilians. In some conflicts, up to 90% of the people killed have been civilians, and no matter how hard we try to not kill civilians in war, many civilians will die. This is due to the chaotic and confusing nature of war, along with human fallibility and the fallibility of technology.

The organizations that are best trained to combat criminal networks are the FBI and police. The FBI helped stop terrorists such as Ted Kaczynski and Timothy McVeigh, and serial killers such as Jeffrey Dahmer and John Wayne Gacy. In the past, international police work has been used to arrest wanted criminals on foreign soil such as the Nazis who escaped from Germany following World War II. After September 11th, the whole world's sympathy went out to us, and we had an opportunity to treat the attacks on September 11th as a horrible criminal act and work with other countries to go after Al Qaeda the way we went after Timothy McVeigh, the Nazis who fled from Germany after World War II, and other criminals.

Will the military be able to adapt to a changing world?

Anyone who thinks the military isn't capable of adapting its tactics and methods in order to meet the challenges of a new era should remember that militaries around the world used to fight with swords and ride horses into battle, but they adapted as technology and the world changed. During World War I, trench warfare was the norm, but again the military adapted and fought much differently during World War II. Today, the military is already adapting and evolving in ways many people don't realize. For example, due to the urban terrain where modern wars are often fought, many U.S. Special Forces soldiers spend more time fighting like a sophisticated SWAT team than the soldiers who invaded the beaches of Normandy or the soldiers who went on long patrols in the jungles of Vietnam. Today the U.S. military has adopted tactics used by law enforcement officers and humanitarian aid organizations, and I think this trend will continue in the coming years because this is how we must adapt in order to confront the threats of the 21st century.

The U.S. military is the only organization in the world that can deploy tens of thousands of physically fit, mentally tough, well trained people to any spot on the globe in a matter of days. Shifting its mission further in the direction of humanitarian aid and disaster relief would not only better protect America by winning hearts and minds around the world, it would also greatly reduce the military budget which can in turn be used to help the American people, because much of the military budget is spent on a vast array of high tech weapons that are becoming more and more obsolete in our modern conflicts. It will also give many soldiers what they truly want. Military recruitment ads appeal largely to young people's idealism, yearning for self-improvement, and desire to do good around the world. The new navy motto is "a global force for good," and have you ever seen a military recruitment commercial that makes any reference to killing? As General Douglas MacArthur reminds us, "The Soldier above all other people prays for peace, for he must suffer and bear the deepest wounds and scars of war."

The United States can implement this new and more effective security strategy, because we have many security advantages that other countries don't have. As a country, we cannot be successfully occupied by a foreign military power. How do I know this? I know this is true, because the United States, which has the most powerful military in human history and the support of NATO allies, cannot successfully occupy or achieve military victory in Afghanistan, which is a small and impoverished country. According to high ranking military commanders such as Admiral Mullen and General Petraeus, military victory is not possible in Afghanistan, because victory must be achieved politically by creating a functioning government that the local people support, not militarily through a decisive battle. Admiral Mullen and General Petraeus believed they could use the U.S. military to provide a level of security that would allow a functioning government to emerge in Afghanistan, but one thing we know from history is that every government that cooperates with a foreign occupying power is corrupt. Think of the Indians who cooperated with the British. The Afghan government is notoriously corrupt, so the question is whether corruption can be stopped and if it can happen quickly enough before our country goes bankrupt.

If the most powerful military in human history and our NATO allies cannot successfully occupy or achieve military victory in a country as small and poor as Afghanistan, what country on Earth could possibly invade and occupy the United States? We have a large population, a huge amount of territory, a lot of mountains, and more guns in this country than people. A foreign invading army that landed on the Pacific Coast wouldn't be able to control California — let alone the entire country — and they wouldn't even get to our shore in the first place if we maintained a competent Navy, which would mostly be performing important missions in our new disaster relief and humanitarian aid role.

The greatest threat to our country is actually from within. Our current approach to fighting terrorism not only threatens to bankrupt our country, but it is causing many of our politicians to abandon American ideals. When America sanctions torture, spies on its own people, and takes away the civil liberties of its citizens, it ceases to be the America that can be a beacon of hope, freedom, and justice around the world.

What do you think about the U.S. military using drone attacks, which end up causing civilian casualties?

While I was in the army I worked at DARPA for several months. DARPA is the Defense Advanced Research Projects Agency, which does the high tech research for the military. DARPA helped create the Internet, GPS, Stealth Fighter, M-16, and Predator Drone, which is a small pilotless airplane that can operate anywhere in the world via remote control from the United States. It can perform surveillance missions and launch missiles onto unsuspecting people below. I learned something interesting about the Predator Drone while I was at DARPA. Throughout human history, the bulk of military research has been focused on making weapons deadlier and more destructive. For thousands of years, some of humanity's most brilliant scientific minds were devoted to making sharper swords, bigger guns, and more powerful bombs. But for the first time in history, a large amount of military research is being used to make weapons less destructive and more precise. At DARPA, I learned that a dream of many military researchers is to develop a precision-guided smart bomb that can accurately kill an enemy combatant while leaving innocent bystanders standing only a few meters away unharmed.

Due to the immense growth of mass media that occurred during and after World War II, people all over the world could see pictures and video that revealed the horror of war and the suffering of innocent civilians. During World War II the U.S. government targeted densely populated civilian areas during its bombing campaigns in cities such as Dresden, Tokyo, Hiroshima, and Nagasaki. The intention was to kill as many civilians as possible, and that was the international norm at the time; Great Britain and

Germany did the same thing. But during the late 20th century targeting civilians during bombing campaigns was no longer acceptable within the international community, so the United States had to develop precision-guided smart bombs that minimize civilian casualties. According to the military researchers I spoke with at DARPA, the Predator Drone sounds like a great idea in theory. It has high-tech targeting systems and precision-guided missiles that are designed to kill enemy combatants without hurting innocent civilians, and because it does not have a pilot, an American will not be killed or captured if it is shot down. I got the impression at DARPA that many of the military researchers had good intentions, but the Predator Drone is an example of good intentions gone horribly wrong.

The Predator Drone is being used in countries such as Iraq, Afghanistan, Libya, Yemen, and Pakistan, and wherever it is being used it is killing civilians. This is because military researchers are unable to create a precision-guided smart bomb capable of overcoming two major obstacles — human fallibility and the fallibility of technology. An example of human fallibility could include faulty intelligence reports claiming that an Al Qaeda operative is alone in a house in Pakistan, when in reality the house also contains women and children, or perhaps the Al Qaeda operative is not even there. The Predator Drone launches a missile based on this faulty intelligence, and innocent people are killed. Things like this are happening all the time. Another example of human fallibility could include the person operating the Predator Drone making a mistake. Human beings make mistakes every day. During the Vietnam War, for example, thousands of American soldiers were killed by their own comrades in "friendly fire" incidents due to human error. Another reason the Predator Drones are killing so many civilians is because technology is not always reliable. Think of all the problems people have every day with their computers. When technological problems happen with my computer, it becomes an inconvenience that can cost me time and money, but when technological problems happen with the Predator Drone, innocent people can die.

Brian Fishman, who teaches at the Combating Terrorism Center at West Point, described during his interview on *Bill Moyers Journal* that the old ways of waging war won't work for combating terrorism. He said:

With the [West Point] cadets in class, we walk through some of the jihadi chat rooms that are used to spread propaganda against their fellow soldiers. And they need to understand — there's a photo out there, a very famous photo that's on all of these chat rooms. It's a picture of a bunch of American soldiers taking a rest in a mosque with their boots on. And it's everywhere ... because it's just a symbol of insult to Islam. And the cadets need to understand that even if they are doing something that they think is completely benign, that they don't mean any sort of insult, it can be used against them. And it's that kind of awareness that they need to get to the point where they understand that they could accidentally do something extraordinarily insulting. That photograph is more of a strategic defeat than any sort of tactical engagement on the battlefield. And we need to understand it and the cadets need to understand that... And so what we tell these cadets is, look, this war against Al Qaeda cannot be won or lost in Iraq. Ultimately, this is a fight for hearts and minds around the Middle East. And that's a cliché, but it's true. And that's why these cadets, they can't win that fight with an M-4 [assault rifle].

Is it too late to change course now, and do you have hope for the future?

I have a lot of hope for the future for many reasons. I am half Korean, a quarter white, and a quarter black, and my American ancestors were slaves. My father — who served in the army for thirty years and fought in the Korean and Vietnam wars — was born in 1925 and grew up during the Great Depression in Virginia under segregation. I was born in 1980 and grew up in Alabama, and although things were far from perfect when I was growing up, I had many opportunities my father never had, and he had many opportunities his slave ancestors never had, because patriotic Americans such as Henry David Thoreau, Frederick Douglass, Susan B. Anthony, Mark Twain, General Smedley Butler, Alice Paul, Woody Guthrie, Martin Luther King, Jr., and countless others worked to make our country a better place. Two hundred years ago in America women could not own property, and less than 10% of the American population could vote. African Americans couldn't vote. Women couldn't vote. And most white people couldn't vote because they didn't own land. I — along with many others — am living proof that change is possible.

Our ancestors confronted the problem of American hypocrisy in the past, and they made a positive impact. For example, the *Declaration of Independence* said "all men are created equal," yet the U.S. government sanctioned slavery. Frederick Douglass saw racial inequality as the utmost hypocrisy, and because of him, Martin Luther King, Jr., and countless others, the system of segregation in the South was dismantled. It's as if the *Declaration of Independence* was a document far ahead of its time, and we are still trying to make its ideals a reality today. We have a long way to go as a country before liberty, justice, and peace achieve their fullest expressions around the world, and racism is still a problem in America today, but if we have come so far, why can't we keep moving in a positive direction? Of course, it will require action on our behalf.

What I am offering is a very hopeful message, because if we believe that people in the Middle East hate us because we're free, then we will be at war forever. But if we understand that many people in the Middle East want freedom just like we do, and many of our problems are being caused by mistakes we are making that are within our power to change, then peace becomes a realistic possibility. Also, we should never underestimate the power of human forgiveness. Africans were enslaved in America for hundreds of years and the United States killed millions of Native Americans, but their descendents are not trying to massacre white people today in revenge. We killed two to three million people in Vietnam during the war, but has Vietnam attacked us in order to seek vengeance? Even though the Germans killed millions of Jews and Russians during World War II, are the Israelis or Russians killing Germans in revenge today?

The ability to forgive is powerful, especially as new generations emerge, which gives me a lot of hope for the future. But if we do not change course and implement a new and more effective American security strategy that involves stopping the hypocrisy of our politicians, ending the injustice of our current foreign policy, and confronting the root causes of terrorism, we cannot move forward as a country or a global community. We must also listen to those who disagree with us, and instead of demonizing them we must strive to understand them. For example, I find the "9/11 Truth Movement" — which many people consider a conspiracy theory — to be very interesting. But what interests me the most is why so many Americans believe the September 11th attacks were an "inside job" where the World Trade Center was brought down by controlled demolitions, the Pentagon was hit by a U.S. military missile instead of a hijacked plane, and President Bush and many others planned it in order to justify an invasion of the Middle East for oil profits.

The first time I heard people claim that the September 11th attacks were an "inside job," I was surprised. I don't doubt that there are heartless rulers in power who are capable of killing their own people, but the U.S. government is not very good at keeping secrets. John F. Kennedy couldn't cheat on his wife without the American people eventually finding out about it, and Nixon couldn't even keep the Watergate scandal a secret. Think about all of the lies that were exposed when Daniel Ellsberg leaked the Pentagon papers, and think about the lies surrounding the Gulf of Tonkin incident, the flawed intelligence that led up to the Iraq invasion, and countless other examples. President Clinton couldn't even have sex in the oval office without people finding out.

The "9/11 Truth Movement" became popular for several reasons. It gained a lot of momentum after the invasion of Iraq in 2003, because many Americans saw how the government deceived the public about weapons of mass destruction in Iraq. Many people concluded that if the American government could lie about the reasons for going to war, it could lie about anything. Due to this breach of trust, many people refused to believe anything the U.S. government told them. But believing the U.S. government always lies is as inaccurate as believing it never lies. The U.S. government — like all governments — lies on occasion, and that is why we must be skeptical of what our politicians tell us. But because trust was breached, many people began to assume that everything the government says is a lie, so if the U.S. government says we killed Osama bin Laden, it must be lie. Since the U.S. government was wrong about weapons of mass destruction in Iraq, there has also been an increase in the number of people who believe we never walked on the moon, because anything the government says must be a lie. It's hard to believe that a government so incompetent that it could not successfully lie about weapons of mass destruction in Iraq or at least plant a few weapons there, that so badly mismanaged the initial reconstruction efforts during the war because it did not understand the local culture and had not done proper planning, could pull off an orchestrated internal attack as sophisticated as September 11th and not get caught.

So breach of trust about weapons of mass destruction in Iraq is one reason the "9/11 Truth Movement" gained momentum. Another reason has to do with the helplessness felt by so many Americans. I heard a story on NPR about a study that was done that tried to find if certain personality traits caused people to believe in conspiracy theories, and the study found a correlation between conspiracy theories and feelings of helplessness.

Conspiracy theories tend to focus on supremely powerful governments and secret organizations that have the power to orchestrate incredibly complex events without people finding out. In reality, organizations are capable of doing a lot of bad things, but they have a difficult time keeping secrets. People as powerful as the Roman Emperors, Joseph Stalin, and Adolf Hitler could not keep their crimes hidden indefinitely, and our country has a long history of whistleblowers from Daniel Ellsberg to Bradley Manning who expose government secrets.

I think the "9/11 Truth Movement" is losing a little steam because, if the September 11th attacks were an "inside job," it would be the most highly orchestrated government coverup in history with countless opportunities for whistleblowers, but nothing from Wikileaks has turned up any evidence yet. So let's wait and see if anything turns up, and in the meantime it's really interesting to read — in the pursuit of truth — the many scientific explanations that seem to debunk the theory that the September 11th attacks were an "inside job." It's important to have a "9/11 Truth Movement," but we must be willing to accept the truth if it turns out that we were attacked not by fellow Americans but by people from the Middle East who hijacked planes. Some of the people in the "9/11 Truth Movement" simply want the government to conduct a more thorough investigation, and I think that's a good idea because the lack of an official, credible, and thorough investigation allows rumors and speculation to run wild.

When I gave a talk in Bellingham, Washington, a student from Pakistan told me, "There is something I never understood until I heard your talk. I always saw Americans as being the friendliest people in the world. Americans are so kind, generous, and optimistic, but their government does so many horrible things around the world. I never understood this contradiction. I never understood how the American people could be so wonderful, yet their government could support dictatorships and do so many violent things in other countries. But now I finally understand this contradiction. I finally understand how the American people can be so wonderful, while at the same time their government can be so terrible. Most Americans don't know what their government is doing around the world."

What are some of the challenges ahead?

There are many nuances for putting this plan into action that I have not had time to discuss during this short interview, but I think the hopeful future that I have briefly outlined is both possible and necessary. I am not sure if America will be saved. I only know that it can be saved if enough people become aware and work together to take constructive action. The American citizens who see through the deceptions and myths of war are underdogs in the struggle to put our country on the right path, and I do not underestimate the challenges ahead. There is a lot of money to be made from war and maintaining the status quo, and many people in America are blinded by ideology and their minds are clouded by fear and anger. But I have seen how my own viewpoints have dramatically changed in recent years, and I believe in the power of the American people to survive, endure, and move closer toward fulfilling the ideals embodied in our *Declaration of Independence*. Solving our national and global problems is a challenging and worthy struggle, and I think the democratic ideals and the dream of peace are stronger than the obstacles we are facing today.

To solve our national and global problems in the interconnected world of the 21st century, we must create a peaceful revolution in human thinking, which includes recognizing our shared humanity and understanding that the life of every human being has as much dignity as the life of every American. As this new awareness spreads, what once seemed impossible will become possible.

During one of General MacArthur's last speeches — given at the 101st commencement at Michigan State University — he shared some useful insights about the challenges ahead. I think his words are more relevant now than ever:

The great question is: Can global war now be outlawed from the world? If so, it would mark the greatest advance in civilization since the Sermon on the Mount. It would lift at one stroke the darkest shadow which has engulfed mankind from the beginning. It would not only remove fear and bring security — it would not only create new moral and spiritual values — it would produce an economic wave of prosperity that would raise the world's standard of living beyond anything ever dreamed of by man. The hundreds of billions of dollars now spent in mutual preparedness [for war] could conceivably abolish poverty from the face of the earth. It would accomplish even more than this; it would at one stroke reduce the international tensions that seem to be insurmountable now, to matters of more probable solution ... Many will tell you with mockery and ridicule that the abolition of war can be only a dream — that it is but the vague imagining of a visionary. But we must go on or we will go under. And the great criticism that can be made is that the world lacks a plan that will enable us to go on. We have suffered the blood and the sweat and the tears. Now we seek the way and the truth and the light. We are in a new era. The old methods and solutions for this vital problem no longer suffice. We must have new thoughts, new ideas, new concepts ... We must have sufficient imagination and courage to translate this universal wish for peace — which is rapidly becoming a universal necessity — into actuality.

Paul K. Chappell graduated from West Point in 2002. He served in the army for seven years, was deployed to Baghdad in 2006, and left active duty in November 2009 as a Captain. He is the author of *Will War Ever End?: A Soldier's Vision of Peace for the 21st Century* and *The End of War: How Waging Peace Can Save Humanity, Our Planet, and Our Future*. He is the Peace Leadership Director for the Nuclear Age Peace Foundation.

V. WHAT TO DO

Questions

By Tony Russell

Where is the military-industrial complex vulnerable?

What are the hidden strengths of the progressive movement?

How will moral energy be generated and harnessed?

How do you prepare the ground for change?

What strategies for change are inefficient or unproductive?

What strategies will capture the imagination of others and empower them?

Are progressives willing to pay the price?

(These questions were used to begin group discussions at the MIC-50 conference.)

Tony Russell lives in Charlottesville, Virginia. A naturalist, poet, photographer, and peace activist, he has worked as a carhop, as a busboy, as foreman of a crew clearing fire lanes, as a day care provider, as an Upward Bound director, as an advocate for senior citizens, as an administrator, as manager of an apartment complex, as a laborer in a glass factory, as a teacher, and as an outreach worker for a health care center. He also served as a Peace Corps Volunteer in Sierra Leone, West Africa.

Moving from a War Economy to a Peace Economy

By Mary Beth Sullivan

It is my intention to stimulate some conversation about economic conversion — that is, planning, designing and implementing a transformation from a war economy to a peace economy. Historically, this is an effort that would include a changeover from military to civilian work in industrial facilities, in laboratories, and at U.S. military bases. To that end, I intend to bring to you all what I've learned from reading Seymour Melman, the most prolific writer on the topic. Seymour Melman was a professor emeritus of Industrial Engineering at Columbia University. He joined the Columbia faculty in 1949, and by all reports, was a popular instructor until he retired from teaching in 2003.

Melman was also an active member of the peace movement. He was the co-chair of the *Committee for a Sane Nuclear Policy* (SANE), and the creator and chair of the National Commission for Economic Conversion and Disarmament. It is reported that Melman was under surveillance by the FBI for much of his career because of his work criticizing the military-industrial complex — a sure sign that there must be something worth hearing in his work. What did he say that the power structure feared?

The economic conversion movement in past decades played a valuable role in bringing together the peace movement and union leadership to do the heady work of imaging how this country could sustain industrial jobs when, as it was envisioned, the U.S. would stop production of the weapons of the Cold War. It is a history that should not be forgotten.

Melman noted that U.S. industry had historically followed an established set of market rules: industry created products consumers needed, sold those products, made a profit, and turned those profits into improving production by upgrading the tools for more efficient production.

Military production for World War II began to change these rules of industry, which were then institutionalized in the 1960's when Robert McNamara was Secretary of Defense. McNamara, who came to the Pentagon having been an executive at Ford Motor Company, implemented some critical changes.

Within the Pentagon, civilian and uniformed Pentagon officials were in conflict about the procedures for how to determine the costs of weapons to be contracted for manufacturing. On the one side, led by an industrial engineer, the idea was to base costs on the formulation of alternative designs and production methods, etc. — a competitive approach that promoted economy.

The other side proposed generating costs based on what was previously spent. For the Pentagon, this meant following the "cost-plus" system used during World War II, also known as "cost maximizing." As Melman put it, "contractors could take the previous cost of making a product for the Pentagon and simply add on an agreed-upon profit margin. The more a product cost, the more [a contractor] stood to earn."

McNamara opted for this second option. The result was that by 1980, the cost of producing major weapons systems had grown at an annual rate of 20%. Melman observed that by 1996, "the cost of the B-2 bomber ... exceeded the value of its weight in gold."

McNamara went on to model the Pentagon after a corporate central office, defining policy, appointing chiefs of subordinate units, maintaining accounting and management functions with huge discretion. Each military service participated in the process of acquiring materiel and weapons. This process resulted in the tens of thousands becoming hundreds of thousands of employees, paid for by America's tax dollars, to maximize the profits of weapons producers. Melman minced no words in articulating the consequences:

> *An industrial management has been installed in the federal government, under the Secretary of Defense, to control the nation's largest network of industrial enterprises … the new state-management combines … economic, political, and military decision-making. … Nowhere in the Constitution is top economic power conferred by the Constitution.*

> *The operation of a permanent military economy makes the president the chief executive officer of the state management controlling the largest single block of capital resources, including the largest aggregation of industrial facilities in the economy. Thereby, a core feature of a Leninist state design was installed in the federal government — top economic, political and military power in the same hands, often unconstrained by law. …[T]his combination of powers in the same hands has been a feature of statist societies — communist, fascist, and others — where individual rights cannot constrain central rule … .*

Among the many critical consequences of this state controlled industry described by Melman, I'll mention a few:

- Firms were no longer efficiency orientated — rather, industry produced increasingly complicated goods.
- Production had nothing to do with meeting the needs of ordinary consumers. Melman pointed out that a nuclear-powered submarine

was a "technological masterpiece," — but consumers can't eat it; can't wear it; can't ride in it; can't live in it; and can't make anything with it.

- Labor lost control of any decision-making it had over production. With the influx of capital came an influx of white-collar middle managers, and an alienation — or disempowering — of workers.

- Where the U.S. was once a top producer and exporter of tools needed for production of consumer goods, the complexity of military production focused industry on specialized machinery and tools that have no utility in meeting consumer needs.

- The Pentagon consumed the talents of our scientists and engineers whose skills were needed in other sectors of our society.

In one of Melman's last articles at the dawn of the 21st Century, his frustration was palpable. He noted that New York City put out a request for a proposal to spend about $3 billion to $4 billion to replace a number of subway cars. Not a single U.S. company bid on the proposal — in part because the U.S. no longer had the tools it needed to build its subway trains. In this article, titled "In the Grip of a Permanent War Economy," Melman calculated that if this manufacturing work were done in the U.S., it would have generated, directly and indirectly, about 32,000 jobs.

Melman shared his vision:

The production facilities and labor force that could deliver six new subway cars each week could produce 300 cars per year, and thereby provide new replacement cars for the New York Subway system in a 20-year cycle — for the 6,000 railcar fleet of the NY subway system. … Well-trained engineers are required to design the key subway transportation equipment. Therefore, we must note that it is almost 25 years since the last book was published in the U.S. on [this topic.] … [This] is also true for every one of the industries targeted for deindustrialization during the second half of the 20th Century.

There was an alternative vision that was percolating within the *economic conversion movement* in decades past with an intent to create and begin the process of reducing the economic decision-power of the war-making institutions. This was to be done by mandating a planning process for the changeover from military to civilian work in factories, laboratories, and military bases.

The plan was to set up a highly decentralized planning process based on "alternative-use committees" to do the necessary blueprinting. Half of each alternative-use committee would be named by management; the other half by the working people. There would be support of incomes during a changeover.

Nationally, a commission chaired by the Secretary of Commerce would publish a manual on local alternative-use planning. It would also encourage federal, state, and local government to make capital investment plans, creating new markets for the capital goods required for infrastructure repair.

Three principal functions would be served by economic conversion.

First, the planning stage would offer assurance to the working people of the war economy that they can have an economic future in a society where war-making is a diminished institution.

Second, reversing the process of economic decay in U.S. manufacturing in particular (and in the rest of the U.S. economy) the National Commission would be empowered to facilitate planning for capital investments in all aspects of infrastructure by governments of cities, counties, states and the federal government, which would comprise a massive program of new jobs and new markets.[145]

Third, the national network of alternative use committees would constitute a gain in decision-making power by all the working people involved.

Melman worked with students, union leaders, the peace movement and with Congress to create momentum around these ideas. There were some key events along the way.

In 1971, George McGovern included the idea of economic conversion when he announced his candidacy for the Democratic Presidential nomination. His statement included this position:

> *Basing our defense budget on actual needs rather than imaginary fears would lead to [budget] savings. Needless war and military waste contribute to the economic crisis not only through inflation, but by the dissipation of labor and resources and in non-productive enterprise. ...*

> *For too long the taxes of our citizens and revenues desperately needed by our cities and states have been drawn into Washington and wasted on senseless war and unnecessary military gadgets .... A major test of the 1970's is the conversion of our economy from the excesses of war to the works of peace. I urgently call for conversion planning to utilize the talent and resources surplus to our military ... for modernizing our industrial plants and meeting other peacetime needs.*

In 1976, SANE held a conference in New York City entitled "The Arms Race and the Economic Crisis." Melman was a featured speaker. This conference was instrumental in winning an economic conversion plank in the Democratic Party platform that year.

In 1988 and '89, Melman had several meetings with then Speaker of the House, Rep. Jim Wright. Wright convened a meeting of congressmen who were committed to support the economic conversion bill proposed by New York's Rep. Ted Weiss. Speaker Wright told Melman that, in his opinion,

> *the arms race had taken on not only dangerous but also economically damaging characteristics, ... and that spending on the military was a burden that sapped the strength of the whole society.*

On the first day of the opening of the 101st Congress, Speaker Wright convened a meeting of members who had proposed economic conversion legislation, and their aids. The purpose was to ensure that all proposals be joined into one, and that this legislation be given priority. To dramatize the importance of this bill, it would be given number H.R. 101. Melman and SANE were elated. And then reality hit. As Melman reported:

> *Supporters of such an initiative did not reckon with the enormous power of those opposed to any such move toward economic conversion. In the weeks that followed, these vested interests waged a concerted and aggressive campaign in Congress and the national media to bring down Jim Wright over allegations of financial misconduct.*

The allegations had little substance, but Newt Gingrich, representing a headquarters district of Lockheed Martin, led the Republican attack. Sadly, they won. According to Melman, "Their media campaign drowned out any further discussion of economic conversion .... A historic opportunity had been destroyed."

I found an article written in 1990 from the *LA Times*, which reported about economic conversion plans developing in California and beyond. It included the following hopeful news:

> *Irvine, California Mayor Larry Agran, planned to make his home town a national model for economic conversion by using*

what all presumed would be "under-worked" defense companies to build a major monorail project. He envisioned a major local mass-transportation industry. His proposed Irvine Institute for Entrepreneurial Development would also look for ways to push local rocket scientists toward environmental cleanup, health care and other such enterprises.

In Los Angeles, Councilwoman Ruth Galanter, with the support of the International Assn. of Machinists, convened a committee to study prospects for converting aerospace jobs to establishing an electric car-manufacturing industry. They argued that there were linkages in technologies and skills across industries.

On the state level, California Assemblyman Sam Farr promoted a package of bills that required the governor to 1) convene an "economic summit" on conversion, 2) appoint a council to study the issue and 3) come up with a means of facilitating the transfer of military technology to the civilian sector.

Finally, at the federal level, Representative Ted Weiss from New York continued to push economic conversion legislation until his death in 1992. To my knowledge, no other Congressperson has taken on this issue.

George H.W. Bush's attack on Iraq in the 1990 Persian Gulf War was a critical nail in the coffin of the national economic conversion movement.

There are some in the peace movement who continued to keep the embers of economic conversion alive. Many years ago in Groton, Connecticut, the local peace community organized a "listening project" to engage the community in conversation about what economic conversion might look like for General Dynamic's Electric Boat Company, builder of submarines for the U.S. Navy. For more than 30 years, the Peace Economy Project in

St. Louis has been advocating for conversion from a military to a more stable peace-based economy locally. The Woodstock peace community held a conference in 2009 focused on the conversion of Ametek/Rotron, a Woodstock manufacturer that makes parts used in F-16 fighter planes, Apache attack helicopters, tanks, and missile delivery systems. Certainly there are others out there engaging their home communities in envisioning alternatives to continued production for endless war.

My partner, Bruce Gagnon, is the coordinator of the Global Network Against Weapons and Nuclear Power in Space. He has been organizing around conversion since the 1980s. His typical question to any audience is: "What is the U.S's number one industrial export?" Audiences across the country shout out "weapons." He then asks, "When weapons are your number one industrial export, what is your global marketing strategy?" "Endless war" becomes the refrain.

In 2003, Bruce and I moved to Maine, in part to be near Bath Iron Works (BIW), the General Dynamic's owned production facility for naval destroyers that are deployed with Aegis weapons systems. These Aegis destroyers are part of the "Star Wars" or "missile defense" vision; they rely on space satellites when launched toward their targets. Bruce and I joined the vigils that peace groups organized in Bath, and Bruce organized some vigils for the Global Network. We would hold signs critical of the purpose of the Aegis destroyer (Aegis is not about defense; Aegis destroys) and would offer an alternative vision for the factory (build wind turbines, not destroyers).

Initially, people laughed, scoffed, scorned, and some spewed hateful things at us.

In 2007, Bruce and I moved to Bath with our friend Karen Wainberg. We bought a big old house; tore down a wall to create a community room; and began conversations in our home about the idea of economic conversion. We interviewed people who had lived in the community for a while. We interviewed some workers at BIW.

In fact one worker, Peter Woodruff, joined our "conversion study group" early on. Broken-hearted by the role of the Aegis destroyers in the shock and awe campaign on Iraq, Peter has been a brave and creative organizer inside BIW. He plays with designs for creating energy through using tidal power; he has been an avid supporter of wind power using offshore wind turbines. Peter has bravely organized petition drives, created bumper stickers, publicly posted articles that educate his colleagues to the reality of the situation. He also spends two hours a week, with Bruce Gagnon, hosting a radio show on the campus of the local private college that espouses an anti-war theme, including conversations about economic conversion.

As BIW copes with episodic layoffs, a diminishing need for more U.S. war ships, and workers are feeling some job insecurity, fewer people scoff at our signs and message. Envisioning a future for BIW in a peace economy is an essential asset to the community.

Meanwhile, there is momentum in Maine to generate wind power options. A professor at the University of Maine is experimenting with composite materials to create a prototype for an offshore wind turbine, and a former governor has created a private company to put wind turbines throughout the state. As a friend who was an employee at BIW many years ago points out, BIW *did* convert years ago — from making commercial ships to naval destroyers. Can it experience another conversion now, making wind turbines and other renewable energy products?

What if BIW converted to making hospital ships? Paul Chappell talked to us here at this conference about transforming the U.S. military into a humanitarian relief organization. Maine author Kate Braestrup spoke at

Maine's Veteran's for Peace PTSD conference this year. She told the story of her Marine son who has experienced a number of deployments focused on disaster relief. She asked him how he can do humanitarian relief when the equipment they carried were instruments of war? He told her it took some creativity, but they were able to transform their equipment to rebuild infrastructure. Braestrup then asked this question: given that devastating extreme weather events will continue to occur, why don't we build hospital ships at BIW to meet the need in disaster relief — and if we need to adapt the materiel to fight wars, we can figure out how to do that?

It behooves the peace movement to create a vision that the populace can get excited about — a vision that will capture people's imagination. A vision that sees skills and talents of our engineers and scientists creating the renewable energy infrastructure that is critical to surviving the 21st Century; a vision that engages peace activists, environmentalists, labor, students, artists, and food security folks in creating plans for how we will heat homes, feed people, transport people in the year 2040. This is the true security need for the U.S., and the world.

Karen Kwiatkowski shared an important admonition at the conference. The MIC culture of cost maximizing/ cronyism/ lack of accountability (and, as Melman noted, worker alienation) makes its factories an unlikely location for the rebuilding of a worn-out infrastructure and creating the new energy models. Perhaps we are talking more about reconstruction than conversion. But it behooves each of us — locally — to look around, determine the needs, create the collaborations, and wrestle the funds away to start building a survivable future.

Economic conversion is an idea whose time has come. As evidence, I submit that we have an ally in none other than Deepak Chopra, the preeminent leader in the field of mind-body medicine. Few people know that, after the 2008 election, Dr. Chopra sent a public letter to Barak Obama which he called "Nine Steps to Peace for Obama in the New Year." Asserting that it was an anti-war constituency that elected Obama, Dr. Chopra invoked the spirit of Dwight D. Eisenhower in insisting Obama move from an economy dependent on war-making to a peace-based economy. Dr. Chopra's recommendations included: writing into every defense contract a requirement for a peacetime project; subsidizing conversion of military companies to peaceful uses with tax incentives and direct funding; converting military bases to housing for the poor; phasing out all foreign military bases; and calling a moratorium on future weapons technologies.

The vision is clear, it is obvious, it is mainstream. An important next step for us is to determine what we can do in our home communities to empower local unions and workers, environmentalists, health care workers, social workers, spiritual leaders, and the neighbors next door to engage the debate.

References for this article from Seymour Melman

"In the Grip of a Permanent War Economy," *Counterpunch*, March 15, 2003.

The Demilitarized Society: Disarmament and Conversion. Montreal: Harvest House, 1988.

After Capitalism: From Managerialism to Workplace Democracy. New York : Knopf., 2001.

See *Economic Reconstruction* and Seymour Melman website at http://globalmakeover.com/SeymourMelman.

War, Inc., an unpublished book, 2008.

Interview on Public Access Television, 1989.

Mary Beth Sullivan is a social worker from Brunswick, Maine, who acts as part-time Outreach Coordinator for Global Network Against Weapons & Nuclear Power in Space.

Time for an Economic Bill of Rights

By Ellen Brown

Henry Ford said, "It is well enough that the people of the nation do not understand our banking and monetary system, for if they did, I believe there would be a revolution before tomorrow morning." We are beginning to understand, and Occupy Wall Street looks like the beginning of the revolution.

We are beginning to understand that our money is created, not by the government, but by banks. Many authorities have confirmed this, including the Federal Reserve itself.[146] The only money the government creates today are coins, which compose less than one ten-thousandth of the money supply. Federal Reserve Notes, or dollar bills, are issued by Federal Reserve Banks, all twelve of which are owned by the private banks in their district. Most of our money comes into circulation as bank loans, and it comes with an interest charge attached.

According to Margrit Kennedy, a German researcher who has studied this issue extensively, interest now composes 40% of the cost of everything we buy.[147] We don't see it on the sales slips, but interest is exacted at every stage of production. Suppliers need to take out loans to pay for labor and materials, before they have a product to sell.

For government projects, Kennedy found that the average cost of interest is 50%.[148] If the government owned the banks, it could keep the interest and get these projects at half price. That means governments — state and federal — could double the number of projects they could afford, without costing the taxpayers a single penny more than we are paying now.

This opens up exciting possibilities. Federal and state governments could fund all sorts of things we think we can't afford now, simply by owning their own banks. They could fund something Franklin D. Roosevelt and Martin Luther King dreamt of — an Economic Bill of Rights.

A Vision for Tomorrow

In his first inaugural address in 1933, Roosevelt criticized the sort of near-sighted Wall Street greed that precipitated the Great Depression. He said, "They only know the rules of a generation of self-seekers. They have no vision, and where there is no vision the people perish." Roosevelt's own vision reached its sharpest focus in 1944, when he called for a Second Bill of Rights. He said:

> *This Republic had its beginning, and grew to its present strength, under the protection of certain inalienable political rights. … They were our rights to life and liberty. As our nation has grown in size and stature, however — as our industrial economy expanded — these political rights proved inadequate to assure us equality in the pursuit of happiness.*

He then enumerated the economic rights he thought needed to be added to the Bill of Rights. They included:

- The right to a job;
- The right to earn enough to pay for food and clothing;
- The right of businessmen to be free of unfair competition and domination by monopolies;
- The right to a decent home;
- The right to adequate medical care and the opportunity to enjoy good health;
- The right to adequate protection from the economic fears of old age, sickness, accident, and unemployment;
- The right to a good education.

Times have changed since the first Bill of Rights was added to the Constitution in 1791. When the country was founded, people could stake out some land, build a house on it, farm it, and be self-sufficient. The Great Depression saw people turned out of their homes and living in the streets — a phenomenon we are seeing again today. Few people now own their own homes. Even if you have signed a mortgage, you will be in debt peonage to the bank for 30 years or so before you can claim the home as your own.

Health needs have changed too. In 1791, foods were natural and nutrient-rich, and outdoor exercise was built into the lifestyle. Degenerative diseases such as cancer and heart disease were rare. Today, health insurance for some people can cost as much as rent.

Then there are college loans, which collectively now exceed a trillion dollars, more even than credit card debt. Students are coming out of universities not just without jobs but carrying a debt of $20,000 or so on their backs. For medical students and other post-graduate students, it can be $100,000 or more. Again, that's as much as a mortgage, with no house to show for it. The justification for incurring these debts was supposed to be that the students would get better jobs when they graduated, but now jobs are scarce.

After World War II, the G.I. Bill provided returning servicemen with free college tuition, as well as cheap home loans and business loans. It was called "the G.I. Bill of Rights." Studies have shown that the G.I. Bill paid for itself seven times over and is one of the most lucrative investments the government ever made.

The government could do that again — without increasing taxes or the federal debt. It could do it by recovering the power to create money from Wall Street and the financial services industry, which now claim a whopping 40% of everything we buy.

An Updated Constitution for a New Millennium

Banks acquired the power to create money by default, when Congress declined to claim it at the Constitutional Convention in 1787. The Constitution says only that "Congress shall have the power to *coin* money [and] regulate the power thereof." The Founders left out not just paper money but checkbook money, credit card money, money market funds, and other forms of exchange that make up the money supply today. All of them are created by private financial institutions, and they all come into the economy as loans with interest attached.

Governments — state and federal — could bypass the interest tab by setting up their own publicly-owned banks. Banking would become a public utility, a tool for promoting productivity and trade rather than for extracting wealth from the debtor class. Congress could go further: it could reclaim the power to issue money from the banks and fund its budget directly. It could do this, in fact, without changing any laws. Congress is empowered to "coin money," and the Constitution sets no limit on the face amount of the coins. Congress could issue a few one-trillion dollar coins, deposit them in an account, and start writing checks.

The Fed's own figures show that the money supply has shrunk by $3 trillion since 2008.[149] That sum could be spent into the economy without inflating prices. Three trillion dollars could go a long way toward providing the jobs and social services necessary to fulfill an Economic Bill of Rights. Guaranteeing employment to anyone willing and able to work would increase GDP, allowing the money supply to expand even further without inflating prices, since supply and demand would increase together.

Modernizing the Bill of Rights

As Bob Dylan said, "The times they are a'changin.'" Revolutionary times call for revolutionary solutions and an updated social contract. Apple and

Microsoft update their programs every year. We are trying to fit a highly complex modern monetary scheme into a constitutional framework that is 200 years old.

After President Roosevelt died in 1945, his vision for an Economic Bill of Rights was kept alive by Martin Luther King. "True compassion," King declared, "is more than flinging a coin to a beggar; it comes to see that an edifice which produces beggars needs restructuring."

MLK too has now passed away, but his vision has been carried on by a variety of money reform groups. The government as "employer of last resort," guaranteeing a living wage to anyone who wants to work, is a basic platform of Modern Monetary Theory (MMT). An MMT website declares that by "[e]nding the enormous unearned profits acquired by the means of the privatization of our sovereign currency ... [i]t is possible to have truly full employment without causing inflation."

What was sufficient for a simple agrarian economy does not provide an adequate framework for freedom and democracy today. We need an Economic Bill of Rights, and we need to end the privatization of the national currency. Only when the privilege of creating the national money supply is returned to the people can we have a government that is truly of the people, by the people and for the people.

Ellen Brown is an attorney, author, and president of the Public Banking Institute, http://PublicBankingInstitute.org. In *Web of Debt*, her latest of eleven books, she shows how the power to create money has been usurped from the people, and how we can get it back. Her websites are http://webofdebt.com and http://ellenbrown.com.

What Needs Changing
By Jonathan Williams

Thanks to everyone for organizing this conference. I appreciate the opportunity to speak with you today. How do we win? How do we get our demands met? We need *power*. But what is power? How do we get it? Simply put, *power is the ability to act*; the ability to end the wars, the ability to convert our economy, the ability to change the world. But how do we get that kind of power?

A lot of my mentors have said there are two kinds of power in this world: there's *organized money* and there's *organized people*. Which one do you think I'm here to talk about? So how do we organize people? We can't get that organized money, but we have the other kind of power. We have the numbers. We have the majority of people on our side.

There's a great quote that goes something like this: *we have to stop thinking that we're going to win because (1) the majority of people are on our side, (2) the facts are on our side, or (3) because we're morally right. Our opponents have none of these things, and they are consistently winning.* How are they winning then? It's because they have *power*. So how do we get that kind of power?

In my organization, Civilian-Soldier Alliance, we talk a lot about leadership. In our work, leadership and relationships are what we think actually organizes people. That's where you get people power. So how do you become a leader for social change? None of us are born as social change organizers. We don't pop out ready to change the world. That's not how it works. It is a process of transformation. It's a transformation of an individual to become a leader, and in turn, transforming lots of individuals transforms society. We call this *transformational organizing*.

It's important to note that this is a *process* and a process takes time. Transformation is a process for the individual and it's a process for society. But it is one that can be very intentional.

This is as opposed to *transactional organizing*. Transactional organizing depends on the self-interest of those being organized. Unions often use this model. They organize workers in the work place by promising higher wages or better working conditions. This is different from transformational organizing, which asks you to organize together for the larger goal of changing society.

So where did we learn this model of organizing? I started out as a student organizer. I organized a five-day student hunger strike on my campus. I don't know if you noticed, but the war didn't end. That's in part because we didn't have an analysis of our own power. We did a lot of *mobilizing*. We ultimately had hundreds of others on the campus participate in our fast. Students on twenty other campuses joined our effort. We raised thousands of dollars for UNICEF and held alternative classes about the Iraq war taught by veterans, military families, and even Iraqi civilians. However, this did not *organize* the campus. This was *mobilizing*. This effort got lots of people involved for a short period of time. This is different from organizing, and it's an important distinction.

In my own history, I grew up watching major mobilizations, such as the Seattle protests of 1999 against the World Trade Organization. I watched flash points like this and like Tahir Square with lots of people mobilized. I asked myself, how do we do that? I was really infatuated with these flash points and missed the years of organizing work it took to create these flash points. However, flash points such as major mobilizations alone are not what create change. I can't just call for a huge student strike, for instance, and expect the war to end. They are only one piece of a larger process of transformation.

I often give this example to explain my infatuation with flash points such as big protests. It's like I was watching someone build a house. I watched them for only a few minutes, saw them hammer some nails, and thought to myself, "I want a house like that. I know, I'll get a hammer!" I was so infatuated with the one tool that I was ignoring all of the other tools. I was ignoring the carpentry required to build the house. So *organizing* is like carpentry, while *mobilizing* is like the hammer; it's only one tool among many in your tool box.

In order to learn about transformational models of organizing, I had to look outside of the peace movement. In the peace movement, I was organizing event after event, protest after protest, lobby visit after lobby visit. I would lobby with the same few folks with the same demands. I wasn't actually organizing *people power*. This became very frustrating for me because I wasn't making change.

Outside of the peace movement, we can take leadership from movements that are winning. In particular, leadership from poor people's organizations, such as United Workers. United Workers uses transformational organizing, which is where my organization, Civilian-Soldier Alliance, learned the model. In turn, United Workers learned a lot from organizations such as Coalition of Immokalee Workers (CIW) and Student/Farmworker Alliance (SFA). These are very successful organizations. In the case of CIW, they've won every campaign they've ever started — a major achievement. In the case of United Workers, in three years they won a living wage for all the day laborers at Camden Yards, where the Baltimore Orioles play.

These organizations win because they focus on leadership development. In the case of United Workers, they ultimately won by doing a hunger strike, but they did not start with a hunger strike. It would be inappropriate to look at the example of the United Workers and think, "I know, I'll do a hunger strike and then I'll win a living wage." The hunger strike was the flash point. It took years of organizing to reach that point. It took years of going to Camden Yards and doing outreach to the workers, and undergoing leadership development with those workers.

In the end, there were about 30 individuals fasting in the hunger strike. Many of them no longer worked at the stadium. A living wage for stadium workers was no longer in their self-interest. They were participating because they had been transformed, they wanted to see Baltimore transformed, and they wanted poverty to end. That's the ultimate goal of the United Workers. United Workers used a focus campaign to develop the leadership of an affected community to win victories. If the name of the game is leadership development, campaigns are the vehicle by which we develop leaders.

The United Workers ultimately won a living wage, benefits, and a union for the workers at Camden Yards. Workers went from earning less than minimum wage to over $12 an hour. But this wasn't the United Workers victory per se — the ultimate victory was there were now 30 new leaders. Thirty new leaders to go on and continue organizing. They are now actively organizing another campaign declaring the Inner Harbor a "Human Rights Zone." They're hosting a conference on Fair Development to explore development of Baltimore city through a human rights framework.

We learned from these folks and from folks like Coalition of Immokalee Workers, tomato growers in Immokalee, Florida, who are organizing as well. They've teamed up with students in Student/Farmworker Alliance to boycott companies that purchase their tomatoes at unfair prices. Students are using their power on their campuses in solidarity with workers in Immokalee who are also organizing.

In looking to the peace movement for these examples, I'm very excited lately, particularly with what's going on with *Bring the War Dollars Home*, and with the *Move the Money* campaign. This is a big part of my work at

Peace Action. One example I'm sure you're familiar with is the *Fund Our Communities, Bring the War Dollars Home* coalition in Maryland. This is a coalition initiated by members of Peace Action Montgomery who started out two years ago by setting their sights on military recruiters in schools. They went to the state legislature and tried to lobby to protect student's rights. They identified clearly as the peace movement and anti-recruitment. This didn't get them anywhere. The next year, they went back to the State legislature but this time formed a coalition of groups, including right-wing, left-wing, and no-wing, under the banner of "Protect Student Privacy." Recruiters consistently violate the privacy of students, but we can get into that later. They ultimately won legislation that has ostensibly banned the ASVAB test (Armed Services Vocational Aptitude Battery) in public schools.

They won in part because they got smart. They didn't identify as an anti-recruitment or peace organization. They recognized that they needed a broad cross-section of Maryland in order to win this legislation, so they went out and did it. Now, many of those relationships are what's behind the *Fund Our Communities, Bring the War Dollars Home* coalition.

I went to their first meeting and the President of the local United Food and Commercial Workers union stood up and said, "we'll put $10,000 up for this right now. Who's with us?" This was a union jumping on board with this. Peace Action Montgomery and others are leading the way in building a new cross-section coalition of Maryland.

This is an example of *coalition building*. This is going to organized sectors of a community and working together around issues that affect everyone. They're going to church groups, unions, high schools, etc. They're hosting a Town Hall on September 20th, they have members of the government speaking, and they're even having break-out groups and doing some organizing. This is very exciting to me. But that's an example of *coalition building* within the peace movement. This is organizing organized people.

I'd like to give another example which is our work with Civilian-Soldier Alliance on Operation Recovery. This is a campaign in which we are using transformational organizing to develop the leadership of active-duty service members and veterans, as well as civilian allies.

Operation Recovery is a *base-building* campaign. This is different from a *coalition-building* campaign, which organizes organized sectors. While the military is highly organized, we can't simply go to an active-duty unit and ask for their endorsement on an antiwar campaign. That's obviously not going to work, so we have to go to *individuals* within the military community — individual active-duty service members and individual veterans. This is called *base building*. We're going into a community and trying to build up a base of leaders. This doesn't mean we go in and say, "hey aren't you against the war as much as we are? I know you just got back" — this does not work.

We spent years thinking about an outreach strategy that would work. I'm sure many of you are familiar with Iraq Veterans Against the War, who initiated Operation Recovery. They began as a speakers bureau of veterans willing to speak out about their experiences. They highlighted stories of war resistance, of service members refusing orders, this kind of thing. This is still ongoing and important work. These veterans, together with allies from Civilian-Soldier Alliance and others, developed a campaign over a long, four-day process of consensus. What we landed on was Operation Recovery. Operation Recovery seeks to stop the deployment of service members diagnosed with trauma such as Military Sexual Trauma (MST), Post-Traumatic Stress Disorder (PTSD) or Traumatic Brain Injury (TBI) as a result of their service.

How is this an antiwar campaign?

Currently, 20-50% of all service members deployed to Iraq or Afghanistan right now suffer from PTSD. A large number of these troops are also on psychotropic drugs. While in combat, there is no reporting on how these drugs are prescribed or taken. Military medics for instance are not required to write scripts, they simply hand out the drugs. In effect, we are arming traumatized troops, dosing them up and sending them back in.

Our campaign is focused in Killeen, Texas right now in partnership with a coffeehouse down there called Under the Hood. We also work with another coffeehouse just outside Joint Base Fort Lewis-McChord called Coffee Strong. In the case of Under the Hood, we actually go on base to Fort Hood and talk to soldiers. We invite them to come out to the coffee shop. We don't ask them if they are against the war. We have a campaign based on the experiences of service members and veterans because it was service members and veterans that said we needed to do something about this trauma.

This becomes an antiwar campaign because without 20-50% of the fighting force, the occupations of Iraq and Afghanistan become untenable. You can't keep a war going without soldiers to fight it. In some cases, the military is violating many of their own policies by deploying troops diagnosed with trauma.

In Fort Hood, for example, there were 22 suicides last year alone. In Joint Base Fort Lewis-McChord, there were 4 suicides on post last month alone. This is an epidemic that the military is refusing to deal with.

We are organizing active-duty service members and veterans to fight. We have a long-term campaign, which is the vehicle by which we develop the leadership of these service members and veterans. We're not asking them to protest with us immediately. We're asking them to do things like come to the coffee shop on Thursday nights for "Ribs and Rights" to learn about G.I. rights and have free barbeque. We ask them to come to Women's

Night on Mondays and these kind of things. At Coffee Strong, they offer free coffee to anyone with an enlisted ID. They like to say that officers have to pay double. The whole idea here is that Operation Recovery develops the leadership of those directly impacted by the wars. We are withdrawing consent from the wars. When a service member withdraws his/her consent from the war and refuses to participate, this ultimately depletes the power of the military to maintain these wars.

This is, as you might imagine, a long haul campaign. This is not us planning a protest in three months and hoping the war will end. We make our plans in multi-year timelines. We learned much of this from United Workers, including how to phase campaigns, set goals, and develop tactics to achieve that goal. This is what works and this is where we're seeing victories.

It's also important to uplift the role of civilians whose experience is not in the military, who have not been to Afghanistan and seen this first hand, who maybe arrive at an antiwar or peace politics as a result of their own analysis and not their direct experience. For others, it is indeed from a direct experience. We have a member whose brother served in Iraq, and this largely influences her perspective.

It's important to have a role for allies in order to uplift our experience as well. This is where groups like Civilian-Soldier Alliance come from. We are civilian allies to service members and veterans. Student/Farmworker Alliance is the same thing; they are students using their power on their campuses to stop buying tomatoes grown under poverty conditions in Immokalee. Simultaneously, the farm workers are organizing in the fields. These kinds of connections create victories.

In conclusion, the title of my talk is "What Needs Changing." I think aside from our economy, perhaps the peace movement itself needs changing. We need to be building leadership. We need to not only do coalition building, in which we go after the low-hanging fruit by trying to get all of the peace organizations together to form a coalition, but we actually need to be doing base building as well. According to polls, the majority of people are on our side, yet we never talk to them. I went on post and spoke with service members in uniform in Fort Hood about Operation Recovery and it was not difficult to get signatures on a pledge about that. The hard part is developing their leadership and creating pathways for involvement. The sentiments are there, and we need to be doing base building, we need to do campaign organizing, and most importantly, we need to take leadership from movements that are winning, in particular poor people's movements. Thank you.

Jonathan Williams, is a program associate at Peace Action and Student Peace Action Network Coordinator. He is the co-founder of Civilian-Soldier Alliance, a national, membership-based organization of civilian organizers working with service members and veterans to stop the deployment of traumatized troops.

Activism and the M.I.C.

By Ray McGovern

The past 50 years have shown that President Eisenhower was spot on, as we would say today, about the Military Industrial Complex and what to expect if Americans were not vigilant, which, of course, we have not been — until maybe now. An endless train of outrages and indignities can be traced to the inordinate influence of the MIC. And a truly formidable challenge awaits those of us determined not to let our democracy be taken away from us by the greed of a small minority.

So here we are, cooped up, by choice, indoors, talking about these dismal matters on a glorious late-summer afternoon. Don't know about you, but I found myself sorely tempted to channel today's activism into a brisk swim in that beautiful little lake just outside. And yet, perhaps, like me, over the past two days you have seen more good news than bad. And the view from where I stand at this podium evokes a powerful feeling of enthusiastic anticipation. The challenges presented by the MIC seem not so daunting as I look out on all you activists!

Activists

I'll confess, it took me a while to become comfortable with the sobriquet commonly used these days to introduce me: "intelligence analyst turned activist." In the circles in which I moved for 30 years, the epithet "activist" was usually hurled in a condescending, what-can-activists-accomplish tone. But, there was Vietnam, no? Often it takes a while, but activists do change things. In an interview a couple of months ago, former President George W. Bush referred sneeringly to "activists." Like you all, I have become accustomed to the customary sneers and smears. And that's precisely why standing here is so important to me. For those given the privilege of looking out at so many gutsy "activists" for Justice, the sneers, smears, and spears lose all their sting. Hope is reborn, because you give flesh to that hope. What I think has been especially great is that, over the past days, so many of you have also had the opportunity to be encouraged, fortified by the view from this podium. Perhaps you, too, have found the experience an effective inoculation against despair and a fillip to action.

Paying the Rent

No one has put it better than a precious new friend I met on a "cruise" in the eastern Mediterranean — Alice Walker, who said it this way: "Activism is my rent for living on this planet." As some of you know, that attitude found her a passenger on *The Audacity of Hope* — the U.S. Boat to Gaza — this past summer. On July 1ˢᵗ, we made an activist break for the open sea and Gaza but were able to sail only nine nautical miles out of Athens before the Greek government, under extreme pressure from the White House and Israel, ordered its Coast Guard to intercept us, threaten to board us, and eventually impound our boat.

It turned out not so bad. We raised a lot of interest, calling attention to how the Likud government in Israel, supported by the taxes we pay, seals off and oppresses 1.6 million Gazans in the largest open-air prison on the planet. And, for those who care to look, we exposed our President kow-towing, for the umpteenth time, to Israeli Prime Minister Benjamin Netanyahu. Obama could not get him to promise not to shoot up our boat, as the Israeli navy did the Mavi Marmora in May of last year. So the White House decided to take the easy way out and bully Greece into issuing an unprecedented edict that no boats could leave Greek ports for Gaza. You learn a lot, and often you expose a lot, when you accept the challenge of being an "activist!"

Anger? or "Unreasoned Patience?"

I find that people often are conflicted about whether or not to allow themselves to be angry. Thomas Aquinas, who wrote a lot about virtue, got quite angry when he realized there was no word in Latin for just the right amount of anger — for the virtue of anger.

Thomas cited what a famous fourth-century theologian said on the subject: "He or she who is not angry, when there is just cause for anger, sins. Why? Because anger *respicit bonum justitiae*, anger looks to the good of Justice, and if you can live among injustice without anger you are unjust." Aquinas added his own corollary; he railed against what he called "unreasoned patience," which, he said, "sows the seeds of vice, nourishes negligence, and persuades not only evil people but good people to do evil."

As we look at the effects of the military industrial complex, who will deny that there is just cause for anger — just the right amount of anger — the virtue of anger. And the fact that this is part of what motivates us — well that's as it should be. Frankly, I have not thought of us activists being virtuous — but maybe we are, at least in our willingness to channel our anger into challenging and changing the many injustices here and around the world. There should be no room these days for "unreasoned patience."

Prophets/Activists and Cads

The Hebrew Scriptures feature the witness of prophets channeling the virtue of anger into speaking truth to power. Many of the prophets were eccentric — from the Greek *ek kentron*, off center, out of the mainstream — and they were generally not welcome in their hometowns. Is this beginning to sound a little like you, maybe?

Happily, we don't have to go back to the eighth-century Hebrew prophets for example. We are surrounded by prophets, although the ones I have in mind would be the last to claim that title. Earlier today I did a little review of the prophets I've run into over the last decade; curiously, all of the ones who first came to mind turned out to be women.

Ann Wright, who keynoted us so well on Friday evening, was the first prophet I thought of. One of the three U.S. diplomats who quit when the U.S. attacked Iraq; mayor of Camp Casey in Crawford, Texas; inspirer and fund raiser for the U.S. Boat to Gaza, with the creative suggestion that we name it —I think after some sort of book — "The Audacity of Hope."

I've had the pleasure of watching Ann up close, and have gotten into the same kind of activist trouble she has. I remember as one of her finest hours, the one during which she sat quietly as the Senate Judiciary Committee deliberated pompously over whether to approve the appointment of Rumsfeld's Pentagon lawyer William J. Haynes, II — an Eagle Scout from Waco, alumnus of Harvard Law, and more recently a "justifier" of torture — to be a federal judge. (The pattern had already been set when Jay Bybee of the Justice Department, who signed off on John Yoo's many mafia-style memoranda approving torture, was given a life-time appointment as a federal judge.)

Ann can be quiet in such circumstances for, well, not very long. She stood up and loudly warned those august Senators that they were about to give a judgeship to a felon. The committee adjourned that day before it was supposed to, and I think it's pretty clear that the ruckus Ann made was instrumental in defeating Haynes' appointment. The findings of a subsequent Senate Armed Services Committee report on torture provide chapter and verse about why Haynes and his boss Rumsfeld should be behind bars.

Mentioning John Yoo evokes the example of West Coast prophet Susan Harman, who has made it her business to cling to Yoo like chewing gum. Seeing Susan's familiar face, Yoo now says, "Hello there". Susan responds, "Torture there". Yoo has enough friends in high places that there are many charlatans to choose from, were we as brave and conscientious as Susan in bird-dogging. Let's each of us choose just one.

And how could I not mention the gutsy women who lead World Can't Wait's watchdog group "War Criminal Watch." It was the World Can't Waiters who got me a ticket to Donald Rumsfeld's speech in Atlanta five years ago. And they did the same to get me into the same auditorium with him just ten days ago at a forum run by the Jewish Policy Center at the 92nd Street Y in New York. (This time I was unceremoniously seized and thrown out by the NYPD before I could ask Rumsfeld a question. The wounds and bruises, though, were minor compared with those inflicted by the thugs who brutalized me as I stood silently with my back to Secretary of State Hillary Clinton during a speech she gave in February.)

More Prophets

How about Rae Abileah, who was brutalized when she called for justice for Palestine as Israeli Prime Minister Benjamin Netanyahu was receiving fulsome applause from our bought-and-sold Congresspeople in May. Or the Code Pink women in the belly of the beast in Dallas, who do something imaginatively pointed and conspicuous whenever George W. Bush surfaces for air.

Or Jesselyn Radack, Esq., fired from the Justice Department for insisting that John Walker Lindh, labeled for political purposes as "The American Taliban," be granted his rights as an American citizen. After being blacklisted by Justice from her profession, Jesselyn has landed on both feet as National Security and Human Rights Counsel at the Government Accountability Project, which focuses on protecting/defending whistleblowers. Jesselyn also was a terrific support to the successful defense of Thomas Drake, ex-NSA senior executive who was recently subjected to a three-year long witch-hunt aimed at dissuading anyone else from blowing the whistle.

And then there's Cindy Sheehan, who had the courage to ask Bush to explain to her what "noble cause" had taken the life of her son Casey. And former FBI special agent/attorney Coleen Rowley, who took a huge risk

— just one year short of retirement — in blowing a loud whistle about FBI shortcomings before 9/11, and who continues to work, in a variety of imaginative ways, for Justice. (Warning: do not, within earshot of Coleen, call her a prophet.) Of women prophets/activists I have gotten to know over the past 10 years I could go on forever.

The Shibboleth of Success

One trait peculiar not only to the Hebrew prophets of the eighth century but to the ones I just mentioned is that they did not get hung up on the all-too-familiar drive for success. That drive, I think, is a distinctly American trait. We generally do not want to embark on a significant course or action without there being a reasonable prospect of success, do we? Who enjoys becoming the object of ridicule?

The commonly felt imperative to be "successful" can be a real impediment to acting for Justice. A prophet/activist from whom I have drawn help and inspiration on this is Dan Berrigan. I'd like to share some of the wisdom that seeps through his autobiography, *To Dwell in Peace*. Berrigan writes that after he, his brother Phil, and a small group of others had used homemade napalm to burn draft cards in Catonsville, Maryland in May 1968 at the height of the Vietnam War, Dan mused about why he took such a risk:

> *I came upon a precious insight. … Something like this: presupposing integrity and discipline, one is justified in entering upon a large risk; not indeed because the outcome is assured, but because the integrity and value of the act have spoken aloud. … Success or efficiency are placed where they belong: in the background. They are not irrelevant, but they are far from central. I was in need of such reflections as we faced the public after our crime. … All sides agreed — we were fools or renegades or plain crazy. … One had very little to go on; and one went ahead nonetheless. Still, the 'little,' had at least one advantage. One was free to concentrate on the act itself, without regard to its*

reception in the world. Free to concentrate on moral preparation, consistency, conscience. Looked at in this light, the 'little' appeared a treasure. The act was let go, its truth and goodness were entrusted to the four winds. Indeed, good consequences were of small matter to me, compared with the integrity of the action, the need responded to, the spirits lifted. ...

The more recent prophets and activists I have known have generally been able to do this — to release the truth of the act to the four winds. And I think that helps them avoid taking themselves too seriously. It seemed to work that way with Dan Berrigan. Here's how he recounts the immediate aftermath of the action at Catonsville:

We sat in custody in the back room of the Catonsville Post Office, weak with relief ... Three or four FBI honchos entered portentously. Their leader, a jut-jawed paradigm, surveyed us from the doorway. His eagle-eye lit on Philip. He roared out: 'Him again! Good God, I'm changing my religion!' I could think of no greater tribute to my brother.

The Berrigans help affirm for me that this God of ours is a merry God, and we are the entertainment. And that's just one of the reasons a light touch is very helpful.

Code Pink knows this well. Watch, for example, the intervention team from War Addicts Anonymous as they engage President Obama outside the White House. Obama says, "I can quit anytime I want!" But can he? (http://codepink.org/article.php?id=5916)

How I look forward to descending on our own "Tahrir Square" at Freedom Plaza in Washington, D.C., starting on October 6th. In the final analysis we will be confronting the "upper crust," which my Irish grandmother described as "a bunch of crumbs held together by a lot of dough."

But will we be successful? Wrong question. We will be faithful — and, I am sure — have a lot of fun in the process. For I believe it is true: the good is worth doing because it is good. Feels good, too.

Ray McGovern, after serving in the Army as an intelligence officer, joined the CIA. His duties eventually included preparing daily intelligence briefings for Pres. Reagan and the first Bush. He works with Tell the Word, the publishing arm of the Church of the Saviour in Washington, D.C. He recently attempted to sail to Gaza on *The Audacity of Hope.*

Imperial Collapse in the Middle East

By Helena Cobban

Thank you, Clare. Thank you to all the organizers. This is a great, a really wonderful initiative. It follows on the initiative earlier this year in January in Greensboro, NC, and I was just kind of transported back there mentally because I recall as I drove from Charlottesville down to Greensboro, NC, back in January, I was listening to the BBC on the satellite radio and they were giving live blow-by-blow accounts of what was happening in Tunisia at the time. It was so exciting.

I got to the conference, and when it came time to speak I got to speak about the Middle East. And I said, "You know, as we are sitting here speaking, the U.S. military empire in the Middle East is starting to collapse." And sure enough, you know, that was about the time that the long-time dictator of Tunisia supported by the U.S. military, Zine el Abidine Ben Ali, left his country under the pro-democracy activism, and then about a month later the same happened to President Hosni Mubarak of Egypt. And the popular movements that forced those two dictators from power were something quite new and wonderful in the Middle East, and I'll come back to that later.

My major thing that I want to talk about this afternoon is the need for us all to, as American citizens, challenge our fellow citizens to reconsider this whole ideology of American exceptionalism which is one of the things that keeps the military industrial complex in power, that keeps us fearful that we might lose our special place in the world, and that we as five percent of humanity need to find a way to deal with the other ninety-five percent on the basis of the equality of all human persons.

So, it sounds like a huge challenge because when people have privilege, it's hard to invite them, or urge them, or push them, or persuade them to give it up. On the other hand, what has that privilege and the way that our government has sought to hang onto it, what has that actually done for the lives of Americans and for the insecurity that we as American citizens feel whenever we go outside our borders and encounter people from other countries? It has not made us safer. It has made us a lot less safe.

In connection with this whole theory of American exceptionalism or manifest destiny or whatever, I think it's at this point absolutely incontestable that the ideology of the ruling elite in Israel has played a huge part. And I know this is a difficult topic to talk about because there is always, there is always the fear of anti-Semitism and arousing anti-Semitic, the anti-Semitic currents that flow so deep in Christian society and have done historically. But at this point, I think we need to come straight out and say that Israeli exceptionalism has been a major motivating and inspiring and supporting feature of American exceptionalism, especially over the past fifteen to twenty years, and that the Israeli military industrial complex and political elite have shown the way to the American military industrial complex in so many different ways.

Now to point this out is not to point a finger at Jewish people in general, because the Israeli political elite does not represent Jewish people in general. They do not represent my wonderful daughter-in-law Liz Jackson who has been at the forefront of Students for Justice in Palestine over in Berkeley along with just about all of her wonderful Jewish family — very strong supporters of equal rights for Palestinians and the Israelis. There are so many wonderful Jewish people in the forefront of the movement for Palestinian equality that I think that those of us who happen to be Christian can be absolutely in solidarity with those wonderful Jewish and Palestinian activists. And we don't need to be cowed or scared by the charge of "Oh, you're just anti-Semitic." No, we're not anti the Jewish people as such. We're anti certain policies of this ruling elite in Israel just as we are anti certain policies, many policies, of this ruling elite here in America.

I want to point out just a few of the ways in which the Israeli political elite has actually led the way in enabling whole new practices on behalf of the American military industrial complex. One is extrajudicial killings, that is assassinations — killing of people around the world based on the suspicion that they might be about to do something. Not based on the rule of law and bringing the evidence out, but based solely on suspicions that may, and as we know in Iraq and Afghanistan and elsewhere, often the suspicions are just based on the hearsay of a jealous neighbor or whatever who goes to the American military and says, "Oh, you know, that sheikh down the road he's been involved with al Qaeda." And then the American military will not have any kind of a judicial process. I mean, it's bad enough here in Virginia where we have a so-called "judicial process" and end up executing somebody. How much worse is it when, based on hearsay and secret evidence, they take out somebody overseas who has no recourse. That policy of extrajudicial executions was introduced by the Israelis back in the 1980s in their dealings with the Palestinians and has continued since.

The use of drones, the use of these horrible, remotely piloted killing vehicles, pioneered by the Israelis. The use of pre-emptive wars, or as they are now called preventive wars, pioneered by the Israelis. The defiance of international law saying, no, we can't be members of the International Criminal Court because that would imply that our servicemen and -women might be tried by foreigners; our generals might be tried by foreigners; our decision-makers who took us into a completely illegal and immoral war might be tried by foreigners. The defiance of international law is something that the Israeli elite pioneered and have pursued for many years, and they made it OK for our country to do the same. If you look at all the list of advisors and people who would justify the Bush administration's defiances of international law, you'll find that many of them were amongst the longest-running pro-Israeli activists in Washington, DC, people like Doug Feith, Paul Wolfowitz, John Hannah. The list is extremely long.

Then the whole ideology of exceptionalism is something that, of course it runs long and deep in American history. The idea that you can wipe out the native peoples here because we have some kind of, white folks have some kind of manifest destiny, is something that has happened and been part of our history, a shameful aspect of our history for so long. But it's also been pushed by the Israelis who have their own form of exceptionalism, who think, who portray themselves, present themselves as representing some kind of civilizational force amongst people who are backward and primitive and, as it happens, mainly Muslim, although there are many Christians in Arab countries. And so, that ideology, and especially the way that it's come back home here in terms of islamophobia, an exaggerated and completely manipulated fear of those of our fellow citizens in this country and people around the world who follow the religion of Islam.

That's in a sense the bad news, you know, how we've gotten to this stage where because of the political power of the pro-Israeli forces in Washington, DC, many of Israel's worst practices have become embedded in the practice of our country and our military industrial complex.

The good news is what I talked about at the beginning about what's been happening in Egypt and Tunisia, so many other countries in the Middle East where the people whose governments for decades have been supported by our military at the expense of their own, you know, internal democratic accountability. The people just finally rose up and went to the public square and said we've had enough. We've had enough of the oppression. We've had enough of the torture that was often carried out by their governments at the express request of our government under the renditions policy. The oppression, the torture, the mind control, the lying, all of that — people went out to the public square and said we've had enough of that. It was so inspiring.

I was there, actually. I was in Tahrir Square in June, and I was lucky enough to get to Gaza in June as well. I went in overland from Cairo. It takes about five hours if there's no security checkpoints but there are lots of security checkpoints. Anyway, it was a very long trip; it was a very difficult trip. I got there and we spent three days with our friends in Gaza which is this tiny little enclave that we have been told in this country is a source of violence and oppression of women and just rockets —t hey fire rockets for no reason whatsoever at the Israelis, those peace-loving Israelis. And we're told this completely nonsensical story about what's happening in Gaza.

I was there. All the stories that were in the Western media about Gaza are completely untrue. I've been to Gaza many times before. On this occasion we were told there's no need for flotillas and such because the borders of Gaza are open. Not true. Absolutely not true. We're told that the people who are ruling Gaza, who were the elected authorities (they were elected in 2005) are irrational, Islamist madmen who want to oppress women. Not true.

I met four of the elected Hamas women parliamentarians — extremely intelligent, well-educated, professional women who get great support from the Hamas party in their endeavors. One of them is the head of the Human Rights Committee in the elected parliament. We had a lot of discussions about Western policy and Palestinian policy. Very smart women. I went to a media center where there were people from Hamas and from other parties and there was very open discussion about policies. There are young women there who are on Twitter all the time and they are tweeting internationally and in touch. It's just like night and day compared with what we are told in the Western media.

And, you know, they have tried to have a ceasefire with Israel, and by and large the ceasefire has worked since the end of the terrible war of 2008-2009. The ones who keep breaking it are the Israelis, and as a result you have deaths in Gaza, maybe two or three every month, people killed and many more wounded and maimed as a result of these killings by Israel. They normally have drones that kill automatically from the air, but they have machine gun nests on the walls around the edge that if the farmers go closer than 500 meters, the machine guns automatically fire so the farmers cannot approach. It's an extremely constrained area. They need every square inch of farming land they can use. If they go closer than 500 meters to the border the machine guns fire automatically.

But they have pulled themselves together after the war of 2008-2009. Things were functioning very well at a low economic level but with great social solidarity. You don't see a lot of gunmen on the streets, for example. I go to Ramallah which is run by an unelected, U.S.-supported Palestinian Authority. There are a lot of gunmen on the streets there; there is a lot of insecurity there.

So then, we spent a little bit of time in Cairo. We went to Tahrir Square. There weren't big actions in Tahrir Square when we were there. There were a couple of small actions. But we talked to so many of the people who had participated in it. One of the things one of my friends said there that really struck me was that what happened in Tahrir Square seemed to be the end of the neoliberal sort of approach to economics, the kind of "me first" and "me for myself." He said there was a whole new moral economy there on Tahrir Square that rich people, poor people would come along, they would bring whatever they had and share it. They would bring their skills, whether they were dentists or doctors or barbers or cooks, they would bring whatever they had and share it freely and create this whole new idea of a society.

They were challenging the authority. They were challenging the military authorities who had ruled there for so long through a combination of fear and spreading distrust. They were standing together whether they were Islamists or secularists. You'd see them all together on the square, and they talked about national unity as being one of their key assets. Most of all they were asserting the end of the humiliation that they had experienced as a result of being ruled by this U.S.-supported, U.S.-imposed leadership. Hosni Mubarak was the president since 1981. He had completely fake elections every so often, and the most recent of those elections was at the end of last year actually, in September 2010. Once again his electoral shenanigans got a complete pass from Washington who said, well, it's OK; it's imperfect as a democracy, but what can you expect.

And that, I think the fact that Washington just kept him in power and turned a blind eye to all his excesses ... not just turned a blind eye. We were sending him people for him to torture. We were supporting his torture machine completely. So when the people rose up against him they were also rising up against that assertion of American power, and we have to understand that and respect it. It's not an anti-American sentiment as such; it's an anti-oppression sentiment. Personally I felt quite safe walking around and talking to people and, you know, it was a wonderful feeling to be there with my friends who had been part of that movement.

I think, and really it's going to come on more with this very soon, what we need is a Tahrir moment, a Tahrir movement here in the United States. The word "Tahrir" actually means liberation. And so it was wonderful that both in Tunis and in Cairo the central square where people gathered was already called Tahrir Square because it was a tahrir, it was a liberation of an earlier era that didn't work out totally well, but they had named their square Tahrir Square. Well, we need to have a Tahrir moment, a Tahrir movement here where we liberate ourselves from all these sick ideologies of American exceptionalism of me firstism, of a kind of ideology, I think it's based on fear. It's based on fear and guilt.

We kind of know that our military industrial complex, our country's government, have actually inflicted a lot of harms on other peoples around the world, most of all in Iraq. I don't believe there is anybody sane in this country who think that what we did in Iraq turned out well. I understand that many of the people who argued for the, and they call it intervention but of course that's a mealy-mouthed word for a war and a brutal invasion. I don't think anybody who supported that … no, that's not true. Most of the people who supported that did so from good motivations, I think. They thought that Saddam Hussein is a brutal dictator, that we are supporting the Iraqi people by launching this war. Or they thought that he's about to develop nuclear weapons because they believed everything that the government told us (wasn't that a mistake), and so they thought they were making the world safer by supporting the invasion. None of that was true. It was all completely a lie.

It's not a lie that Saddam Hussein was oppressive, but what is a lie is that what came after has been any better, as we know from the stories from 2004 onwards from Abu Ghraib; from the terrible, terrible internal social breakdown that our military oversaw in Iraq in 2006-2007 in the course of which hundreds of thousands of Iraqi citizens lost their lives while we were "in charge." And it continues today if you read the newspapers. Day after day after day there are mass killings, usually on a sectarian basis, that were part of a process that our military accelerated.

So, I don't think that many people now can stand up in this country and say that that was a great idea — invading Iraq. What's more we know what the costs have been in terms of purely financial and, as we heard yesterday again and again, the terrible human costs.

But just imagine if we had taken that $3 trillion and put it into, over this past 10 years, put it into rebuilding schools and hospitals, infrastructure, a decent train system in this country, green energy. Three trillion dollars, what could we have done? Instead of which it all ended up with Halliburton, with the contractors, with General Dynamics, with very corrupt Iraqi and Afghani subcontractors, with Saudi Arabian arms dealers, with Israeli so-called security consulting companies that put in place all the mechanisms of human control, or tried to, in Iraq with retina scans and all of this fine stuff.

Three trillion dollars, I mean, you know, that's why we need, that's why we need to transform our relationship with the rest of the world. And that's why we have the opportunity now because we have a very powerful story to tell. You know, you don't actually persuade people by and large by throwing figures at them. You persuade people if you can tell them a story that connects with something inside them. And we have a very powerful story to tell about the folly of war, about the way that that war in particular and the war in Afghanistan . ...

Do you know it costs $1 million a year to keep one American service member in Afghanistan. The gasoline that they use there, and they use a lot in those big tanks and MRAPs and other vehicles that they use, it costs $400 a gallon. To get it there, if you look at a map, I mean, it's not easy to get gasoline into Afghanistan. That's where our money is continuing to drain. That's why we have to say enough. We have the evidence, we have the story, we have the compelling case to make.

You know I've been working on my Southern drawl for fifteen years, but I have to tell you I did grow up in England. I know that will come as a surprise to you. But I grew up in the 1950s and 1960s at a time of decolonization there, when Britain was under the pressure of self-bankruptcy that had happened to the country as a result of a series of imperial wars, including one against Egypt in Sinai and Gaza in 1956. The UK, the British people were having to draw back and completely re-imagine themselves. What does it mean to be British? Until then, to be British meant we have an empire. In the 1950s and 1960s we stepped back and I was part of this as a child — a new process of what it means to be British. Actually, interestingly, one of the things it meant was that we had a National Health Service.

But what I want to say is that for the UK, ending imperialism and empire was OK. You know, the British people are OK. For South Africa, ending apartheid was OK. The white people have not been wiped out. The white people are doing very nicely in South Africa, thank you. If we transform our relationship with the 95 percent of the world who are not Americans into one of human equality and mutual respect, we will not only be OK but we will be a lot better off than we are now. Thank you.

Helena Cobban has been a reporter for ABC News and the BBC, as well as a columnist for the *Christian Science Monitor*. Her area of special expertise is Middle Eastern diplomacy and politics. She has written seven books of her own, and was a key contributor to *When the Rain Returns: Toward Justice and Reconciliation in Palestine and Israel*, published by the American Friends Service Committee. She recently launched JustWorld Books.

It Would Grind to a Halt Tomorrow

By Lisa Savage

Following on Ray McGovern's call to action for October 6 in Washington DC, the website for info is October2011.org. Thank you conference organizers, and to everyone for taking time to be here today. When I reflect on activism and the military-industrial complex (MIC) I think of a video made by a friend, Pete Sirois, of Bruce Gagnon in front of Bath Iron Works speaking about conversion. Bath Iron Works is where they build the Aegis destroyers that are to be docked on South Korea's Jeju Island that Ann Wright spoke about last night. Bruce's speech mentions the Pollin and Garrett-Peltier study about the relative number of jobs generated by investment in various sectors of the economy, which sounded interesting. So I contacted Bruce and got a link to the study, done at UMass Amherst in 2007. This led to my husband Mark and I starting to organize with Bruce and Mary Beth Sullivan in Bath. Which led eventually to joining others in a statewide, and now a national campaign, to Bring Our War $$ Home.

Pete at the time was an amateur videographer with a local access tv cable show. He grasped early what potential this communication channel offers at a very low cost. His willingness to challenge himself and take risks to do the work has really helped get the word out, and been a catalyst for all kinds of activism.

My Maine grandmother told me things that have stuck with me, and two of them are: "Fools' names and fools' faces are often seen in public places," and "Pretty is as pretty does." I had to overcome that first admonition in order to do the activism that I do. And I have come to a deeper understanding of the second one.

Bruce has told how as a young "true believer" serving in the Air Force and stationed in California, he and the others would see protesters at the gate of the air base. This led the people inside the base to have long debates over whether the signs were right or wrong. These conversations changed Bruce's understanding and brought him over to the side of demanding military cuts to fund domestic needs.

So don't ever think, just because you don't get to see their effects, that your messages don't matter. They matter a lot. People today lack good information and you are helping to address that problem with well thought out messaging.

Using the power of branding is also effective and this is one thing that I love about CodePink. Also choosing a short phrase that conveys the essence of the message in a way that most people are likely to understand. Bring Our War $$ Home is all short, simple words that even a young kid can understand. I wish I could take credit for penning the phrase, and its author remains anonymous. Then repeating the phrase in as many ways as you can think of while also thinking carefully about the explanation that backs up the slogan. Knowing it's possible your understanding of the phrase will evolve. When this "headline" has clear meaning to your audience, it becomes the work horse of the campaign.

The most important aspect of communication is listening. We have to listen to the audience if we are to know whether our message was received. And we communicate effectively when we understand the needs of the listener. Then, as we devise ways to address some of those needs, and build relationships, we can keep using listening to get feedback in order to try new things.

We've used many communication strategies in our current campaign: radio ads by a well-known comic personality are running now on right wing talk radio stations; we've had signature ads and community event listings in newspapers; and with the Union of Maine Visual Artists we've conducted Draw-a-thons and Draw-ins at various places, including our state capitol building, where artists interact with the general public. These resulted in a group of strong poster designs for war $$ home available on our website, designs that are now on t-shirts. We have shirts here at the conference, and gave two of them as participation prizes yesterday during the federal budget activity at the conference. And so the message goes forward.

Currently I'm seeking support for the development of a digital game that offers the chance to convert war spending in a community to other needs, because I think that could be a powerful communication device. Imagining conversion as utopia could be addicting if visually appealing and properly designed. Young people with all that college debt and no real jobs are the audience I want to reach.

I don't play such games but I do tweet, facebook, and skype in the course of my activism. Most of you here have stretched and learned new technology tools. I have been helped immensely in learning these by younger members of CodePink who are very patient with us oldsters. Blogging is something I've added lately and I've had some good mentors who encouraged me as I was getting started. I often learn and get ideas from other blogs. Getting real information is almost a full time job in this day and age. Thankful for the Internet while we still have it.

What else are we up against? I think Americans — that is, people in the U.S., because America is a continent, not a country — are scared. Maybe more scared than we give them credit for a lot of the time. I'll tell two stories to illustrate.

The last time Social Security was on the chopping block, back when George W. wanted to "privatize" it, a woman who worked at my school as an ed tech told me in the hall that she appreciated my letter to the editor about how families who have a parent die depend on S.S. The woman told me that her mother had used her father's S.S. to help feed their family after he died, and had a hard enough time even with that income. I told my co-worker that people needed to hear her story, and to please consider a letter of her own. She reacted with alarm and said, "Oh I don't think Dr. ____ would appreciate that," referring to our superintendent. He had never said anything negative to me about my letters, and I told her so. "Oh but that's you," she said as if perhaps her status as an ed tech without a continuing contract was much different than mine as a teacher.

Just this summer I was at a conference and I needed a ride to Rockland at the end, in order to meet my husband to stand with local organizers opposing an Islamophobic group that was going to be protesting a speech by the Al Jazeera Bureau Chief in Washington. When I briefly stated my reason for needing a ride, the other teachers and librarians in the room froze like deer in headlights. No one said a single word in response. I think I had violated the unspoken dictum of life in our nation, that as long as we don't rock the boat that nothing bad will happen around us. Bad things are happening elsewhere, but not right where we are. And hoping to keep it that way.

So people are frightened, and they are bewildered by misinformation, and we offer them our message. The Bring Our War $$ Home coalition in Maine has benefited from a good faith approach of supporting one another to bring an accurate explanation for budget cuts and funding shortfalls in our communities, cooperating across what is a large if not very populous state. The Care-a-Van began on September 10th at Unity College with WERU Community Radio's Grassroots Media Conference as we silkscreened the t-shirts we have here today. It continues to many venues including five other college campuses in our state, with a teach-in at Bowdoin, and a stop in support of on-campus peace group P.A.inT for a concert at the University of Maine, Farmington.

Because I am also deeply involved with CodePink as a Local Coordinator two of the co-founders, Medea Benjamin and Jodie Evans, picked up on the campaign and asked if they could adopt it nationally. Adopt away, we said, with the result that the campaign is now being waged in California, New York, and Texas among other places, and that the U.S. Conference of Mayors passed a resolution to bring the war dollars home this summer.

If people stopped cooperating with and supporting the MIC, it would grind to a halt tomorrow. People just don't know it yet. Some do — right now there are youth occupying Wall St. in a show of nonviolent methods that remind me of the great untapped power of human stubbornness. I was lucky enough to meet Gene Sharp and Jamila Raqib of the Albert Einstein Institution a couple of years ago, and Sharp said in response to my question that the antiwar movement lacked an overall strategy. I can see several heads nodding in the audience.

Now is the time in the program where we will have some time for planning and I'm going to read you a list of questions developed by the organizers of the conference, questions that can inform this part of our work today: Where is the MIC vulnerable? What are the hidden strengths of the progressive movement? How will moral energy be generated and harnessed? How do you prepare the ground for change? What strategies for change are inefficient or unproductive? What strategies will capture the imagination of others and empower them? Are progressives willing to pay the price?

Now we are going into self-selected groups.

Thank you.

Lisa Savage is Maine coordinator for Code Pink and coordinator of a model statewide campaign to move money from wars to human needs at BringOurWarDollarsHome.org.

Stop Deceptive Military Testing in Schools

By Pat Elder

The Armed Services Vocational Aptitude Battery (ASVAB) is the military's entrance exam that is given to fresh recruits to determine their aptitude for various military occupations. Soon after young men and women enlist in the U.S. military they are brought to the nearest Military Entrance Processing Station to take the ASVAB. Although it is somewhat similar to the SAT, the ASVAB also includes sections on Auto and Shop, Assembling Objects, and Mechanical Comprehension. The military relies on ASVAB results to place fresh recruits into Military Occupational Specialties, or jobs.

The test is also used as a recruiting tool in 12,000 high schools across the country. The 3 hour test is used by military recruiting services to gain sensitive, personal information on more than 660,000 high school students across the country every year, the vast majority of whom are under the age of 18. Students typically are given the test at school without parental knowledge or consent. The school-based ASVAB Career Exploration Program is among the military's most effective recruiting tools.

The Department of Defense promotes the ASVAB in high schools across the country without revealing its tie-in to the military or its primary function as a recruitment tool. School counselors and administrators encourage students to take the test that many claim assists students in matching their abilities with certain career paths. The US Army Recruiting Command's School Recruiting Program Handbook says the primary purpose of the ASVAB is to provide military recruiters "with a source of leads of high school juniors and seniors qualified through the ASVAB for enlistment into the Active Army and Army Reserve."

The military uses the four-hour exam to gather a treasure-trove of information to use in a sophisticated recruiting program. After the test is administered, military representatives typically meet with youth at school to discuss their scores and suggest career paths. Later, recruiters make calls to the students, using individualized profiles gathered from test data and other sources.

Let's be clear. The U.S. Military Entrance Processing Command collects information on American youth from a thousand sources today. The list is staggering. From electronic trolling of social websites to yearbook and ring companies — the military knows what's in Johnny's head, even if Johnny has a girlfriend and what she thinks of his decision regarding enlistment. The laptops of local recruiters are loaded with personal information. Before first contact, today's military recruiter knows our boy reads wrestling magazines, weighs 150, can bench press 230, drives a ten year-old Chevy truck, listens to "classic rock," and enjoys fly fishing. But the ASVAB opens the door to our boy's cognitive abilities, something recruiting services can't purchase or find on line. Our child's social, intellectual, and mechanical dimensions are merged to create a precise virtual portrait. It's an insidious game; a psychological mismatch. Advantage: Recruiter.

Federal and state laws strictly monitor the release of student information from the schools, but the military manages to circumvent these laws with the administration of the ASVAB. The Family Educational Rights Protection Act and the Elementary and Secondary Education Act both contain requirements for opt-out notifications in releases of student information. Parents are given the right to stop their child's personal information from being released to third parties, but there are no such requirements in the ASVAB student testing program. The Pentagon claims that ASVAB results do not constitute student information. Rather, they argue, The ASVAB is administered by military officials so the test materials are military records, not school records.

Aside from managing to evade the constraints of federal privacy laws, the military is also violating many state laws on student privacy when it administers the ASVAB in public high schools. Students taking the ASVAB are required to furnish their social security numbers for the tests to be processed, even though many state laws specifically forbid such information being released without parental consent. In addition, the ASVAB Answer Sheet requires under-aged students to sign a Privacy Statement, a practice that is also prohibited by many state laws. Department of Defense regulations, however, allow the test to be administered while precluding test results from reaching recruiters. Our collective experience across the country has revealed that few school administrators are aware of the option. Nationally, only 12% of all students tested during the 2009-2010 school year had their privacy protected.

U.S. Military Entrance Processing Command (USMEPCOM) Regulation 601-4 identifies several options schools have regarding the administration and release of ASVAB information. These options range from Option 1, which permits test results and other student information to be released to military recruiters without prior consent, to Option 8, the only one that prevents test results from being used for recruiting purposes. Inaction on the part of a school will cause USMEPCOM to automatically select Option 1. Students and parents may not determine which release option is used; therefore they cannot opt out of releasing the information individually.[150] Nationally, the selection of ASVAB Option 8 has climbed from less than 1% in 2005 (our estimate) to 4.4% in 2007 to 8.6% in 2009 to 12.2% in 2010.

Year	Schools	Students	Schools Mandatory	Students Mandatory	# Opt. 8	%Opt. 8
06-07	11,847	617,799	---	---	27,026	4.4
08-09	12,158	643,642	---	---	55,585	8.6
09-10	12,247	661,555	1,058	59,018	80,423	12.2

Source: United States Military Entrance Processing Command

Mandatory Testing

The data reveals the existence of mandatory testing in more than a thousand schools across the country, and although the invasion of student privacy associated with ASVAB testing in the high schools has been well documented by mainstream media sources, the practice of mandatory testing has never been covered. Consider this announcement from a high school in New York:

> *All Juniors will report to the cafeteria on Monday at 8:10 a.m. to take the ASVAB. Whether you're planning on college, a technical school, or you're just not sure yet, the ASVAB Career Exploration Program can provide you with important information about your skills, abilities and interests — and help put you on the right course for a satisfying career.*

This announcement or one very similar to it greets students in more than a thousand high schools across the country.[151]

The military prefers to test juniors because ASVAB scores are good for enlistment purposes for two years and because it's easier to corral a higher percentage of 11th graders to take the test. Imagine you're Captain Eric W. Johnson, United States Navy, Commander, United States Military Entrance Processing Command, Little Rock Arkansas and you had the complete cooperation of the Arkansas Department of Education to recruit high school students into the U.S. military. The first step you might take is to require juniors in public high schools to take the ASVAB. ASVAB results are good for enlistment purposes for up to two years. The ASVAB allows the state's top recruiter to pre-screen the entire crop of incoming potential recruits. "Sit down, shut up, and take this test. That's an order!"

142 high schools forced more than 10,000 children to take this military test without parental consent in Arkansas last year and all results were

shared with recruiting services. "We've always done it that way and no one has ever complained," explained one school counselor.

The Army recruiter's handbook calls for military recruiters to take ownership of schools and this is one way they're doing it. The U.S. Army Recruiting Command ranks each high school based on how receptive it is to military recruiters. Schools are awarded extra points when they make the ASVAB mandatory. Meanwhile, USMEPCOM regulation 601-4 specifically prohibits recruiters from imposing mandatory testing, "School and student participation in the Student Testing Program is voluntary. DOD personnel are prohibited from suggesting to school officials or any other influential individual or group that the test be made mandatory. Schools will be encouraged to recommend most students participate in the ASVAB CEP. If the school requires all students of a particular group or grade to test, the MEPS will support it." It's a pretty thin line and it appears the military has crossed it. How else can we explain the existence of 1,000 schools that require students to take the ASVAB?

Whose schools are they?

Examine the data on the website, http://studentprivacy.org listing the high schools in your state where the military is allowed to administer the ASVAB. You can double check the Pentagon's listing of schools where the ASVAB is mandatory. There are hundreds of schools that require testing in states across the country that are not identified as being mandatory in the USMEPCOM data. For instance, the information released by the DoD for the '09-'10 school year shows there is no mandatory testing in Ohio, however, it is possible, using a simple Google search, in this case -- ("k12.oh.us" asvab "all juniors"), to uncover hundreds of schools that require students to take the ASVAB that are not reported by the Pentagon. Simply substitute the abbreviation for your state. This contradictory evidence must be collected and disseminated to activists, policy makers, and local and national media outlets.

The ASVAB Campaign

Although the National Coalition to Protect Student Privacy is an organization formed in 2011, many of our members across the country have been working to educate school officials about the Pentagon's invasion of privacy associated with the ASVAB Career Exploration program since 2005. In that year activists began applying pressure on school officials in more than two dozen states urging them to .select Option 8 for students taking the ASVAB, thereby prohibiting the automatic release of test data to military recruiting services. The issue has steadily gained traction and has found a place on the agendas of civil rights and peace and justice organizations.

In the next few years, loosely coordinated campaigns helped to launch successful programs that resulted in hundreds of schools, as well as several of the nation's largest school districts, including those in Montgomery County, Maryland; New York City; San Diego; and Los Angeles to select Option 8 for all students taking the ASVAB. The L.A. Chapter of the National Lawyers Guild wrote a compelling legal brief that identified ASVAB testing in the schools as a civil rights issue. Campaign successes through 2008 attracted national media attention, particularly a story in the *Philadelphia Inquirer* that published a database acquired from the DoD through a Freedom of Information Act (FOIA) request.

Individuals affiliated with ASVAB campaigns in Hawaii, Maryland, and California set their sights on statewide initiatives to mandate the universal selection of Option 8. Hawaii's Department of Education implemented the nation's first statewide policy. Next, the California legislature passed an Option 8 measure in 2008, but it was vetoed by Gov. Arnold Schwarzenegger.

In 2010, a campaign directed by the Maryland Coalition to Protect Student Privacy resulted in Maryland becoming the first state to enact a law that prohibits the automatic release of student information to military recruiters gathered as a result of the administration of the ASVAB. The

NAACP, MD-PTA, ACLU-MD, Peace Action, and several privacy groups lobbied for the passage of the bill. The law requires that each public school that administers the ASVAB shall choose "Option 8" as the reporting option for military recruiter contact to prohibit the general release of any student information to military recruiters. Stories in several national media outlets, including *USA Today* and NPR Radio brought additional national attention.

The ASVAB Campaign of the National Coalition to Protect Student Privacy is not an anti-military operation. We acknowledge federal laws that guarantee military recruiters' access to public high school children. We're simply calling for the universal selection of ASVAB Option 8 for all students who participate in the high school ASVAB testing program. This may be achieved by administrative policy changes at the school, school district, or state level, or through the passage of laws similar to the one passed in Maryland.

Although Maryland's law sets the gold standard, the focus of The ASVAB Campaign is to educate the educators. The operation in Maryland taught activists the national initiative would have to be launched under the umbrella of student privacy rather than being associated with a "counter-recruitment" or "anti-military" campaign.

The debate in Maryland's General Assembly over the passage of the Option 8 legislation is best understood by examining the testimony of Lt. Col. Christopher Beveridge, Commander, 12th Battalion, U.S. Military Entrance Processing Command, the state's top military recruiter, and Ms. Merry Eisner, President of the Maryland Parent Teacher Association. Lt. Col. Beveridge opposed the universal selection of Option 8, arguing that the military, not parents, should ultimately decide on the release of student information gathered through the administration of the ASVAB. Ms. Eisner testified that parents should make these decisions. The legislation carried.

There is great potential here. The ASVAB Campaign has several components.

FOIA's

Colleagues affiliated with the coalition in Oregon have received a series of responses to FOIA requests pertaining to ASVAB testing over the last few years. This data is crucial in allowing us to track our progress. When presented with the data, school officials often have different numbers for mandatory testing, students tested, and their release options. As a result of our annual FOIA requests, we've received three separate years of data. Recently, the Pentagon has been resisting our FOIA requests. We relied on the help of Sen. Ron Wyden, (D-OR) in receiving last year's information. We're still waiting for the 2010-2011 school year data. FOIA results provide grist for the press release mill while much of this story still has not been told.

Outreach to Educational Professionals

Opening up a dialogue with local and state educational professionals is crucial. Typically, school administrators fail to select Option 8 because they don't realize the option exists. Thus, the thrust of this campaign is to inform educational policy makers. State superintendents of schools and members of state boards of education are being methodically approached.

Catholic Schools

The ASVAB is administered to more than 10,000 students in 200 Catholic high schools across the country, numbers roughly approximating the average state. 20.4% of the students in Catholic schools taking the ASVAB had Option 8 selected for them. There are at least 17 Catholic high schools that require students to take the ASVAB. A campaign enlisting the help of several Catholic groups is picking up momentum, and contact has recently been made with several bishops.

Documenting Abuses

The campaign collects and catalogs press reports of abuses and gathers the names of students and parents who feel they've been victimized by the ASVAB program and are willing to go on record. These accounts provide a human face to the campaign and are indispensible in dealing with the press.

We worked with students in North Carolina who went to school determined not to take the ASVAB and wound up in detention. We also coached their parents on how to deal with the media and how to bring about the cessation of mandatory testing and the selection of Option 8. We coached the students in Colorado who blew the whistle when the recruiter called them "f*ing faggots" while 500 were assembled to take the mandatory test. Amazingly, the press reports never addressed the injustice of forcing 500 students to take a military test without parental consent. We worked with a young woman and her mother who started the firestorm in Florida when they publicly objected to mandatory testing. We worked with the parents and students in Tennessee when military officers hijacked a school board meeting that was intended to discuss the privacy implications of ASVAB Testing. We organized students in Georgia to use FaceBook to resist mandatory testing. There are a hundred episodes that haven't appeared in the press. It seems there are two echelons of courage; one is the courage to resist; the other is to tell the world. See ASVAB in the News for more: http://www.studentprivacy.org/news.htm.

ASVAB As a Civil Rights Issue

An analysis of ASVAB testing in Maryland's schools reveals that the "Career Exploration Program" was practically nonexistent in any school in areas with median family incomes above $90,000 and there was a direct correlation between the numbers tested in a particular high school and deteriorated socio-economic conditions. Inner-city youth in Baltimore take the test; not the upper-middle class kids in Bethesda. This explains why the NAACP was a coalition partner and their leadership was eager to testify in Maryland's General Assembly.

ASVAB is Sexist

A recent study published in *Perspectives on Psychological Science* joins the chorus of leading academics to question the validity of the ASVAB as a predictor of career aptitudes, but the study also provides a compelling argument that the ASVAB has a built-in bias against women. Women perform poorly on a high number of ASVAB test items pertaining to mechanical skills because the questions measure a person's past experience, not their actual potential. Thus, women may be advised against choosing certain occupations because of socially-determined factors rather than a true assessment of their ability to learn and do well in them.

The ASVAB Campaign is directly responsible for the selection of Option 8 by several hundred schools and school systems. In the last year and a half we've been successful in attracting substantial national mainstream media attention, including stories in several dozen major dailies, *USA Today*, and NPR, as well as numerous radio talk programs. Perhaps more importantly, the issue has routinely appeared in widely circulated educational and legislative journals. Passing the law in Maryland was a watershed event.

You can stop it.

Visit http://studentprivacy.org and consider sending an email to your state's school officials requesting they select Option8 for children taking the ASVAB.

Pat Elder is the Executive Director of the National Coalition to Protect Student Privacy pelder@studentprivacy.org

Ready to Rumble for Jobs, Not War and More Weapons?

By Judith Le Blanc

Something is missing in the swirl of news reporting on the debt ceiling deal struck on August 2 by the Congress and the President for close to $1 trillion in cuts in discretionary programs over the next decade. Will the 58% of discretionary spending that goes to the Pentagon take a hit in the name of deficit reduction?[152]

The short answer is not necessarily, not unless we are ready to rumble. Even the Senate Armed Services Committee leaders Sens. Carl Levin and John McCain have no idea what the deal does to the Pentagon budget.[153] The cruel irony is the debt ceiling deal exempts spending on the wars in Afghanistan and Iraq, even though war costs are one of the biggest factors driving up the national debt by over a trillion dollars.[154]

Caps have been set for "security and non security" spending. The cuts will follow. The security category lumps together the Pentagon with the State Department, Veterans Affairs, Homeland Security, and nuclear weapons systems. Right now cuts to the Pentagon budget are not guaranteed. It is threat. Without a grassroots rumble the ax won't fall on the Pentagon or weapons of mass destruction, it will land on veteran's benefits or diplomatic efforts. It's a fight, not a discussion.

The military budget has doubled in the last 13 years. Up until now there has been a bottomless till for weapons and wars. Lawrence Korb, former assistant secretary of Defense under President Reagan, says, "in real or inflation adjusted dollars it is higher than at any time since World War II, including the Korean and Vietnam wars and the height of the Reagan buildup."

Secretary of Defense Leon Panetta released a statement stirring up fear about the threat of across the board cuts if the "sequester mechanism" took effect and the Committee of 12 Congressional representatives fail to reach a compromise on how to make the next $1.5 trillion in cuts.

He also said, "We must be accountable to the American people for what we spend, where we spend it, and with what result. While we have reasonable controls over much of our budgetary information, it is unacceptable to me that the Department of Defense cannot produce a financial statement that passes all financial audit standards."

That's our mandate to rumble. The Pentagon and the Congress must be made accountable to us for what they cut, spend, and the result. Pouring scarce resources into the Pentagon is not a jobs program.

Unemployment has become a constant. CNBC, the business news website, reported on August 2, "The job cuts were up 60 percent from June, and 59 percent higher than the 41,676 layoffs recorded in July 2010. It was the largest monthly total since March 2010, and the first month this year that the government was not the biggest job cutter."

Cuts in "non security" discretionary spending means layoffs. The 26 million people unemployed or underemployed in our communities can't afford for that to happen.

Nick Johnson of the Center on Budget and Policy Priorities notes that the deal "inevitably will lead to large federal cuts in programs for state and local governments," and that these cuts will begin "in the middle of the worst year for state budgets." State and local governments have eliminated more than 400,000 jobs since the start of 2010.

So let's rumble. Take the facts to our Congressional representatives. We can and must cut the Pentagon budget to fund jobs and services in our communities.

Although the National Commission on Fiscal Responsibility and Reform, the bipartisan commission chaired by former Senator Alan Simpson and Erskine Bowles, did not have many recommendations to cheer about, it got one thing right. Cutting military spending is possible.

They proposed closing one third of U.S. bases around the world as an immediate savings. Not only is it a wise budget cut, it fits with how U.S. foreign policy needs to change in the 21st century. We can't afford a militarized foreign policy of endless wars and occupations and the modernizing of nuclear weapons systems.

In The Hill, Tom Colina, the research director at Arms Control Association wrote, "By carefully reducing our nuclear forces and scaling back new weapon systems, the United States can save billions. Moreover, by reducing the incentive for Russia to rebuild its arsenal, these budget savings can make America safer."

In June, 2010,the bi-partisan Sustainable Defense Task Force initiated by Rep. Barney Frank (D-MA), working in cooperation with Rep. Walter B. Jones (R-NC), Rep. Ron Paul (R-TX), and Sen. Ron Wyden (D-OR), proposed ways to cut Pentagon spending in their report "Debt, Deficits and Defense: A Way Forward." It can be done if the political will is mustered.

That's where the peace and economic justice movements come in: generating the political will.

Alongside of the misery of the budget cuts, there is an opportunity to win real cuts in military spending. Joel Rubin in *Ploughshares Blog* wrote, "There is still much to be defined, yet the inherently competitive situation now shaping up on defense spending is welcome news to those who have been long seeking to get rid of the bloated weapons systems that weaken our economy while doing scant little to advance our national security."

The President said in April when he announced his framework for dealing with the federal budget that "we're going to have to conduct a fundamental review of America's missions, capabilities, and our role in a changing world."

New movements are taking the opportunity for such a fundamental review and a change in the spending priorities. On August 4th, the AFL-CIO issued a statement, "Fake Political Crisis and Real Economic Crisis — A Call for Leadership and Action." The AFL-CIO Executive Council said, "It doesn't have to be this way. There are real solutions to the job crisis, but real solutions require government action."

They also noted, "There is no way to fund what we must do as a nation without bringing our troops home from Iraq and Afghanistan. The militarization of our foreign policy has proven to be a costly mistake. It is time to invest at home."

It's going to take a an adamant, militant grassroots rumble to demand demilitarization of U.S. foreign policy, to end the insanity of endless and countless wars draining the scarce resources needed for people, the world over, to have jobs and a decent life.

Judith Le Blanc is the Field Director for Peace Action.

Political Passivity, Anti-Authoritarianism, and Building a Base

By Bruce Levine

I want to begin by explaining how a clinical psychologist ends up giving the final talk at a conference on the military-industrial complex. Actually, for many years now, I've been writing and speaking about — and fighting against — another industrial complex, the pharmaceutical-industrial complex, specifically the psycho-pharmaceutical-industrial complex.

All these industrial complexes are painful similar in their revolving doors of employment. So, for example, the National Institute of Mental Health (NIMH) is the leading government agency on mental health and funds research. People at the NIMH who have has been friendly to drug companies have been rewarded by drug companies with a high-paying job after they leave NIMH. And just about every influential mental health institution takes money from drug companies. The National Alliance for the Mentally Ill, a consumer group, takes millions of dollars from drug companies, and so does the American Psychiatric Association, which is the professional organization of America's psychiatrists.

The American Psychiatric Association publishes the official diagnostic manual for the mental health profession. It's called the DSM. They're up to the DSM-4 revision, and they're working on the DSM-5. Each revision gets larger and larger. When I was watching Eugene Jarecki's documentary about the military-industrial complex, *Why We Fight*, I remember Chalmers Johnson saying, "I guarantee you when war becomes that profitable, you are going to see more of it." Same is true in my profession. The more profitable mental illness has become, the more you are seeing of it.

So, lots of my activism really starts with embarrassment with my own profession. One of the things that I became initially embarrassed by was its pathologizing and medicating normal human behavior in order to make a buck. They turned shyness into "avoidant personality disorder," and turned temper tantrums of three-year olds into "pediatric bipolar disorder" and now give three-year olds heavy-duty antipsychotic drugs. What has especially troubled me has been the increasing pathologizing of stubbornness, resistance, rebellion, and anti-authoritarianism, especially in children and teenagers.

There are several subtle examples of this kind of pathologizing of rebellion, but the most obvious one is something called "oppositional defiant disorder" (ODD), which when it first appeared in the DSM-3, I told my colleagues that this must be a joke. Symptoms of ODD include "often actively defies or refuses to comply with adult requests or rules" and "often argues with adults." I have spent a great deal of time with these previously labeled ODD kids. While some of them may be a "handful" for their parents, many are the hope of the nation. I tell my colleagues, "Don't you realize that damn near every well-known activist in American history — from Tom Paine, to Emma Goldman, to Malcolm X, to Saul Alinsky — would have been diagnosed with ODD. And sadly, increasing numbers of these kids are being medicated, often on heavily tranquilizing antipsychotic drugs, and this is especially true for more impoverished kids on Medicaid. That's one reason why the antipsychotic industry is now the largest grossing class of all drugs in the United States.

So, I became very much concerned that my profession had become one more spoke in the wheel that is politically pacifying Americans. There are other spokes that I will also talk about. When I talk about these pacifying forces, it's not to depress us but so that we recognize that there are multiple "democracy battlefields" — not just national elections and demonstrations — to fight each day and to get back our strength.

Another step in getting me to this conference was my working on individual depression, which was once called melancholia. Depression results from our attempt to shut down overwhelming pain, which causes us to shut ourselves down, often to a point of immobilization. So, why is it that there has been a tenfold increase in depression in the United States in the last 50 years? Why is it that 10 percent of Americans are now on antidepressants? Why is it that the World Health Organization is predicting that depression will become the world's second leading illness by 2020. It seems obvious that there are major cultural, societal, economic, and political transformations that are making us more depressed. This epidemic of depression is not exactly being caused by Al Qaeda sucking the serotonin out of us.

It doesn't take that much in America to get labeled a "dissident psychologist." You just heard what it takes.

The major step in getting me closer to this conference, however, came at the end of 2009. For the previous decade, I had been watching increasing American politically passivity that paralleled increasing American individual depression and immobilization. I found it remarkable that in the face of senseless wars and a loss of liberties and economic and social injustice that — compared to other periods of American history and compared to many other nations today — there was so little political resistance in the United States.

The area of "disputed presidential elections" got me thinking in 2009. In 2009 in Iran, in response to their disputed presidential election, despite hearing that they would be shot at — and some were killed — two to three million Iranians hit the streets of Tehran. Same thing in Mexico when their more progressive guy lost in their disputed presidential election of 2006 — millions hit the streets of Mexico City, some surrounding foreign-owned banks. And in the Ukraine in 2004, when their more progressive guy lost in a disputed presidential election, not only did millions demonstrate, there were general strikes that basically closed down the county; their "Orange Revolution" forced the Ukraine's Supreme Court to call for new elections, and ultimately this Orange Revolution succeeded in righting an election wrong.

But then take a look at the response to U.S. disputed presidential elections. There was relatively little resistance to the 2004 disputed election, but the one that I really thought about was our response to the disputed 2000 presidential election, the one where Al Gore, undisputedly, received a half million more votes than George W. Bush. Now, I'm not this big fan of Al Gore, but more than 50 million people voted for him. You probably remember that there was a major dispute over the Florida vote, and so a recount was ordered, but the U.S. Supreme Court overturned the Florida Supreme Court and basically handed the election over to Bush in December. One of the dissenting U.S. Supreme Court Justices, John Paul Stevens, by no means a radical — he was appointed by Gerald Ford — was so disgusted with his fellow Supreme Court Justices that he said, "Although we may never know with complete certainty the identity of the winner of this year's presidential election, the identity of the loser is perfectly clear. It is the nation's confidence in the judge as an impartial guardian of the rule of law." This was widely reported. So what was the American response? Well, a handful demonstrated outside the Supreme Court, and a month later at Bush's inauguration there were maybe 50,000 people angry with Bush, but there was never any real public battle to dispute this election. And I remember thinking that if I were Bush or Cheney, the lesson that I would have learned was, "We can get away with just about anything," and that seems to be the lesson that they learned.

Americans' response to these ongoing wars is also remarkable. What's remarkable to me is that as these wars in Afghanistan and Iraq have become more *unpopular* in the polls, there has been less resistance than when these wars were more popular.

So, in late September 2001, when over 80 percent of Americans favored going into Afghanistan — as they believed that this was just about getting Bin Laden and those responsible for the World Trade Center and other attacks — 20,000 Americans in Washington, D.C., still protested against our imminent invasion.

And I'm sure many of you remember the major protests in February 2003 against the then imminent invasion of Iraq. Even though a slight majority of American favored the war in the polls — believing the government propaganda about WMDs and other lies — 500,000 showed up in New York City to protest. And there were other major demonstrations all over the United States. I should say that there were even larger protests in Europe, with the largest protest of any kind in London's history, and millions more protested in Spain, Italy and other parts of Europe. But the remarkable thing is that as these wars have gotten more *unpopular* in the polls — with now, depending on the poll question, at least 60 to 65 percent of Americans opposing these wars — there has been diminished resistance.

And there are several other areas — from the Wall Street bailout, to other corporate welfare, to health care — where the majority of Americans clearly oppose the policy of the corporate-controlled government, but there has been relatively little resistance.

So, in late 2009, I decided to write some articles about this issue of American political passivity in places that would publish me — certainly not the *New York Times*. I get published in *AlterNet*, *Z Magazine*, *CounterPunch*, *Truthout*, sort of anti-authoritarian left places. I wanted to see if other Americans also thought that this passivity was remarkable. In these articles, I talked about some of the psychological reasons. For example, the idea of learned helplessness in our presidential elections, in which no matter which party wins, we still get senseless wars and corporate control. And I also talked about the abuse syndrome. I've been working with abused people for over 25 years, and when you eat too much crap — physical, emotional abuse — for too long, you can grow weak. I talked about some of the societal and cultural reasons for this passivity, and began to talk about some of the solutions.

I received an overwhelming response to those pieces, more than I had ever received before in terms of comments, emails, response articles, and media requests from people across the political spectrum. David Swanson wrote an excellent response piece that was helpful, and I incorporated some of his ideas in *Get Up, Stand Up*. I also received several media requests from the libertarian anti-war world. Now, there is a big difference between these people and those bigoted-militarist Tea Partiers. Many of these libertarian anti-war folks like me. I'm not exactly sure why. I think it's because they are happy that somebody writing in these left publications is comfortable with anger and is talking about this issue of passivity. And so, I am able to have enough glue with them so that we can actually have a dialogue and discuss issues that we disagree on, such as healthcare.

Because of this huge response, and because I really felt that I only had touched on some of the reasons for this political passivity, and mostly because I wanted to talk about solutions, I decided to write a book. So I spent a good deal of 2010 researching and writing it.

One area I wanted to research was the history of democratic movements, especially American democratic movements, not just to examine their strategies and tactics but to take a look at the psyche of these movements. In that kind of research, it doesn't take long to come across the work of

Lawrence Goodwyn, a journalist who became a historian and one of the foremost scholars on democratic movements. Goodwyn wrote a book about Solidarity in Poland, but he is most famous for his work on America's Populist Movement, which was the agrarian revolt in the 1880s and 1890s against the crop lien system and the moneyed elite of that era — the railroads, the banks, the exploitative merchants, and so on — in which the farmers were losing their farms because they owed more than they could make farming. In *Get Up, Stand Up*, I talk about the great lessons to be leaned from these Populists in terms of strategies and tactics. But for now, I just want to stick to something else that Goodwyn talked about.

Goodwyn observed from his study of democratic movements that successful or near successful ones had two important psychological and cultural building blocks — "individual self-respect" and "collective self-confidence." Individual self-respect means that one believes that one is worthy of power and one does not accept a role of being a subject of power. One does not accept "one's place in the bequeathed social hierarchy." Those farmers in the Populist movement rejected the idea that because they didn't have much money or much schooling that they were not entitled to their fair share of power. Collective self-confidence simply means that a group believes that it can win, that it can succeed in overcoming oppression and exploitation. It was clear to me that these are two important building blocks that had been lost in America, and that we had to recover them in order to create democratic movements.

There are other important cultural and psychological building blocks that are unquantifiable but vital for every democratic movement. These include *courage, guts, determination,* and *solidarity.*

Another important element of democratic movements that I want to spend a little time on is *anti-authoritarianism. Authoritarianism* is simply the unquestioning obedience to authority. Anti-authoritarians assess whether authorities are legitimate or illegitimate. Does that authority know what they are talking about or not? Does the authority lie or tell the truth? Does that authority actually care about those who are taking their authority seriously, or is that authority on some financial or ego trip? If one judges that authority to be illegitimate, then anti-authoritarians challenge and resist it.

Anti-authoritarianism is not only intellectually vital for democracy, it is emotionally vital for democratic movements as it creates enormous energy. That is why an authoritarian society tries to crush it.

A person I think about here is Tom Paine. Paine, a working-class guy, was different from many of the elitist aristocratic founding fathers. When Paine came to America in 1774 he was intoxicated by the colonials' anti-authoritarianism. Paine assessed correctly that many of these colonials were actually way ahead in terms of their anti-authoritarianism than many of these future "founding fathers" who were mostly just speaking out against the British Parliament's "taxation without representation." George Washington was still toasting King George in 1775. But Paine viewed the entire British authority — Parliament, the monarchy, the British East India Company — as illegitimate, and he voiced the then taboo word of *independence*. His pamphlet *Common Sense*, which was published in January of 1776, was ultimately read by an estimated 500,000 out of 3 million colonials, which is the equivalent of over 50 million Americans today. And so Jefferson knew he had a pretty big market share for the *Declaration of Independence*, which came out about 6 months later.

Beyond emotionally energizing us, anti-authoritarianism also does something else. It helps create those strong bonds of solidarity. Specifically, when one actively, in the flesh, supports others who are challenging and resisting illegitimate authority, that's how we get those strong bonds of solidarity, which are hugely necessary when authorities strike back, which they always do.

So, I am very much interested in those institutional, societal, and cultural forces that are reducing our anti-authoritarianism, individual self-respect, collective self-confidence, courage, determination, and solidarity, and increasing our fear. There are many spokes in this problematic wheel. I talk about them not so as to depress us, but for us to gain awareness that there are many "democracy battlefields" going on each and every day.

(Audience member shouts out, "TSA"). Yes, okay, you want to start with surveillance. That's important. Surveillance, or more specifically the fear of surveillance, has pacified many of us. You might guess that lots of the libertarian anti-war world rails a great deal about surveillance, but they usually only talk about government surveillance. While government surveillance is a reality for many of the activists at this conference, a more pervasive kind of surveillance for more Americans that also creates fear is workplace surveillance, with cameras in warehouses and managers checking out people's company computers. Libertarians are not exactly pro-labor union folks, but when I talk to them about the decimation of labor unions — another spoke in the American political passivity wheel — in the context that unions are the *only* protection against workplace surveillance, some working-people libertarians are more open to the idea that union decimation is problematic for the cause of freedom and democracy. And so this becomes another way to open up a dialogue to create solidarity.

Another area that weakens democratic movements is social isolation, caused by our suburbanized-television-car-consumer culture that sociologist Robert Putnam talks about in *Bowling Alone*. 25 percent of Americans do not have a single confidant in their lives, and this is up from 10 percent just 25 years ago. And so of course this isolation creates more fear and reduces our chances for solidarity.

There are several other spokes in the wheel that break our spirit of resistance that I talk about in *Get Up, Stand Up*. There are many aspects of our society and our institutions that create fear, as fear breaks people's spirit of resistance. So, there are democracy battlefields in many areas of our lives.

A special area of concern of mine are those spokes that affect young people. So, while many older activists lament the lack of young people in the anti-war and other democracy movements, I am impressed that there are any young people involved at all, because our society has thrown a great deal of impediments against young people resisting. It is so much harder for young people today to resist than it was in my generation.

One big thing is the student-loan debt issue. Debt creates enormous fear which kills resistance. If I had the kind of debt that most young people have today, it would have dampened my desire to speak our and fight against injustices and lies. When I was going to college, if you were working class like I was, there were great public universities and colleges in which you could get a B.A. and even graduate degrees either free or for very low cost. I went to Queens College at the City University of New York for free, and later for free at the University of Cincinnati to get my Ph.D. It was easy to graduate with all kinds of degrees without debt. This is still the case in much of the rest of the world. And in the recent Arab spring, while there was huge unemployment in Egypt, those young people didn't have student debt, as universities are free throughout the Arab world. And higher education is either free or very close in much of the rest of the world. And so I talk a lot about it in my book about the political actions as well as the individual and family ways of reducing and eliminating this debt. This is important to reduce fear, and to create strength and build a larger base.

Also, standard schooling has always been a problematic spoke in the wheel. Despite well-meaning teachers, institutions often care more about obedience than creating an education for democracy — the kind of education which inspires curiosity, a love of independent learning and reading, critical thinking and questioning authority.

However, the problems of authoritarian schooling have gotten much worse, thanks to another Democratic-Republican bipartisanship. Watch out when those guys get together, as you get senseless wars, Wall Street bailouts, and other corporate welfare. You also get bipartisan education policies such as "No Child Left Behind" and "Race to the Top," which are essentially about standardized testing tyranny. Administrators, teachers, parents, and students live in fear of these corporate-created standardized tests. And of course fear kills curiosity, love of learning, and critical thinking, and fear kills the kind of education you need for democracy.

The good news is that as a society and its institutions become more authoritarian, many ordinary nonpolitical folks get radicalized. An example of that in American history is the Fugitive Slave Act, which made lots of regular abolitionist folk into lawbreakers, and then made them question and challenge many other things. So, I see this kind of thing with many teachers I talk with. Before, they never really seriously challenged the authoritarian aspects of standardized schools, but when this standardized-testing tyranny made their classrooms so miserable, some of those 3 million teachers have started becoming more politicized, speaking out publicly against this stuff. Some teachers are even going into their classroom and telling their students that they aren't getting educated for democracy, that what they are receiving by incessant test preparation is only making these test-producing corporations richer.

And as I mentioned before, my mental health profession is also a major spoke in the wheel, especially for young people. There are about one million of us mental health professionals — psychologists, social workers, psychiatrists, counselors, paraprofessionals — who see over 20 percent of U.S. kids. And I can tell you, from over 25 years of private practice, that those kids are not being dragged into shrinks' offices for being excessively compliant and conformist. No, most of those kids are disrupting something, sometimes selfishly, but often these kids have a passion for justice and feel that there is some family or school or other injustice going on, and they are reacting in the only ways they know how.

In the 1950s, the left-humanist psychoanalyst Erich Fromm was already speaking about his concern that the mental health profession was going to be used to help people adapt and adjust to society, regardless of how dehumanizing, anti-democratic, and authoritarian that society had become. And this is now clearly the case. This is especially obvious today as mental health professionals are used to help soldiers adapt and adjust to senseless wars, including giving them drugs to numb them, nowadays even in battle zones.

So, in response to what mainstream mental health has become, I have been talking to my colleagues and to the general public about another kind of psychology, what I call a "liberation psychology." I thought I had invented this term, but I quickly realized that somebody else years before me had popularized it, and he certainly deserves all the credit. That person was the El Salvadoran social psychologist and priest Ignacio Martin-Baró. Martin-Baró should certainly be given credit for popularizing the term *liberation psychology*, as he lost his life because of his liberation psychology, liberation theology, and activism for the people of El Salvador. In 1989, Martin-Baró, together with several others, was assassinated by a U.S.-trained El Salvadoran death squad.

Along with Martin-Baró, many other social scientists in Central America, South America, Africa, and the Caribbean have understood that when people become subjugated and externally depressed for too long, they develop an internal oppression, a defeatism, a fatalism, a helplessness, a demoralization, and a hopelessness. Bob Marley — the poet laureate of oppressed people around the world — called it "mental slavery," and he sang about emancipating yourself from mental slavery.

This phenomenon of subjugation resulting in demoralization and defeatism has also now happened in the United States, but it is more difficult for many Americans to see it, as our oppressors are not obvious tyrants such as a Pinochet or a Mubarak but instead are the more impersonal corporate state, the corporatocracy, or what George Carlin called, "the owners of this country." We must first acknowledge the reality that for millions of Americans, subjugation has in fact resulted in demoralization and fatalism. Then, we can begin to liberate ourselves from what I call "corporatocracy abuse" and "battered people's syndrome."

There are actually parallels to other abuse syndromes in terms of how one helps oneself and each other recover from corporatocracy abuse and battered people's syndrome. It's about getting people to let go of their fear and gain their strength back. It is certainly about coming out of denial that one is being abused. That means letting go of the shame that comes from being a victim, and this means forgiving oneself, especially for believing the lies of the abuser.

We also need to forgive one another for continuing to buy into crap. We need to remember that all abusers — whether it is a spouse abuser or Dick Cheney — are liars. Even if the liar is not brilliant, if they are practicing lying all the time, which is what abusers do, they become very proficient at it. And so there is no great shame in having bought into some of their lies.

Another aspect of liberation psychology that I think about a great deal is how we can create greater solidarity among people. The polls show that the vast majority of Americans oppose these senseless wars and corporate welfare, but most are not battling against it. So, I want to talk about some ways that we can go back to our community and help expand the base.

What tyrants and dictators have always done is use the "divide-and-conquer" strategy on the rest of us. Historically in the United States, they have tried to divide us racially and ethnically, and they have used religion as well. The tactic that they are using a great deal lately is to try to divide us among union workers versus nonunion workers. So, it's always important to be aware of this and confront this.

However, even more empowering is seeing how we divide ourselves, which we can change. I want to talk about a couple ways we do this, so that when we leave this conference and go back into our communities, we can unite rather than divide, and build a larger base. There are several areas in which we divide ourselves, but I want to talk about two important ones.

One divide among us is what I call the divide between the "comfortable anti-authoritarians" and the "afflicted anti-authoritarians." I don't use the term comfortable anti-authoritarians pejoratively. The reality is that some of us who are critically thinking anti-authoritarians are in a lot less pain than others. Some of us may be lucky enough to have a few bucks in the bank or have a decent paying job, maybe a prof job or we may have a decent pension. And pain is reduced by other things, such as work that feels meaningful. Pain is also reduced by having social support. And pain is also reduced by having a public platform in which one feels through one's books, articles, talks and so on that one is having an impact.

The vast majority of anti-authoritarians in America are in the afflicted zone. They oppose these senseless wars and corporate welfare. They are on our side, but they are often politically passive. They are overwhelmed by the pain of their lives. The pain of severe money problem. The pain of unemployment, watching foreclosure and bankruptcy closing in on them. The pain of holding on to a meaningless job just for health insurance. The pain of alienation and isolation. The pain of nobody giving a damn about what they have to say.

In my life, like many of you, I've traveled across this afflicted-comfortable continuum, though not at the extremes of either. There is a very different psychology that people have depending on where they are on this continuum. So, if you are in the afflicted zone, much of what you are trying to do each day is to keep the pain of your life from overwhelming you. That might mean drinking a few more beers than you should or watching too much stupid television. You are often looking for anything to take the edge off of your pain so that you can function at all.

When you are in that afflicted zone, and people come at you with all the truths of how you are getting victimized and what you have to do, that can feel like just more pain. It can feel like a painful lecture or a scolding. It can even feel shaming. So, what do the afflicted do? They walk away. It is a turnoff. People say, "I don't need that." These lectures can also create resentment, as it feels like an assumption that one's political passivity has to do with ignorance and laziness, and not overwhelming pain. And so these kind of lectures can be divisive. So, if we want to expand the base, we have to realize that we have to try to reduce the afflicted's pain. If we don't do it, some demagogue will come along and exploit their pain.

One of the great examples of a non-demagogic way of reducing the afflicted's pain — a way that helped create a huge democratic movement — was what the Populists did. They created the first large-scale working people's cooperatives that helped farmers get a better price for their crops and so reduced their financial pains. GI coffeehouses that Jonathan spoke about are another great way to reduce people's people, as free coffee and some fun socializing can be a great pain reducer. At the very least, we need to offer respect and empathy, as that helps reduce the pain. And by respecting and not exploiting people's pain, we draw people to democratic movements and build a base.

Another divide that is close to my heart is around hope. Now this divide is not only among us, but it is also internal, within many of us. That's the case with myself, as I sometimes move into hopelessness. I personally don't know any Pollyannaish critically-thinking antiauthoritarians. The divide around hope is more between those who are completely hopeless and believe that there is no chance in hell we can eliminate something as huge and powerful as the military-industrial complex versus those who do have some hope and think that there is at least one chance in hell that we can succeed.

So, as we go back into our community, we might want to think about how we can approach the hopelessness of critically-thinking anti-authoritarians in a way that doesn't insult theirs — or our own — intelligence.

One thing that is helpful for me is my work with depressed people. Research tells us that people who are more critically thinking are more susceptible to depression. In the late 1970s, there were a bunch of studies where people were given rigged games in which they had no power over winning. Those who were more astute in assessing the truth of their powerlessness — the more critically thinking subjects — were those who were more likely to be depressed. And so like every trait, critically-thinking is a double-edged sword. I think this is relevant to political passivity, in that many people who see the enormity of the military-industrial complex and other industrial-complexes' power over us can move into defeatism. And so they become part of a self-fulfilling prophesy.

One of the things I often need to tell myself and which I talk about with critically-thinking anti-authoritarians who move into hopelessness is, "While you may in fact be better able than many other people to see ugly truths, you cannot, if you are human, see *everything*." In other words, critical thinkers must learn to have critical thinking about their own critical thinking, and have some humility.

One example that is interesting for me is Abraham Lincoln, who many historians consider our most critically-thinking president, certainly one of the best writers. What most Americans don't know is that Lincoln was a major depressive. When he was a young man, he became so depressed that his friends twice had to form suicide watches over him. In the 1850s in the United States, the major battle was not so much over abolishing slavery as stopping the spread of slavery. In 1856, Lincoln, who fought politically to stop the spread of slavery, wrote this pessimistic economic analysis of how the South had far more to gain by spreading slavery than the North had to gain by stopping the spread of slavery. As critically thinking as Lincoln was, he could not possible have foreseen that he — with his checkered political career in which he lost more than he won — would become the presidential nominee of this upstart third party called the Republican Party; and that in a three-way race and with less than the majority of votes that he would win the presidency; and that this would so piss off the South that — even though Lincoln did not campaign on abolishing slavery — most of the southern states would secede; and that a bunch of boys in South Carolina would get so incensed that they world fire on a federal fort, Fort Sumter; and other events would follow, so that ultimately within less than decade of his pessimistic analysis of how it would be difficult to stop the spread of slavery, slavery would be abolished. So, critical thinkers need to keep in mind that while they may see more than others, they don't see everything.

There are lots of other examples of this kind of thing in history, even in recent times. One recent example is of course the Arab spring, as lots of critical thinkers who I've talked with from that part of the world are amazed at what happened in Egypt.

I saw evidence of this kind of thing when I was younger. Even up until shortly before it occurred, the collapse of the Soviet empire seemed an impossibility to most Americans, who saw only mass resignation within the Soviet Union and its sphere of control. But the shipyard workers in Gdansk, Poland, did not see their Soviet and Communist Party rulers as the all-powerful forces that Americans did. And so Polish workers'

Solidarity, by simply refusing to go away, provided a strong dose of morale across Eastern Europe at the same time other historical events weakened the Soviet empire — such as their own stupid Afghanistan war — and then the Soviet Union just collapsed.

So, there are lots of examples from history that challenge the hopelessness and fatalism of critically thinking people and compel them to rethink whether they are actually seeing all the possibilities. One lesson from history is that tyrannical and dehumanizing institutions are often more fragile than they appear, and with time, luck, morale, and the people's ability to seize the moment, damn near anything is possible.

Going back to our communities, it is important to emotionally validate people's feelings of hopelessness — that feeling is a legitimate one, and you will simply turn people off by invalidating their feelings. But it is possible to validate that feeling while at the same time challenging the wisdom of inactions based on hopelessness, and to challenge it in a way that doesn't insult the intelligence of critical thinkers.

History tells us that empires ultimately fall, and I think it is pretty safe to say that the U.S. military-industrial complex will also one day fall. It may be transformed by our own efforts or, perhaps more likely, it will fall under the weight of its own stupidity.

However, in order to either transform undemocratic institutions or to have what it takes to create and maintain a democratic society after that undemocratic institution falls under the weight of its own stupidity, we must be working each day on all those democracy battlefields to regain our anti-authoritarianism, individual self-respect, collective self-confidence, courage, determination, and solidarity.

Thank you.

Bruce Levine is a clinical psychologist in private practice in Cincinnati, Ohio. He has been in practice for more than two decades. Levine's most recent book is *Get Up, Stand Up: Uniting Populists, Energizing the Defeated, and Battling the Corporate Elite.*

VI. SING

When Bradley Comes Marching Home

By John Heuer

with Stu Hutchison, Wally Myers, and Pete Seeger

For Bradley Manning

When Bradley comes marching home again Hurroo, hurroo

When Bradley comes marching home again Hurroo, hurroo

We'll charge the war makers with their crimes

Put 'em in the dock, make them pay for those crimes

When the peace is won and Bradley comes marching home

For Molly Ivins

When Molly comes marching home again Hurrah, hurrah

When Molly comes marching home again Hurrah, Hurrah

We'll win the peace, just you see

The world will have a chance to be free

When the peace is won and Molly comes marching home

For Dr. King

When Martin comes marching home again Hurray, Hurray

When Martin comes marching home again Hurray, Hurray

We'll put our conscience to the test

And lay the war machine to rest

When the peace is won and Martin comes marching home

When Bradley comes marching home again Hurray, Hurray

When Bradley comes marching home again Hurray, Hurray

We'll start with a truce, don't you see

No more war, that's the key

When the peace is won and Bradley comes marching home

John Heuer is a member of the Eisenhower Chapter of Veterans for Peace and serves as chair of North Carolina Peace Action. He lives in Chapel Hill and can be reached at heu93@aol.com.

Appendix: Sample Resolution

CALLING ON CONGRESS TO REDIRECT MILITARY SPENDING TO DOMESTIC PRIORITIES

WHEREAS, the severity of the ongoing economic crisis has created budget shortfalls at all levels of government and requires us to re-examine our national spending priorities; and

WHEREAS, every dollar spent on the military produces fewer jobs than spending the same dollar on education, healthcare, clean energy, or even tax cuts for household consumption[*]; and

WHEREAS, U.S. military spending has approximately doubled in the past decade, in real dollars and as a percentage of federal discretionary spending;

WHEREAS, well over half of federal discretionary spending is now spent on the military [**];

WHEREAS, we are spending more money on the military now than during the Cold War, the Vietnam War, or the Korean War;

WHEREAS, the U.S. military budget could be cut by 80% and remain the largest in the world;

WHEREAS, President Dwight David Eisenhower warned us 50 years ago that "In the councils of government, we must guard against the acquisition of unwarranted influence, whether sought or unsought, by the military-industrial complex. The potential for the disastrous rise of misplaced power exists and will persist";

WHEREAS, the National Commission on Fiscal Responsibility and Reform proposed in both its Co-Chairs' proposal in November 2010 and its final report in December 2010 major reductions in military spending[***];

WHEREAS, the U.S. Conference of Mayors passed in June 2011 a resolution calling on Congress to redirect spending to domestic priorities;

WHEREAS, the people of the United States favor redirecting spending to domestic priorities[****];

WHEREAS, the people of the United States in numerous opinion polls favor withdrawing the U.S. military from Afghanistan;

WHEREAS, the United States has armed forces stationed at approximately 1,000 foreign bases in approximately 150 foreign countries;

WHEREAS, the United States is the wealthiest nation on earth but trails many other nations in life expectancy, infant mortality, education level, housing, and environmental sustainability, as well as in non-military aid to foreign nations;

NOW, THEREFORE, BE IT RESOLVED, that [**your club, organization, town, city, county, or state**] calls on the U.S. Congress to end foreign ground and drone wars and reduce base military spending, in order to meet vital human needs, promote job creation, re-train and re-employ those losing jobs in the process of conversion to non-military industries, rebuild our infrastructure, aid municipal and state governments, and develop a new economy based upon renewable, sustainable energy.

* See "The U.S. Employment Effects Of Military And Domestic Spending Priorities: An Updated Analysis," by Robert Pollin & Heidi Garrett-Peltier, Political Economy Research Institute, University of Massachusetts, Amherst, October 2009, http://www.peri.umass.edu/fileadmin/pdf/published_study/spending_priorities_PERI.pdf.

** See "People's Guide to the Federal Budget," by the National Priorities Project, http://nationalpriorities.org/resources/federal-budget-101/peoples-guide/#spending.

*** See http://www.fiscalcommission.gov.

**** See "American Public Shows How It Would Cut the Budget Deficit," by World Public Opinion, February 3, 2011, http://www.worldpublicopinion.org/incl/printable_version.php?pnt=677.

Notes

1.   Dwight Eisenhower, Farewell Address, 1961. Video accessed November 28, 2011, http://www.youtube.com/watch?v=5pWAGgLSCSQ.

2.   Thomas Jefferson, Letter to Henry Lee, August 10, 1824.

3.   Thomas Jefferson, Letter to Joseph Cabell, February 2, 1816.

4.   Thomas Jefferson, Letter to Nathaniel Macon, 1821.

5.   Thomas Jefferson, Letter to William Johnson, June 19, 1823.

6.   Thomas Jefferson, Letter to John Taylor, May 23, 1816.

7.   Thomas Jefferson, Letter to Nathaniel Macon, January 12, 1819.

8.   Martin Luther King, Jr., Nobel Lecture, December 11, 1964.

9.   Martin Luther King, Jr., "Beyond Vietnam: A Time to Break Silence," April 4, 1967. Video accessed November 28, 2011, http://youtube.com/watch?v=Q5VhCvrEcPY.

10.   Thomas Jefferson, Letter to John Taylor, May 28, 1816.

11.   Thomas Jefferson, Sixth Annual Message to Congress, December 2, 1806.

12.   Dwight Eisenhower, Speech in Ottawa, January 10, 1946.

13.   Dwight Eisenhower, "The Chance for Peace," speech given to the American Society of Newspaper Editors, April 16, 1953.

14.   Martin Luther King, Jr., "Beyond Vietnam: A Time to Break Silence," April 4, 1967. Video accessed November 28, 2011, http://youtube.com/watch?v=Q5VhCvrEcPY.

15.   Thomas Jefferson, Letter to William Short, November 28, 1814.

16.   Martin Luther King, Jr., Nobel Lecture, December 11, 1964.

17.   Dwight Eisenhower, "The Chance for Peace," speech given to the American Society of Newspaper Editors, April 16, 1953.

18.   *Ibid.*

19.   Martin Luther King, Jr., Nobel Lecture, December 11, 1964.

20.   Martin Luther King, Jr., Farewell Statement for All India Radio, March 9, 1959.

21.   Thomas Jefferson, Letter to John Gassway, February 17, 1809.

22.   Thomas Jefferson, "Declaration of Independence," July 4, 1776.

23.   Martin Luther King, Jr., "Beyond Vietnam: A Time to Break Silence," April 4, 1967. Video accessed November 28, 2011, http://youtube.com/watch?v=Q5VhCvrEcPY.

24.   Dwight Eisenhower, "The Chance for Peace," speech given to the American Society of Newspaper Editors, April 16, 1953.

25. Dwight Eisenhower, Speech in Ottawa, January 10, 1946.

26. Thomas Jefferson, Letter to Samuel Kercheval, January 19, 1810.

27. Martin Luther King, Jr., Nobel Lecture, December 11, 1964.

28. Dwight Eisenhower, Farewell Address, 1961. Video accessed November 28, 2011, http://www.youtube.com/watch?v=5pWAGgLSCSQ.

29. Koohan Paik, "True Defenders," *The Garden Island,* September 4, 2011. Accessed on November 28, 2011, http://thegardenisland.com/news/opinion/mailbag/article_16c56936-d6d5-11e0-8938-001cc4c03286.html.

30. Greg Miller and Julie Tate, "CIA Shifts Focus to Killing Targets," *Washington Post,* September 1, 2011.

31. Harlow was Eisenhower's speechwriter and congressional liaison reputed to have coined the "military-industrial complex" label. Williams was an Eisenhower speechwriter who co-authored this presidential valedictory (with fellow speechwriter Malcolm Moos).

32. This is usually termed the *Keynesian consumption function,* described explicitly in the *General Theory* as a "fundamental psychological law." It is my contention that popular criticisms of this fundamental concept fall very short, especially with regard to its significant *macroeconomic* implications (how redistribution affects aggregate consumption and saving and the overall level of economic activity). For cogent early, later, and recent defenses of the Keynesian consumption function, see Gardner Ackley, *Macroeconomic Theory* (New York: MacMillan, 1961), 208-251; James S. Duesenberry, *Income, Saving and the Theory of Consumer Behavior* (New York: Oxford University Press, 1967); Gardner Ackley, *Macroeconomics: Theory and Policy* (New York: MacMillan, 1978), pp. 157-70, 533-73; George Hadjimatheou, *Consumer Economics After Keynes; Theory and Evidence of the Consumption Function* (New York: St. Martin's, 1987); Karen Dynan, Jonathan Skinner, and Stephen Zeldes "Do the Rich Save More?" Working Paper 7906, National Bureau of Economic Research, 2000.

33. For a glimpse of the skeptical or disdainful reaction of American general officers to Eisenhower's New Look strategy, see Lewis Sorley, *Honorable Warrior: General Harold K. Johnson and the Ethics of Command* (Lawrence: University Press of Kansas, 1998), pp. 112-114. For persuasive analyses of the Eisenhower years in Vietnam and the unique vulnerabilities of the New Look strategy, see David L. Anderson, *Trapped by Success: The Eisenhower Administration and*

Vietnam, 1953-61 (New York: Columbia University Press, 1991); and Seth Jacobs, *America's Miracle Man in Vietnam: Ngo Dinh Diem, Religion, Race, and U.S. Intervention in Vietnam* (Durham: Duke University Press, 2004).

34.   See, for example, Seymour Melman, *The Peace Race* (London: Gollancz, 1962); Melman, *The Defense Economy: Conversion of Industries and Occupations to Civilian Needs* (New York: Praeger, 1970); Melman, *Pentagon Capitalism: The Political Economy of War* (New York: McGraw-Hill, 1970); and Melman, *The Permanent War Economy: U.S. Capitalism in Decline* (New York: Simon and Schuster, 1976).

35.   Lyndon Johnson to Andy Hatcher, 23 December 1963, 10:15 p.m., Tape K6312.16, PNO 20 and 21, Robert David Johnson and David Shreve, editors, *The Presidential Recordings: Lyndon B. Johnson: The Kennedy Assassination and the Transfer of Power: Volume II* (New York: W.W. Norton, 2005), p. 773.

36.   Lyndon Johnson to Walter Reuther, 23 December 1963, 9:18 p.m., Tape K6312.16, PNO 6, Robert David Johnson and David Shreve, editors, *The Presidential Recordings: Lyndon B. Johnson: The Kennedy Assassination and the Transfer of Power: Volume II* (New York: W.W. Norton, 2005), pp. 745-48. The "WPA" reference, of course, was to the New Deal program LBJ greatly admired, the Works Progress Administration, which ran from 1935-1943, and which, in its National Youth Administration subdivision, employed Johnson as Texas state director, from 1935-7. Its principal aim was to employ millions of unskilled American workers in useful public works projects.

37.   Quoted in Larry Berman, *Planning a Tragedy: The Americanization of the War in Vietnam* (New York: W.W. Norton, 1983), p. 34.

38.   Quoted in Eric F. Goldman, *The Tragedy of Lyndon Johnson* (New York: Knopf, 1969), p. 383.

39.   Walter Heller, "Getting Ready for Peace," *Harper's*, April 1968, p. 57.

40.   John Maynard Keynes, *The General Theory of Interest, Employment and Money* (London: Macmillan, 1936), p.129.

41.   *Ibid.*

42.   Robert Pollin and Heidi Garrett-Peltier, "The U.S. Employment Effects of Military and Domestic Spending Priorities," (Washington, D.C.: Institute for Policy Studies, 2007). In a different context, such as the one that prevails in 2011—where debates revolve around what and how much to cut rather than spend—a corollary lesson

can be derived from this study: all cuts would reduce employment levels and harm the economy, but cuts to military spending would raise unemployment and dampen economic activity *less than* corresponding cuts to education, transportation, and other non-military outlays.

43.   For a persuasive historical analysis of the rise of the "gunbelt," see Ann Markusen, Peter Hall, Scott Campbell, and Sabina Deitrick, *The Rise of the Gunbelt: The Military Remapping of Industrial America* (New York: Oxford University Press, 1991).

44.   Only in the rare case of a state like Hawaii, which finances public education within a unified state system, or in a few other states, which have made an effort to displace local funding with a generous state funding formula, has this been avoided to some degree.

45.   Keynes, *The General Theory*, p.159.

46.   *Ibid.*

47.   Spencer Ackerman, "Defense Industry: Keep Paying Us or the Economy Dies," *Wired*, 27 October 2011.

48.   Dean Baker, "The Military Spending Fairy," Center for Economic Policy and Research blog, 26 October 2011, http://www.cepr.net/index.php/cepr-blog. Accessed October 28, 2011.

49.   Dwight Eisenhower, "The Chance for Peace," speech given to the American Society of Newspaper Editors, April 16, 1953.

50.   Martin Feldstein, "The Economy Is Worse Than You Think," *Wall Street Journal*, June 8, 2011. Accessed November 28, 2011, http://online.wsj.com/article/SB10001424052702303657404576363984173620692.html?KEYWORDS=feldstein.

51.   "Federal Budget Pie Charts," *War Resisters League*, 2011. Accessed November 28, 2011, https://www.warresisters.org/category/catalog/federal-budget-pie-charts.

52.   Lloyd J. Dumas, "Finding the Future: The Role of Economic Conversion in Shaping the Twenty-first Century," *utwatch.org*, 1995. Accessed November 28, 2011, http://www.utwatch.org/war/21stcenturyeconomics.html.

53.   "Chalmers Johnson Interview: Conversations with History," *Institute of International Studies*, UC Berkeley, 2004. Accessed November 28, 2011, http://globetrotter.berkeley.edu/people4/CJohnson/cjohnson-con3.html.

54.   Bruce Gagnon, "Global Warming or Conversion of Military Industrial Complex?", *War Is A Crime .org*, May 16, 2007. Accessed

November 28, 2011, http://warisacrime.org/node/22546.

55. Seymour Melman, "In the Grip of a Permanent War Economy," *CounterPunch*, March 15-17, 2003. Accessed November 28, 2011, http://www.counterpunch.org/2003/03/15/in-the-grip-of-a-permanent-war-economy.

56. Lloyd J. Dumas, "Finding the Future: The Role of Economic Conversion in Shaping the Twenty-first Century," *utwatch.org*, 1995. Accessed November 28, 2011, http://www.utwatch.org/war/21stcenturyeconomics.html.

57. *Ibid.*

58. Seymour Melman, "Disarmament, Economic Conversion, and Jobs for All," *Uncommon Sense*, October 8, 1995, republished by *National Jobs for All Coalition*. Accessed November 28, 2011, http://www.njfac.org/us8.htm.

59. Bruce Gagnon, "Global Warming or Conversion of Military Industrial Complex?", *War Is A Crime .org*, May 16, 2007. Accessed November 28, 2011, http://warisacrime.org/node/22546.

60. Robert Pollin and Heidi Garrett-Peltier, "The U.S. Employment Effects of Military and Domestic Spending Priorities," Department of Economics and Political Economy Research Institute, University of Massachusetts, Amherst, October 2007. Accessed November 28, 2011, http://www.ips-dc.org/reports/071001-jobcreation.pdf.

61. Nicholas D. Kristof, "Our Lefty Military," *New York Times*, June 15, 2011.

62. "On the Japanese Threat: An Interview With Chalmers Johnson," *The Multinational Monitor*, November 1989. Accessed November 28, 2011, http://multinationalmonitor.org/hyper/issues/1989/11/interview-johnson.html.

63. Kathy Wolfe, "Hamilton's Ghost Haunts Washington From Tokyo," *American Almanac*, January 1992. Accessed November 28, 2011, http://american_almanac.tripod.com/mejei.htm.

64. Seymour Melman, "Disarmament, Economic Conversion, and Jobs for All," *Uncommon Sense*, October 8, 1995, republished by *National Jobs for All Coalition*. Accessed November 28, 2011, http://www.njfac.org/us8.htm.

65. Ellen Brown, "Cheney Was Right About One Thing: Deficits Don't Matter," *Web of Debt*, April 25, 2011. Accessed November 28, 2011, http://www.webofdebt.com/articles/cheney_deficits.php.

66. Barney Frank, "Cut the Military Budget - II," *The Nation*, March 2, 2009. Accessed November 28, 2011, http://www.thenation.com/

article/cut-military-budget-ii.

67.   *People's Guide to the Federal Budget,* National Priorities Project. Accessed December 6, 2011, http://nationalpriorities.org/resources/federal-budget-101/peoples-guide/#spending.

68.   Steven Kull, Clay Ramsay, Evan Lewis, and Stefan Subias, "How the American Public Would Deal With the Budget Deficit," The Program for Public Consultation, February 3, 2011. Accessed December 6, 2011, http://www.worldpublicopinion.org/incl/printable_version.php?pnt=677.

69.   Bruce Fellman, "Training the Next Leaders," Yale Alumni Magazine, March 2003. Accessed December 6, 2011, http://www.yalealumnimagazine.com/issues/03_03/grandstrategy.html.

70.   Jason Leopold, "Army's 'Spiritual Fitness' Test Comes Under Fire," *Truthout,* January 5, 2011. Accessed December 7, 2011, http://www.truth-out.org/armys-fitness-test-designed-psychologist-who-inspired-cias-torture-program-under-fire66577.

71.   Chris Rodda, "Soldiers Forced to See Chaplain After Failing Spiritual Fitness Test," *Huffington Post,* January 20, 2011. Accessed December 7, 2011, http://www.huffingtonpost.com/chris-rodda/soldiers-forced-to-see-ch_b_810558.html.

72.   Associate Professor of Law, University of Toledo College of Law. This paper is based on a presentation made at the "Military Industrial Complex at 50 National Conference," Charlottesville, Virginia, September 16-18, 2011. All errors are the responsibility of the author. Parts of this paper are derived from "International Law and the American Project since 9/11," dated September 11, 2011 and available at http://jurist.org/forum/2011/09/benjamin-davis-american-project.php and "Bringing Light to Dark Matters: Drones, Torture and Illegal Wars," dated July 20, 2011 and available at http://www.saltlaw.org/blog/2011/07/20/bringing-light-to-dark-matter-drones-torture-illegal-wars.

73.   Hans Fallada, *Every Man Dies Alone* (Michael Hofmann, Translation) (Melville House 2009) (First published in 1947 as *Jeder stirbt fur sich allein*).

74.   Francesco Alberoni, *Movement and Institution* (Columbia University Press 1984).

75.   Article 38, Statute of the International Court of Justice.

76.   Article 27, Vienna Convention on the Law of Treaties and a rule of customary international law.

77.   *United States v. Salim Ahmed Hamdan*, CMCR 09-002, United

States Court of Military Commission Review (June 24, 2011) available at http://www.defense.gov/news/CMCRHamdan.html.

78. *United States v. Ali Hamza Ahmad Suliman Al Bahlul*, CMCR 09-001, United States Court of Military Commission Review (September 9, 2011) available at http://www.lawfareblog.com/wp-content/uploads/2011/09/al-Bahlul-USCt-Mil-Comm-Review-Sept-9-2011-1.pdf.

79. "Billing dispute reveals CIA torture flights," *The Raw Story*, September 1, 2011, available at http://www.rawstory.com/rs/2011/09/01/billing-dispute-reveals-cia-torture-flights.

80. Benjamin G. Davis, "No Third Class Processes for Foreigners," 103 Nw. U. L. Rev. Colloquy 88 (2008).

81. Tara Mckelvey, "Inside the Killing Machine," *Newsweek*, February 13, 2011. Accessed December 7, 2011, http://www.thedailybeast.com/newsweek/2011/02/13/inside-the-killing-machine.html.

82. Or help create the legal basis to prosecute at Nuremberg the international crime of crime against the peace (aggressive war) as did William C. Chanler, a Wall Street lawyer. See Jonathan A. Bush, "The Supreme... Crime And its Origins: The Lost Legislative History of the Crime of Aggressive War," 102 *Columbia Law Review* 2324-2424 (2002).

83. See Pew Research Center for the People and the Press, "Press Accuracy Rating Hits Two Decade Low," September 13, 2009. http://people-press.org/2009/09/13/press-accuracy-rating-hits-two-decade-low.

84. For an account of the development of objectivity, see David Mindich, *Just the Facts: How "Objectivity" Came to Define American Journalism* (New York: New York University Press, November 1998).

85. There is an extensive literature documenting this journalistic practice, including Gaye Tuchman, *Making News: A Study in the Construction of Reality* (New York: Free Press, 1978); Herbert Gans, *Deciding What's News* (New York: Pantheon, 1979); and Mark Fishman, *Manufacturing the News* (Austin: University of Texas Press, 1980).

86. *The Daily Show*, July 12, 2004. http://www.thedailyshow.com/watch/mon-july-12-2004/wolf-blitzer.

87. For an overview, see Michael Massing, *Now They Tell Us: The American Press and Iraq* (New York: New York Review of Books, 2004).

88. Lawrence Soley, *The News Shapers: The Sources Who Explain the News* (New York: Praeger, 1992).

89.   Edward S. Herman and Noam Chomsky, *Manufacturing Consent: The Political Economy of the Mass Media* (New York: Pantheon, 1988).
90.   Garth S. Jowett and Victoria O'Donnell, *Propaganda and Persuasion*, 5th ed. (Thousand Oaks, CA: Sage, 2012), p. 7.
91.   Matthew Creamer, "Obama Wins! ... Ad Age's Marketer of the Year," *Advertising Age*, October 17, 2008. http://adage.com/article/moy-2008/obama-wins-ad-age-s-marketer-year/131810.
92.   Elisabeth Bumiller, "Traces of Terror: The Strategy; Bush Aides Set Strategy to Sell Policy on Iraq," *New York Times*, September 7, 2002, p. A-1.
93.   Dwight D. Eisenhower Farewell Address delivered January 17, 1961. http://www.americanrhetoric.com/speeches/dwightdeisenhowerfarewell.html. Cited September, 2011.
94.   Rich Jones, "Review By NRC Cites Safety Issues At Plant In Erwin," *The Greeneville Sun*, April 8, 2011. Accessed December 12, 2011, http://greenevillesun.com/story/314103.
95.   "INTERIM REPORT: Results for Isotopic Studies of Uranium in Environmental Samples from the Vicinity of the Nuclear Fuel Services Facility, Erwin, TN," November 11, 2010. Prepared by: Michael E. Ketterer, PhD, Professor, Chemistry and Biochemistry, Box 5698, Northern Arizona University, Flagstaff AZ 86011-5698. http://www.nrc.gov/reading-rm/doc-collections/commission/slides/2011/20110527/ketterer-ureport-20110527.pdf.
96.   "Uranium could become explosive issue in Virginia," *Associated Press, The Augusta Chronicle*, February 17, 2008. http://chronicle.augusta.com/stories/2008/02/17/bus_187533.shtml.
97.   "A Proposed Annex to the Wreck Removal Convention Treaty to Address Environmental Hazards of Sunken World War II Naval Vessels, " LT Craig R. Petersen, USCG, University College University of Denver Capstone Project for Master of Environmental Policy and Management, May 15, 2007. http://www.seaaustralia.com/documents/NAVY%20WRECKS-Petersen.pdf.
98.   "Special Report: The Deadliness Below: Of Clamshells, Artillery Shells," John M.R. Bull, *Daily Press,*. Oct. 30, 2005. http://www.dailypress.com/news/dp-chemdumping-stories,0,4442836.storygallery.
99.   "A New Way to Track Debris in Orbit," William Matthews, *Defense News*, February 16, 2009. http://www.defensenews.com/story.php?i=3949244
100. "The Juno Mission: NASA's Solar Probe," Karl Grossman,

Counterpunch, Aug. 3, 2011. http://www.counterpunch.
org/2011/08/03/nasas-solar-probe.
101. "Joint Vision 2020 Emphasizes Full-spectrum Dominance," Jim
Garamone, *American Forces Press Service,* June 2, 2000. http://www.
defense.gov/news/newsarticle.aspx?id=45289.
102. http://www.operationpaperclip.info.
103. http://www.operationpaperclip.info/wernher-von-braun.php.
104. Environmental Working Group, Perchlorate. http://www.ewg.
org/chemindex/chemicals/perchlorate.
105. "Rocket Fuel in Drinking Water, New Data Show Widespread
Nationwide Contamination," Bill Walker, Renee Sharp, Environmental
Working Group, March 2003. http://www.ewg.org/reports/
rocketwater.
106. Fact Sheet, Utah Department of Environmental of
Environmental Quality, October, 2010. http://www.hazardouswaste.
utah.gov/Docs/perchlorate_FS_2.pdf.
107. "Children Consuming Contaminated Tap Water And Food At
Risk; EPA Tap Water Safety Standards Are Critically Needed," Anila
Jacob, Jane Houlihan, Environmental Working Group, January 2008.
108. Representative Bart Stupak, House Energy and Commerce
Committee, June 12, 2006.
109. "Environmental Destruction Caused by U.S. Military Bases
and the Serious Implications for the Philippines," Jorge Emmanuel,
Presented at Crossroad 1991: Towards a Nuclear Free, Bases Free
Philippines An International Conference, May 14 - 16, 1990, Manila,
Philippines. http://guamagentorange.info/yahoo_site_admin/assets/
docs/Environmental_Distruction_By_Military.238134937.pdf.
110. Barry Sanders, *The Green Zone: The Environmental Costs of
Militarism*, AK Press, 2009.
111. "New Office Aims to Reduce Military's Fuel Usage," Lisa Daniel,
American Forces Press Service, July 22, 2010. http://www.defense.
gov/news/newsarticle.aspx?id=60131.
112. Barry Sanders, *op cit.*
113. Encyclopedia of Alabama, Anniston Army Depot, w. Jayson Hill,
January 20, 2010. http://www.encyclopediaofalabama.org/face/
Article.jsp?id=h-1776.
114. "Green and Strong: U.S. Army Project Reduces Waste, Recycles
More Than Six Million Pounds of Steel," *PRNewswire,* July 25, 2011,
http://www.thefreelibrary.com.
115. Eileen Welsome, *The Plutonium Files*, Delta Books, 1999.

116. Alan R Cantwell Jr., M.D., "The Human Radiation Experiments: How Scientists Secretly Used U.S. Citizens as Guinea Pigs During the Cold War," *New Dawn Magazine*. http://www.newdawnmagazine. com/articles/THE_HUMAN_RADIATION_EXPERIMENTS.html (cited September 2011).

117. http://www.youtube.com/watch?v=RIw0RU4JFOA.

118. Michael Renner of the World Watch Institute writing in the 1997 book, *War and Public Health*.

119. Joshua Holland, "The 10 States With the Worst Economies In America," *AlterNet*, August 30, 2011.

120. Mangano, J.J., "Improvements in Local Infant Health After Nuclear Power Reactor Closing," *Environmental Epidemiology and Toxicology* 2(1):32-36, 2000.

121. Diane D' Arrigo and Mary Olson, "Out of Control—On Purpose: DOE's Dispersal of Radioactive Waste into Landfills and Consumer Products," *Nuclear Information and Resource Service*, May 14, 2007.

122. Sue Sturgis, "Radioactive Racism at Tennessee Nuclear Waste Processing Company," *Facing South*, Jan. 26, 2010.

123. Arthur N. Bernklau, "Mushrooming Depleted Uranium (DU) Scandal Blamed for Sec of Veterans Affairs Departure," *Preventive Psychiatry E-Newsletter* No. 169, March 2005.

124. Vincent Warren, "The 9/11 Decade and the Decline of U.S. Democracy," *Center for Constitutional Rights*, http://ccrjustice.org/ the911decade, cited September, 2011.

125. "Caring for U.S. Veterans", *CostOfWar.org*, June 29, 2011. Accessed December 7, 2011, http://costsofwar.org/article/caring-us-veterans.

126. Chuck Fager, "Agent Orange: A Half Century of Pain," *Quaker House*, August 10, 2011. Accessed December 7, 2011, http:// quakerhouse.blogspot.com/2011/08/agent-orange-half-century-of-pain.html.

127. "VA Begins Paying Benefits for New Agent Orange claims," *U.S. Department of Veterans Affairs*, Nov. 1, 2010. Accessed December 7, 2011, http://www.va.gov/opa/pressrel/pressrelease.cfm?id=1991.

128. Jenifer L. Price, "Findings From the National Vietnam Veterans' Readjustment Study," *U.S. Department of Veterans Affairs*, January 1, 2007. Accessed December 7, 2011, http://www.ptsd.va.gov/ professional/pages/vietnam-vets-study.asp.

129. Penny Coleman, *Flashback: Posttraumatic Stress Disorder, Suicide, and the Lessons of War*, Beacon Press, 2006, p. 19.

130. Hearst, et al, "Delayed Effects of the Military Draft on Mortality," *NEJM,* March 6, 1986, pp. 620-624. Accessed December 7, 2011, http://rds.epi-ucsf.org/ticr/syllabus/courses/76/2011/05/25/Lecture/readings/HearstThe%20new%20england%20journal%20of%20medicine1986.pdf.

131. "Vietnam Combat Linked to Many Diseases 20 Years Later," *Science Daily,* November 26, 1997. Accessed December 7, 2011, http://www.sciencedaily.com/releases/1997/11/971126042926.htm.

132. North Carolina Coalition to End Homelessness, "January 27, 2010 — NC Point-in-Time Count Reporting Form." Accessed December 7, 2011, http://www.ncceh.org/attachments/contentmanagers/825/PIT_State_2010-FINAL.pdf.

133. National Coalition for Homeless Veterans, "FAQ About Homeless Veterans." Accessed December 7, 2011, http://www.nchv.org/background.cfm#questions.

134. Ibid.

135. Nora Eisenberg, "10 Hard Truths for Veterans Day (and Every Other Day)", *Alternet.* Accessed December 7, 2011, http://www.alternet.org/story/148818/10_hard_truths_about_war_for_veterans_day_%28and_every_other_day%29.

136. Joseph E. Stiglitz, "The Price of 9/11," *Project Syndicate,* September 1, 2011. Accessed December 7, 2011, http://www.project-syndicate.org/commentary/stiglitz142/English.

137. Ronald Glasser, "A War of Disabilities: Iraq's Hidden Costs are Coming Home," *Harper's,* August 2005.

138. North Carolina Child Advocacy Institute, "Reducing Collateral Damage on the Home Front: Child Homicides within Military Families and Communities in North Carolina: Facts and Recommendations," *Quaker House,* September 2004. Accessed December 7, 2011, http://quakerhouse.org/child-homicides.htm.

139. Crawford Lutz et al., "The Costs of War," *Brown University's Watson Institute for International Studies, Eisenhower Research Project.*

140. Rick Maze, "18 Veterans Commit Suicide Each Day," *Army Times,* April 22, 2010. Accessed December 7, 2011, http://www.armytimes.com/news/2010/04/military_veterans_suicide_042210w.

141. Veterans for Common Sense, "Suicide Remains Sad Legacy of 9/11" September 5, 2011. Accessed December 7, 2011, http://www.veteransforcommonsense.org/index.php/veterans-category-articles/2517-vcs.

142. Ibid.

143. "The Wounded Platoon," *Frontline,* May 18, 2010. Accessed December 7, 2011, http://www.pbs.org/wgbh/pages/frontline/woundedplatoon.

144. Ann Wright, "Is There an Army Cover Up of Rape and Murder of Women Soldiers?" *Common Dreams,* April 28, 2008. Accessed December 7, 2011, http://www.commondreams.org/view/2008/04/28.

145. Melman frequently referred to the annual "report card" published by the society of civil engineers to highlight the declining infrastructure in the U.S. (deteriorating roads, bridges, schools, etc.), a situation that continues to worsen.

146 "Everyday Economics," *Federal Reserve Bank of Dallas.* Accessed Dec.ember 9, 2011, http://dallasfed.org/educate/everyday/ev9.html.

147. Margrit Kennedy, "A Changing Money System: The Economy of Ecology." Accessed December 9, 2011, http://converge.org.nz/evcnz/resources/money.pdf.

148. Deidre Kent, "Margrit Kennedy Inspires New Zealand Groups To Establish Regional Money Systems," *The McKeever Institute of Economic Policy Analysis.* Accessed December 9, 2011, http://www.mkeever.com/kent.html.

149. Zoltan Pozsar, Tobias Adrian, Adam Ashcraft, and Hayley Boesky, "Shadow Banking," *Federal Reserve Bank of New York,* July 2010. Accessed December 9, 2011, http://www.newyorkfed.org/research/staff_reports/sr458.html.

150. USMEPCOM Regulation 601-4, Section 3-2. Accessed December 11, 2011, http://www.mepcom.army.mil/publications/pdf/regs/r-0601-004.pdf.

151. "ASVAB Career Exploration Program Snippets for Announcements, Student Newsletters, School Website or Email Communications." Accessed December 11, 2011, http://asvabprogram.com/downloads/Announcement.pdf.

152. Discretionary Budget FY2011, *National Priorities Project.* Accessed December 11, 2011, http://nationalpriorities.org/en/resources/federal-budget-101/charts/discretionary-spending/discretionary-budget-fy2011.

153. Josh Rogin, "Levin and McCain: We Have No Idea How Much Debt Deal Cuts Defense," *Foreign Policy,* August 2, 2011. Accessed December 11, 2011, http://thecable.foreignpolicy.com/posts/2011/08/02/levin_and_mccain_we_have_no_idea_how_much_debt_deal_cuts_defense.

154. "U.S. National Debt," *White House,* July 26, 2011. Accessed December 11, 2011, http://www.whitehouse.gov/infographics/us-national-debt.

(We'll be billing the Pentagon extra for the blank space on this page.)

CPSIA information can be obtained at www.ICGtesting.com
Printed in the USA
BVOW080007140912

300233BV00008B/3/P